SHAMBHALA DRAGON EDITIONS

The dragon is an age-old symbol of the highest spiritual essence, embodying wisdom, strength, and the divine power of
transformation. In this spirit, Shambhala Dragon Editions
offers a treasury of readings in the sacred knowledge of Asia.
In presenting the works of authors both ancient and modern,
we seek to make these teachings accessible to lovers of wisdom everywhere.

LING CH'I CHING

A Classic Chinese Oracle

o o o o o o

Translated, with commentary, by
RALPH D. SAWYER *and*
MEI-CHÜN LEE SAWYER

SHAMBHALA
Boston & London
1995

SHAMBHALA PUBLICATIONS, INC.
Horticultural Hall
300 Massachusetts Avenue
Boston, Massachusetts 02115

First Edition
Printed in the United States of America on acid-free paper ⊗
Distributed in the United States by Random House, Inc.,
and in Canada by Random House of Canada Ltd

LIBRARY OF CONGRESS CATALOGING-IN-PUBLICATION DATA
Ling ch'i ching. English.
Ling ch'i ching: a classic Chinese oracle/translated, with
commentary, by Ralph D. Sawyer and Mei-chün Lee Sawyer.—1st ed.
p.   cm.—(Shambhala dragon editions)
ISBN 1-57062-083-0 (acid-free paper)
1. Divination—China.   I. Sawyer, Ralph.   II. Sawyer, Mei-chün.
III. Title.
BF1770.C5L55   1995   95-15876
133.3'3—dc20   CIP

In memory of

ZENO THEOPHRASTUS

who trod the path and thereby illuminated the Way

Contents

Contents

Preface

Several decades ago, while still in primary school, I was fortuitously introduced to the mystical world of fortunetelling through watching an irrepressible aunt insightfully manipulate a Tarot-like deck with rather startling results. Thereafter I stumbled on a mass-marketed version of traditional Chinese temple sticks and became intrigued by divination and other human attempts to predict the future. Despite a degree from M.I.T. and many years spent at least partly in the rigorous world of science and engineering, mantic systems have continued to be a focal interest.

Our study of the *Ling Ch'i Ching* dates back to the early 1970s when I first encountered it being profitably employed by a Tokyo street diviner and, eventually, several other highly successful self-styled experts in the bustling night markets of Kyoto and Osaka. During the early years of that troubled decade, I spent many weekends visiting aged practitioners of the mantic arts in Taiwan, Korea, and Japan, particularly those still found in rustic settings and ensconced in temples, as yet unsullied by commercialization or estranged from ancient ways. My wife, Mei-Chün Lee Sawyer, and I also collected countless sets of divination strips from various temples in all three countries, investigated the commonly found systems, and prepared draft translations for several of them which remain in a dusty corner even today. At that time we were fortunate to enjoy the company and friendship of the late Professor Ts'ai Mao-t'ang—and his enlighting insights on many issues of folk religion, including unique sects and esoteric practices. Although the flow of events diverted our attention from the many intriguing questions posed by these mantic systems, Mei-chün and I continued to seek out relevant materials over the past two decades, whenever possible, and even provided consultations under Surquest, our hall name, to gain the insights that can only be wrought by experience. Having pondered the *Ling Ch'i Ching* for several years and circulated a draft translation among our friends that stimulated a surprisingly enthusiastic response, we felt compelled to complete the translation and make it available so that others might learn of another complex and intriguing work from the Chinese divination tradition previously identified solely with the great and justly famous *I Ching*.

In comparison with other divination works in the powerful Chinese tradition, the *Ling Ch'i Ching* is a reasonably accessible text rarely requiring extensive scholarly annotation or apparatus. This is not to say that scholars would not benefit from a careful analytic version with various allusions, textual variations, and poetical images appropriately referenced, supplemented with a lengthy historical introduction setting the work within its context. However, our intent in undertaking this translation has been to make the work accessible to the widest possible audience, one that need not have every unknown term and cultural allusion explained when their general meaning and function are immediately obvious. While it would be impossible to succinctly re-create a meaningful historical context for the casual reader, even without it the book speaks clearly, as witnessed by the many readers of the translation who have offered their reactions and comments.

For the translation itself we have largely retained the original word order and also attempted to preserve some sense of the book's archaic quality. Perhaps when originally created, it reflected vernacular language, but as works of this type are universally felt to benefit from an aura of arcaneness, thereby realizing greater psychological impact, we have opted to employ somewhat stylized terms such as "remain in residence" rather than simply "stay at home"; the "hundred affairs" rather than "everything"; and "baleful" rather than "bad" or simply "inauspicious." (Baleful appropriately evokes a dark and threatening image, in our opinion.)

The translation is based on the *Ssu-k'u Ch'üan-shu* edition, although recourse has frequently been made to the one preserved in the *Tao Tsang* as well as other important versions. Since they are all readily available to scholars and our choice of one or another phrase for purposes of clarity and consistency in a small number of cases is readily apparent, they have not been footnoted. The issues of textual transmission, even of history itself, are murky and need to be addressed; in the absence of articles focusing on these subjects, we intend to offer something in the near future. Meanwhile, it should be noted that none of the academic journals devoted to history, philosophy, or religion published throughout Asia in recent decades— including specialized journals focusing on the mantic arts, and particularly the *I Ching,* in Taiwan and the People's Republic of China—has ever carried even a single article about the *Ling Ch'i Ching.* Clearly this is a situation that needs to be remedied.

In the West the text has been similarly ignored, although translations and studies of the *I Ching* abound. The great James Legge attempted the first full translation of the *I Ching* into English more than a century ago, a work that may still be found in bookstores throughout the country. Richard Wilhelm's famous version, unfortunately translated through the intermediary of German, also remains popular and is generally considered the most erudite edition. However, more recently, John Blofeld produced a convenient reader's translation, and Thomas Cleary has brought forth Buddhist and Taoist versions in modern English, while two or three new translations are apparently in the offing. Moreover, over the decades, Richard Wilhelm and Hellmut Wilhelm have produced a series of contemplative studies on the material and meaning of the *I Ching—Change: Eight Lectures on the I Ching; Heaven, Earth, and Man in the I Ching*; and *Lectures on the I Ching: Constancy and Change*—all of which can be profitably consulted for general and thematic background material.

Modern studies of the Chinese mantic tradition and texts attained a promising foundation in the early 1980s with a flurry of articles in China and several insightful papers by such Western scholars as David Nivison, Paul Serruys, E. L. Shaughnessy, David Keightley, and L. Vandermeersch. These writings on the history of divination in China were largely based on oracle bones, shells, and analytic examinations of concepts found in the *I Ching* itself. Their radical conclusions have caused much consternation because the fundamental assumptions of the *I Ching*, such as the significance and operation of the moving lines and resulting second hexagram, have had to be rethought. Moreover, Werner Banck similarly collected the various temple slips found around Taiwan and other Asian locales, resulting in the publication of a bulky work entitled *Das chinesische Tempelorakel* in 1976; and Michael Strickmann delivered an incisive analysis of temple divination strips in a pioneering paper at the Shang conference in 1983 entitled "Chinese Oracles in Buddhist Vestments." Unfortunately, further elaborations of these original efforts have been scarce and presented only in uncirculated papers at academic conferences; although undoubtedly advancing the field of scholarship, they remain generally inaccessible. However, Nathan Sivin's early ruminations on the *T'ai Hsüan Ching* prompted us to ponder that work for many years, and Michael Nylan's insightful translation has recently appeared, providing Western readers with another text from this vibrant tradition. We have two further works in preparation and hope to bring them forward if the response to the *Ling Ch'i Ching* merits it.

We would like to express our appreciation to a number of people who have been associated with the translation and publication of *Ling Ch'i Ching*. First, to Nathan Sivin for piquing my interest and providing initial orientations; the late Ts'ai Mao-t'ang for his attempts to diminish my opacity; and Paul Gauvin, Shean Sheehan, and Miao Yong-i for meandering but illuminating ruminations. Next, to all those who willingly read and commented on draft translations over the years with a view to identifying problems and guiding its final format: Paul and Bonney Fitzgerald, Tom Tomasian, Ralph Tomasian, Rick and Jo-anne Williams, Cleon Brewer, Guy Baer, and especially Patricia Hans, whose comments and insights are much appreciated. Bernie Flynn of Trident Booksellers offered valuable advice on divination texts and other matters related to the printed word. Fred Marks congenially provided wise counsel over the years. Zhao Yong collected variant editions and collateral materials. Norman Reis labored during auspicious hours to expertly craft numerous sets of research disks. Max Gartenberg and Stuart Miller smoothed the path to publication, while Peter Turner at Shambhala Publications courageously brought it to fruition. Finally, we are honored to have the calligraphy of Lee T'ing-rong throughout the work.

Note to the Reader

The intent of the translators has been to provide an accurate yet accessible translation of an important historical work from the Chinese divination tradition. Although readers may wish to actively explore the oracular and divination possibilities encompassed by the *Ling Ch'i Ching*, no claim is made or implied by the translators or publisher as to the validity and accuracy of the system portrayed in this work. Additional commentary provided by the translators is intended to facilitate understanding and provide contemporary relevance for those who wish to study the Oracle or consult it for the purposes of self-knowledge. No commercial, medical, or other significant life decisions should ever be based on the *Ling Ch'i Ching*, even if all the prerequisites for the creation of the empowered disks (as described by the introduction) are fully satisfied. Assessing and determining the validity of the text, if any, is solely the responsibility of the reader. Those wishing to consult the *Ling Ch'i Ching* are cautioned that, unlike the *I Ching*—which almost always implies that through perseverance and pursuing the course of virtue the querent can escape even the most dire situations unscathed—the *Ling Ch'i Ching* contains many inauspicious predictions, reflecting its author's view of life and reality. While these indications should be understood symbolically and metaphysically as admonitions and warnings rather than a matter of fate, readers potentially troubled by drawing such prognostications should not consult the *Ling Ch'i Ching* as a divination book but instead simply read it as a historical artifact.

Introduction

The *Ling Ch'i Ching* was created by an unknown Chinese scholar who consciously sought to present the literate world with a more accessible oracle than the arcane *I Ching*; it is one of several such attempts. The title, which might be translated as the "Spiritual Chess Classic" or the "Classic of the Empowered Chessmen," refers to the twelve disks—similar to Chinese chess or Western checkers pieces—employed in the divination process. The first character in the title, *ling,* entails the concept of spiritual power, of being numinously empowered; the second, *ch'i,* usually refers to various Chinese chess games or, as here, the pieces themselves. The method for determining the trigraph, the associated images, and the language of the oracle are relatively simple and direct in comparison with the *I Ching.* There are no moving lines to interpret, and concrete pronouncements of a divinatory or fortunetelling nature are provided for numerous categories of ongoing human concern. The *Ling Ch'i Ching* is totally self-contained, requiring no additional specialized knowledge on the part of the inquirer (unlike the Tarot or similar systems) nor the cultivation of ecstatic powers (such as characterizes many African systems). This classic proved extremely popular over the centuries, was highly esteemed by all but the most puritanical officials, and eventually was adopted in Japan as well.

The core of the present text was probably composed early in the Wei-Chin period (222–419 CE), while the four interpretative commentaries were added in subsequent centuries. The work is generally considered to be genuine, although its exact origins remain murky. Tradition variously attributes the authorship to Tung-fang Shuo, a shadowy Han-dynasty figure who earned repute for his wit, repartee, irascible behavior, and skill in guessing the nature of concealed objects; Chang Liang, the famous Han tactician, who is also said to have received it from the apocryphal strategist Huang-shih Kung; and Liu An, best known for the Taoist-oriented *Huai-nan tzu*.

Although the mantic arts seem to have flourished in China virtually since the beginning of time, they probably began in the period of the legendary Sage Emperors (2852–2255 BCE), and certainly by the late Hsia (2205–1766 BCE). In the early Shang dynasty (1766–1045 BCE) scapulimancy and, subsequently, plastromancy—divination by consulting the cracks formed on heated shoulder bones and turtle plastrons, respectively—had become an integral part of the ruling elite's culture. The Shang theocracy, in which the right to perform divination was reserved for the ruler, consulted the oracle for all important matters of state, including military campaigns, trips, appropriate times for sacrifice, political relations, hunting expeditions, likelihood of rain, and other agricultural concerns. In addition, the ruler personally inquired about illness, childbirth, ghosts, and private calamities and enmities.

Divination by bone and shell was, however, largely subject to an expert's interpretative powers in reading the crack patterns. A favorable response was thought to be obtained when two crack lines intersected more or less at right angles, the horizontal one originating in the vertical one. This origin point for the horizontal line was not accidental but was essentially predetermined by skillfully drilling holes partially through the back of the turtle plastrons before they were heated. Over the centuries a considerable body of interpretive knowledge developed; the cracks, readings, and sometimes actual results were all correlated and inscribed onto the plastrons themselves, thereby creating a library that defined the basic parameters and circumscribed the range of future possibilities.

The Chou dynasty, forcefully established by the peripheral Chou state with the dramatic conquest of the Shang in 1045 BCE, developed a different form of divination—one based on the systematic manipulation of yarrow or milfoil stalks to produce the hexagrams now found in the *I Ching*. Although the evolution of this great work remains murky, tradition holds that Fu Hsi created the original trigrams and the hexagrams themselves, King Wen was inspired to append the judgments while he was imprisoned by the Shang, and the Duke of Chou developed the line explanations. Modern studies, however, clearly show that much disparate material was melded to create the present text, including actual historical events, prophetic verses, and common rhymes. Moreover, the material stems from different periods and apparently evolved extensively before attaining its present form.

The *I Ching* may have developed as a more rational, less subjective alternative to the interpretation of bone cracks, as traditionally claimed, or may simply be the product of the Chou culture. In either event, the standardized manipulative procedure, which has also recently come into question, makes the process of obtaining the oracle's pronouncement completely independent of the querent's knowledge and perspective. Moreover, unlike many other systems of divination found in Africa and South America, the querent does not need to have perfected any special skills, cultivated ecstatic powers, or been shamanistically initiated into a set of religious beliefs and practices. This freedom from an innate dependence on any single deity or religious rite, from having transcendental knowledge divinely revealed, pertains not only to the *I Ching*, but also all the works derived from its philosophic content.

The *I Ching* itself almost certainly attained final form sometime during the early Chou period and was widely employed for divination purposes in the Spring and Autumn (722–481 BCE) and Warring States (403–221 BCE) periods. During this time a body of interpretative literature and systematized analytic thought, including highly esoteric views, developed around the text. It was even claimed that Confucius had edited the *I Ching* and penned some of the appendices that transformed the divination work into a cosmological, philosophic treatise. Even though this is unlikely, the complex material that evolved over the centuries provided the philosophic foundation and basic world view for the *Ling Ch'i Ching* and similar works.

By the Han dynasty (206 BCE–220 CE) several schools of interpretation had arisen, and variant texts, as well as other, presumably older mantic writings, seem to have existed. However, other than for the especially erudite, the *I Ching* apparently had become an opaque text, easy to cast but difficult to interpret, subject to widely differing opinions. Consequently, additional writings appeared, such as the *I Lin* (Forest of Change) and *T'ai Hsüan Ching* (Canon of the Supreme Mystery), providing readily accessible or more fully integrated systems for consultation. In general, at a minimum they presupposed much, if not all, of the worldview incorporated into the ever-more contorted body of *I Ching* literature and borrowed from it extensively, frequently alluding to the trigrams, hexagram names, and even individual lines. The *Ling Ch'i Ching* falls somewhere in the middle of this pattern, clearly subsuming the *I Ching*'s worldview and frequently echoing images and lines from it, but without presupposing any actual or detailed understanding of the *I Ching*.

Authorship of the *Ling Ch'i Ching* has traditionally been ascribed to Tung-fang Shuo, a palace retainer in the early years of the powerful Emperor Wu, who vigorously ruled the Former, or Western, Han dynasty from 140 to 86 BCE. Although pedantic Confucians deprecated Tung-fang Shuo for his verbal facility and irreverent approach to the serious, life-defining project of cultivating virtue and vigilantly practicing righteousness, he clearly understood the dangers of inopportunely criticizing of a strong-willed ruler and modified his behavior accordingly. His extensive biography in the *Han Shu*, while ostensibly just the record of clever wit but shallow morals, in fact preserves several strong remonstrances evincing great concern for the welfare of the people, implementation of upright policies, cultivation of virtuous ways, adherence to law, and maintenance of proper order. The first paragraph of this biography apparently preserves his initial submission to the emperor, one that caught Emperor Wu's attention by its lack of prescribed humility and led to Shuo being given a minor palace position:

> Tung-fang Shuo, whose personal name was Man-ch'ien ["handsome"], was a native of Yen-tz'u in P'ing-yüan. When Emperor Wu had just ascended the throne, he directed the realm to recommend gentlemen who were square and upright, worthy and good, or marked by skill in literature or other strengths who would then receive appointment outside the normal bureaucratic hierarchy. Throughout the four quarters many were the gentlemen who submitted missives discussing the virtues and defects of the government. Those who boasted and promoted themselves were numbered by the thousands; the ones who were deemed unworthy for selection were abruptly dismissed with notification that their missives had been considered.
>
> When Tung-fang Shuo initially appeared, he submitted a missive that said: "When I, your subject, was young, I lost my father and mother, and in growing up was nurtured by my elder brother and his wife. When I was thirteen, I commenced my studies, and within three winters my knowledge of literature and history was adequate for ordinary use. When I was fifteen,

I studied swordsmanship. At sixteen, I studied the *Book of Odes* and the *Book of Documents*, committing 220,000 words to memory. When I was nineteen, I studied the tactics and strategies of Sun-tzu and Wu-tzu, the methods for combat deployment, and the instructions for commanding with the gongs and drums, and similarly committed 220,000 words to memory. Shuo, your subject, can now recite 440,000 words. Moreover, I constantly embrace Tzu Lu's aim (to properly order and govern the state). I, your subject, am twenty-two years old, nine [*Han*] feet three inches tall. My eyes are like suspended pearls, my teeth arrayed like shells. I am as courageous as Meng Pen, quick as Ch'ing Chi, incorruptible as Pao Shu-ya, and as trustworthy as Wei Sheng. Accordingly, I can be employed as a great minister to the Son of Heaven. Your subject Shuo, risking death, bows twice in making this submission.

As his own words indicate, and several of his later remonstrances and monologues also record, Tung-fang Shuo was obviously knowledgeable about the military classics prominent in his time, Sun-tzu's *Art of War* and Wu Ch'i's *Wu-tzu*. Furthermore, his skill in applying stratagems to life's rapidly evolving situations can be seen from the following incident:

Sometime thereafter Shuo deceived the dwarfs who exercised [the horses], saying: "The Emperor thinks fellows like you are of no use in local offices; in tilling the fields, even if you fully exert your strength, you certainly will not come up to other men; in administering the masses and holding office, you will not be able to govern the people; and if engaged in military activities and striking the enemy, you will be unequal to the responsibilities of military affairs. You are useless in state activities, and merely deplete its clothing and food. So now he wants to slay all you fellows." The dwarfs, greatly afraid, wailed and cried. Shuo advised them: "When the Emperor comes by, strike your heads on the ground and ask for forgiveness."

Somewhat later when they heard the Emperor coming by, the dwarfs all cried out in tears and bowed their heads down. The Emperor inquired: "What are you going on about?" They replied: "Tung-fang Shuo said Your Majesty wants to execute all of us." The Emperor, knowing Shuo's cleverness, summoned and questioned him: "Why have you put the dwarfs in fear?" He replied: "Whether I am to live or die, your subject Shuo will explain it. The dwarfs, who are more than three [*Han*] feet tall, are each granted a sack of grain and 240 cash as an allowance. Your subject Shuo, who is more than nine [*Han*] feet tall, also receives an allowance of a sack of grain and 240 cash. The dwarfs are sated to the point of death; your subject Shuo is hungry to the point of extinction. If my words can be employed, favor me with different treatment. If they cannot be employed, dismiss me. Do not have me merely deplete Changan's rice." The Emperor was greatly amused and had him thenceforth await future summons at the Golden Horse Gate. Thereafter he gradually became closer to the Emperor.

After his death his name became associated with all sorts of clever arts and magical skills, and he was variously apotheosized as a Taoist immortal. The *Ling Ch'i Ching* apparently became identified with Tung-fang Shuo because he displayed great skill in guessing concealed objects by employing the *I Ching*, thereby establishing his expertise in the peripheral arts associated with the book and profound knowledge of the *I Ching* itself. His biography preserves a famous incident:

On one occasion the emperor had his conjurers guess the identity of concealed objects. He put a gecko beneath the cover and had them guess at it, but no one was able to hit it accurately. Shuo, praising himself, said: "I once studied the *I Ching*. I would like a chance to guess it." Thereupon he manipulated the milfoil sticks, arrayed the hexagrams and replied: "Your subject would have thought it to be a dragon, but it has no horns; he would have termed it a snake, but it also has feet. Scurrying, watchful, adept at wall-climbing—if it is not a gecko, it must be a water lizard." "Excellent," the emperor exclaimed, and bestowed fourteen rolls of silk on him. He then had him guess at other objects; one after another Shuo proved accurate and was awarded additonal silk each time.

The biography continues with Shuo's skill being challenged by a court actor who is then vanquished and subjected to Shuo's clever verbal abuse, as well as being beaten as a penalty. Although these incidents are interesting, the text obviously dates considerably later than the Former Han. However, historically the view has sometimes been held that the *Ling Ch'i Ching*'s original conception or minimal origins might still be properly associated with Tung-fang Shuo. While this is extremely doubtful, it indicates the lore and views traditionally associated with the book's genesis.

THE STRUCTURE OF THE TEXT

As a glance at any of the classic's 125 entries will immediately reveal, each one follows the standard format reproduced below:

number   romanized pronunciation   Chinese characters
                 of characters

○ ○ ○ ○   trigraph name

○ ○ ○ ○   image

                 phase energetics

○ ○ ○ ○   associated trigram ° direction

ORACLE
VERSE
COMMENTARIES

By tossing the twelve inscribed disks as described at the end of the introduction, anywhere from none to twelve characters will become visible. The trigraph is fully determined when the characters are arranged into their respective rows by whether they are *shang* (meaning "above," "top," or "upper"), *chung* ("middle"), or *hisa* ("below" or "lower," or by extension, "bottom.") Consulting the text will then reveal the Oracle, Verse, and other material appropriate to the specific configuration, including the interpretive commentaries, added over the centuries, which make the pronouncements more accessible.

In most civilizations oracles normally provide revealed knowledge, often under the guidance of a particular deity or spirit. However, the *Ling Ch'i Ching* presumes that the disks themselves are empowered;

therefore, it is the act of casting the disks within the flux of the cosmos, oriented and refined by one's concrete situation, that determines the trigraph. Unlike African forms of divination, such as Ifa or Yoruba, there are no taboos, spirits, gods, or concrete spiritual entities to contemplate, fear, or propitiate. The process is completely free from specific spiritual constraints or beliefs, being reduced to a concrete, essentially mechanical manipulation—performed with a sincere attitude after proper contemplation—that invariably produces a visual guide to the situational dynamics.

Unlike the *I Ching*, which integrates multiple layers and much disparate material, the text for each trigraph in the *Ling Ch'i Ching* consistently proceeds from the name through the Image and Verses. The Image's theme is generally expanded or restated in concrete terms in the Oracle, often by introducing new images and analogies. The Verse then recapitulates the thematic content, frequently echoing the key images already employed, but also fashioning emotive pictures for intuitive apperception. The Verse thus supplies a vibrant conclusion that predominately evokes moods or feelings, resulting in a felt emotional response, rather than recapturing the Oracle's essence with statements whose applicability might require ponderous interpretation and yet still yield a simple, perhaps sterile analytic understanding. When required by a dire or baleful situation, the Verse may also conclude with an admonishment, enjoining the querent to adhere to virtue, even advising retirement as a defensive measure against the vagaries of the age or disharmonious tendencies.

Structure of the Trigraph

Each line in the trigraph contains four positions, indicated by the four circles. Any number of these positions may be filled, depending on the cast of the disks, and the line may also be absent, resulting from all four disks turning up blank (obverse side up). When visible results are obtained, depending on the number of disks showing in the line, it is referred to as either yin or yang: yang for the odd numbers of one and three, yin for the even numbers of two and the maximum of four. Moreover, somewhat akin to the dynamics of yin and yang in the *I Ching,* a progression or aging is envisioned as the numbers move from smaller to larger. Therefore the possibilities are characterized as follows:

○   young yang; immature yang; single yang; slender yang
○○   young yin; immature yin; two yin; weak yin
○○○   old yang; mature yang; triple yang; great yang
○○○○   old yin; mature yin; cluster of yin; four yin; doubled yin

The main distinction is between the young and mature, the former being energetic and robust but undisciplined, often too youthful unless appropriately constrained; and the latter—the mature aspect—being powerful but also sometimes viewed as spent and exhausted, incapable of being effective. One of the prefaces of the text observes that "the young makes a match for the young, but old yin and great yang are enemies." Furthermore, according to yin/yang dynamics, young yin progresses to mature yin, young yang to mature yang. However, mature yin then reverts to youthful yang, often in the very next trigraph, and mature yang to young yin. All extremes being unstable, every situation is constantly shifting and evolving. The trigraph provides a static portrait of a momentary situation, conceived in terms of an endless cycle of yin and yang locked in their polar tension, one increasing while the other decreases until the point of mutual reversion is reached.

The Oracle

The trigraph's theoretical basis lies in the concept of the Three Realms of Heaven, Man, and Earth, and each of the three lines is designated by them respectively. Schematically:

Top position	Heaven	上
Middle position	Man	中
Bottom position	Earth	下

The characters for each position, previously noted, are shown on the right, meaning above, middle, and below, respectively. Basic theory holds that when the three positions are all present and mutually in harmony, the portents will be auspicious, as will be discussed later.

Each position is also correlated and spoken about in terms of a hierarchy: Heaven symbolizes the ruler; Man, his ministers; and the bottom line, the people. However, the middle position, being the

Realm of Man, also frequently refers to human activity, and therefore the situation among the people. Because the terms are inherently hierarchically related, interpretative possibilities immediately exist—such as the ministers being too strong for the ruler and usurping power—but they are not invariably pursued.

The themes and images for the Oracle and the Verses, as well as the Images themselves, are generally derived from mundane life situations rather than esoteric realms and imaginary structures. While ghosts, and very occasionally spirits or spiritual beings, are sometimes mentioned to characterize the momentary situation with its inherent tendencies, the writings are oriented to the bitter world of dust and dross rather than ethereal dimensions and fantastic visions. The abstract is thus to be understood in the concrete, frequently by analogy rather than declarative statement, although phase energetics are also depicted. Common themes for the Oracle are family situations; aspects of agriculture; animals and animal behavior, especially horses, dogs, and dragons; natural phenomena, including the appearance of the sun and moon, unusual weather conditions, clouds and rain, and the stars; human activities, particularly those crucial to civilization, such as digging wells, hunting, sleeping, praying, childbirth, and observing the mourning rites; the environment, extending to the mountains, rivers, and lakes; and human difficulties, encompassing the encountering of evil, illness, sorrow, obstacles, and misfortune. Virtue remains paramount, and the Sages who advance civilization and the Worthies (or moral exemplars) who help administer it are crucial. Spiritual immortals who have arduously practiced self-cultivation in their quest to escape the realm of toil and travail sometimes appear, and the need to pray and sacrifice in adverse circumstances is often emphasized. However, the Oracle also frequently discourses on the prospects for advancement or penetration, for achieving or receiving riches and happiness, whether merited or not, invariably advising when indications are contrary, when omens portend lying low and cultivating oneself.

In general the Oracle might be seen as depicting situations along life's path, although not particularly imagized in terms of a journey. The operative assumption is essentially Confucian: effort is required to be human, and work is necessary to make a contribution, to fashion civilization, sustain society, and support one's family and clan. Sometimes the situation proves frustrating, and less active or aggressive courses are necessary, but throughout, the book is oriented toward effort and positive accomplishment rather than merely floating along aimlessly. Recourse to Taoism, in terms of quietude, limiting wants, curtailing the power of desire, even being satisfied in poverty, appears as a placative, particularly when events do not appear promising, and finds greatest expression in the Verses and their images.

The Oracle generally characterizes the dynamics of the present situation, presumably revealing knowledge about it derived through synchronicity. While it often offers encouraging pronouncements about the prospects for attaining riches and honor, it primarily depicts the tendencies of the moment. On this succinct basis, the historical commentators proceed to analyze the image formed by the three lines and offer concrete prognostications for specific categories, such as commercial activities, traveling, seeking office, and resolving legal problems. Thus their writings essentially convert the abstract Oracle into a relatively concrete, accessible work of divination. However, it should be noted that the Chinese character *hsiang*, here translated as "oracle," is actually the same graph translated as "image" in the head material. Although the term *hsiang* primarily means "image," it also entails the concept of an oracle, and insofar as the pronouncements are not generally concrete, such as characterize a work of divination (including the temple strips discussed below), to distinguish the two, "oracle" has been employed.

The Verses

The Verses continue the themes of the name, Oracle, and Image, but depict them more poetically, providing visions for intuitive apperception and felt experiencing of a more nebulous and thus encompassing nature. Apart from those that simply repeat the Oracle's themes or blatantly admonish querents to conduct themselves in a certain—usually restrained—manner, many draw on images also commonly found in the naturalistic or Taoist-influenced poetry that subsequently flourished through the T'ang and Sung dynasties. Seasonal depictions are particularly common, such as of flowers and gardens, the coming of spring or arrival of fall; the sun, moon, clouds, and darkness also appear, casting spells of uplift or sorrow; images of journeying, or rivers and mountains, suggest the human quest, the hustle to achieve and act; wanderings to ethereal realms also appear in a few cases, especially where the prospects for action in the ordinary world are not conducive, while tranquil, idealized lands lure the reader;

beautiful women and their enchantments, perfume and fragrances, beckon suggestively; and of course, menials, kings, and various human activities, such as hunting, chasing, drinking, and celebrating are recounted. Emotions often appear, especially sadness and sorrow, as well as sighs about fate—generally condemned as wasteful—occasionally illness, sometimes dreams, and often prayer. Finally, dragons poke out their heads, and other animals often threaten. However, the underlying spirit or worldview is clearly one symbolized by the act of discovering and polishing a rare jewel. When first found, few recognize its worth; only when cut and hewn, polished and glossed, does everyone finally become capable of perceiving its great value. Even though this is a lament, a paradigm for talents unrecognized, it entails an inherent admonition to make effort, to strive—not necessarily to realize any particular achievement, but because striving is the essence of life and the foundation of society, the family, and state.

The *Ling Ch'i Ching*'s inclusion of verses to summarize the prognostication is not unique and may well have been strongly influenced by an earlier work entitled the *I Lin* (*Forest of Change*), written in the first century BCE by Chiao Kan to provide poetic images for all the possible changing lines in every hexagram. Furthermore, another system of divination found extensively in both Taoist and Buddhist temples over the centuries—one that remains popular in modern, westernized Asia even today—determines the querent's fortune through the selection of a slender bamboo stick from a set of either sixty-four or one hundred. This system probably developed some centuries later than *Ling Ch'i Ching* and became popular because illiterate believers could simply inquire about the stick's significance. A monk or temple caretaker would always be available to supply the faithful—who were seeking an answer from the god at whose temple they were worshiping—with a preprinted answer that could be immediately explained. Even today these divination slips remain essentially unchanged, normally providing a general indication of the querent's short-range prospects, as well as concrete answers to a range of specific questions focused on common concerns, such as the prospects for rain, birth of a son, a successful harvest, or making money. The slips also include a one- or two-stanza poem frequently restating the portent in terms of common images and life situations. Two typical examples are:

When winds quiet and the waves calm, you can put out in your
   boat;
The time just mid-autumn, the moon a great wide circle.
No matter the affair, it's unnecessary to be greatly troubled;
Good fortune and riches will by themselves bless your home.

The flowers opened, but half the fruit has withered.
Regretfully, you have uselessly passed the year in vain.
Gradually the sun is setting behind the Western mountains,
Advising you it's fruitless to proceed along the present path.

The Name

Each trigraph has a two-character name appended to it, as well as its
number in the overall sequence. These names sometimes echo those
for trigrams or hexagrams in the *I Ching*, but more often they characterize the situational dynamics with pithy, often enigmatic phrases.
Their understanding is open to interpretation in many cases, particularly when pondering whether the two characters form a conjoined
pair, indicate an adjective-noun relationship, or describe two stages
in unfolding events. These names were probably part of the core material and are frequently reflected in the Oracles themselves.

The Image

Another two-character pair, marked by the same problems of understanding as the name, the Image characterizes the "image" envisioned
as being formed by the disk array and its dynamics. Generally the
image represents another way of expressing the name, unveiling more
of the forces in tension or another aspect of complexity, but sometimes the relationship is more difficult to perceive, causing the commentators some problems. (In at least one of the book's variant
editions, the name and image have been exchanged, suggesting how
inherently interrelated and interchangeable they normally were.)

Phase Energetics

This brief entry summarizes the trigraph's phase energetics in terms
of yin and yang activity. Their interrelationship, potentially complex,

is reduced to a fairly simple characterization, setting the basis for the commentators' views that follow.

Associated Trigram

For each trigraph in which all the lines have at least one disk showing, a trigram consisting of yin or yang in each corresponding position is immediately generated. For those trigraphs that lack any upturned disks in one or more lines, the text has still assigned a trigram. Apart from providing a convenient visual aid for interpreting the yin/yang dynamics, these trigrams immediately invoke the extensive, complex associations that evolved over the centuries before the founding of the Ch'in dynasty in 221 BCE. Frequently identified with Fu Hsi, and traditionally thought to underlie the evolution or creation of the *I Ching* itself (whose hexagrams consist of two trigrams placed one above the other), in the After Heaven sequence employed by the *Ling Ch'i Ching*'s authors, the most important associations are as follows:

☰	Ch'ien	Heaven	Creative, active, strong, firm, the sky, light, the father, northwest. Heaven rules things.
☷	K'un	Earth	Receptive, responsive, yielding, passive, weak, dark, the mother, sustaining, southwest. Earth stores things.
☳	Chen	Thunder	Spring, active, movement, arousing, wood, east. Thunder moves things.
☵	K'an	Water	Clouds, pit, moon, winter, the abysmal, north. Rain moisturizes things.
☶	Ken	Mountain	Thunder, stubbornness, the immovable, the perverse, northeast. The mountain stops things.
☴	Sun	Wind	Wood, gentle, mild, bland, penetrating; southeast. Wind scatters things.

☲   Li   Fire   Lightning, sun, summer, beautiful, dependent, clinging, weapons, south. The sun warms things.

☱   Tui   Lake   Marsh, rain, autumn, joyful, pleasure, west. The lake gives pleasure to things.

Despite being prominently named just above the Oracle, the role of the trigrams in the *Ling Ch'i Ching* is, however, very circumscribed and largely allusive. Neither the Oracle nor the Verses ever specifically refers to the trigrams, although the commentators obviously draw on the wealthy body of *I Ching* theoretical literature, frequently basing their interpretations on aspects of the trigrams and their internal dynamics.

The Commentaries

The four commentaries found in most of the extant texts have been fully provided in the translation because each of them brings a slightly different perspective and focuses on different issues. Moreover, they reflect four different time periods, although there is some question about Yen Yu-ming, who is generally thought to have lived sometime during the Chin period (265–420 CE). The other commentators are Ho Ch'eng-t'ien, a scholar-official noted both for his writings on the rites and his involvement in military affairs, who flourished in the early part of the brief Sung period (420–477 CE); Ch'en Shih-k'ai, a reclusive figure in the Mongolian Yüan dynasty of the fourteenth century; and Liu Chi, who was active at the end of the Yüan and in the early Ming dynasties, and probably edited the commonly available editions as well as providing his own commentary. Yen, Ho, and Ch'en all lived during periods of upheaval, social discord, frequent battles, barbarian invasions, and even foreign domination, when people turned increasingly to Taoist and eventually Buddhist beliefs as a refuge against the misery and pessimism of the times. Consequently, their commentaries tend to be concerned with misfortune and ill-fortune, with the times being out-of-joint and tendencies truly inauspicious. Liu, however, witnessed the establishment of the great Ming dynasty and might be expected to have a more optimistic outlook. The fifth commentary, our own, attempts to explain obscure issues, provide at least minimal contextual material, and explicate the prognostication in more contemporary terms for the convenience of readers who wish to expore the Oracle more directly.

Analysis of the Dynamics

Materials appended to the *Ling Ch'i Ching* suggest that the trigraph should be auspicious when the positions of Heaven and Man are both yang and that of Earth is yin, corresponding to what is perceived as their inherent appropriateness. Accordingly, throughout the text the commentators discuss the "correctness" or "appropriateness" of the lines against this background. Moreover, there is a considerable body of literature regarding the interrelationship and dynamics of yin and yang in the line positions of the *I Ching*, much of which is felt to apply to the *Ling Ch'i Ching*, although not necessarily with full justification. However, while a simple study of the trigraphs indicates that there are some general tendencies, in most cases the pronouncements obtainable from such tendencies are ambivalent, while the perceived tendencies can be used to justify widely ranging results. Consequently, it is still not possible to predict any specific trigraph's interpretation solely from such abstracted principles. However, for the purpose of understanding the images and dynamics recorded in the *Ling Ch'i Ching*, the conceptual trends described below retain a useful, if circumscribed, validity.

In order to discern the most obvious trends in positional dynamics, the trigraphs were classified into four basic categories for auspiciousness, the possibility of a neutral response being specifically excluded: baleful, inauspicious, slightly auspicious or very auspicious. Several people took part in this simplistic effort, which, although often encountering problems for the less decisive cases, yielded the remarkable result that exactly one-half or sixty-two of the trigraphs were considered auspicious, and one-half inauspicious. The last or 125th trigraph, although falling outside the system because it represents the as-yet-unformed, can also be regarded as generally inauspicious.

For the purposes of analysis and discussion, the trigrams associated with each trigraph can be employed as a convenient classifier, insofar as even the missing line positions are subsumed within them. Four of the trigram groupings do not contain any missing positions and therefore consist of closed sets of eight: Li, K'an, Sun, and Tui. Among the remaining four, the trigrams for Heaven and Earth, Ch'ien (all yang) and K'un (all yin), respectively, each subsume eighteen trigraphs with missing positions, while the mixed trigrams of Ken and Chen subsume twelve each. The 125th, or unformed, trigraph is again outside the system and not associated with any trigram.

As predicted by the *Ling Ch'i Ching*'s appended materials, trigraphs termed Sun, characterized by yang in the realms of Heaven and Man, and yin in the realm of Earth—all the positions thus being appropriate and correct—prove to be auspicious without exception. However, no trigraphs missing any positions are included within this category.

Equally auspicious, without exception, are the eight trigraphs with yang in all three positions, symbolized by Ch'ien, the trigram for Heaven. This is particularly to be noted because such extreme dominance by yang should be unstable. Moreover, yang's presence in the realm of Earth is theoretically inappropriate and should therefore presage difficulties, although, as will be discussed below, it usually turns out to be empowering rather than detrimental. When any one of the three positions is absent in a trigraph classified under Heaven, signifying all yang lines, the results are mixed, though slightly more auspicious than not.

Trigraphs characterized as all yin and therefore subsumed under the category of K'un (Earth) are—contrary to expectation—only slightly more often inauspicious. As the appended materials state: "When yin flourishes, intentions differ and become contrary." However, if one of the positions is absent, the trigraph almost always portends difficulty and misfortune in varying degrees, and many offer very dire predictions.

The other trigram groupings are less definitive but have some tendencies, as follows: Li, consisting of yang in Heaven and Earth, with yin in the middle for Man, is auspicious most of the time. The reverse of this situation—yin in Heaven and Earth, yang in the position of Man—is mediocre at best and tends to have equally distributed results between good and ill fortune. Ken—yang in Heaven over yin in the two lower positions—is almost always baleful, although sometimes just inauspicious. However, when one of the positions is absent, it becomes auspicious, even highly auspicious, twice as often as not, a remarkable if puzzling ameliorating effect. Chen, the inversion of Ken—yin in the upper two positions of Heaven and Man, yang in Earth—tends to be inauspicious when all positions are present, and baleful when any one of them is missing.

The principle is sometimes advanced that yang in the position of Heaven should be very auspicious, perhaps constituting the minimum requirement for a trigraph to portend good fortune. Investigating the effect of yang in the various positions yields the following tendencies:

> Heaven: Single or youthful yang in the position of Heaven is indeterminate, found equally in auspicious and inauspicious trigraphs. Three or mature yang in the position of Heaven is found in predominately auspicious trigraphs, roughly in a ratio of three to one.
>
> Man: Single or young yang is auspicious roughly two out of three times. Three yang are good or excellent approximately 90 percent of the time, indicating that the presence of mature yang in the Realm of Man is a defining attribute, always presaging the ability to advance and even overcome obstacles posed by clusters of yin in the other positions of Heaven and Earth.
>
> Earth: Single yang is indeterminate; mature yang is auspicious almost two-thirds of the time.

From the above it can be concluded that young yang, although energetic and robust, is not powerful enough to define the trigraph's portents, whereas mature yang frequently powers the trigraph to auspiciousness.

Conversely, yin at the top, in the position of Heaven, should theoretically be overwhelmingly strong, even a fatal mismatch for any yang positions, and doom the trigraph to ill potent. Accordingly, mature yin, often spoken of as a "cluster of yin," would be even more baleful. A brief analysis reveals the following tendencies for mature yin:

> Heaven: As predicted, it is usually inauspicious, and often baleful, roughly three out of four times.
>
> Man: Inauspicious or baleful slightly more often than not.
>
> Earth: Generally inauspicious or baleful approximately two-thirds of the time, even though, being yin's optimal position, it should be highly auspicious. In contrast, as noted above, yang in the Realm of Earth, although theoretically mismatched and inappropriate, tends to be found in auspicious trigraphs.

Obviously yin's presence does not bode well for the trigraph's prognostication. Moreover, as might be expected, when mature yin occupies more than one position in the trigraph, the results are almost always baleful and never more than slightly auspicious.

The Effect of a Missing Position

In the *Ling Ch'i Ching,* unlike the *I Ching* or *T'ai Hsüan Ching,* a line may be completely absent, indicating a period before the formation of yin or yang. However, the trigraphs are still categorized for trigram purposes as if the position were present; surprisingly, these trigram classification do not invariably substitute a yin equivalent for the missing line. The effects of yin and yang's complete absence in a line can be summarized as follows:

> Heaven: The results are indeterminate.
> Man: The results are extremely dire, being baleful in almost every case. Clearly, the absence of the position of Man is abysmal, precluding the field of realizable possibility.
> Earth: As with Heaven, the results are indeterminate.

When multiple positions are missing, particularly if Heaven should be one of them, paradoxically the trigraphs tend to be auspicious more often than not, even including those in which Man is absent. However, when Man and Earth are missing and only Heaven is present, Heaven lacks a field for action; therefore the trigraph is essentially sterile and inauspicious. Within a set of trigraphs grouped under a particular trigram, when a position is missing, the otherwise baleful nature of an inauspicious trigraph can also be ameliorated, such as in the case of Ken.

METHODS FOR CONSULTING THE ORACLE

Since the *Ling Ch'i Ching* is a work within the grand tradition initiated and defined by the *I Ching,* it can be assumed that the spiritual preparation and mental concentration appropriate to consulting the *I Ching* should be employed before casting the *Ling Ch'i Ching.* No specific ceremony is recommended by the early text, although rituals and incantations became attached to it at some point. Fundamentally, the Chinese divination tradition is pervaded by an inherent sense that through proper concentration the process will produce truer results, although contemporary theories of synchronicity obviate such concerns. Furthermore, the attitude of modern worshipers casting temple sticks is frequently boisterous, skeptical, even almost playful, while yet maintaining an undercurrent of belief. However, if the *Ling Ch'i Ching* is being employed as a tool for self-cultivation and self-knowledge, for discovering clues to one's situation and subconscious, then concentration and simple rituals emphasizing an attitude of respect and sincerity should prove fruitful.

According to the traditional method (now viewed as being of doubtful validity), orthodox *I Ching* divination should be performed with repetitive manipulations of the yarrow sticks (rather than the convenient but inferior three-coin method that became prevalent in recent centuries). The procedure, requiring some twenty minutes to properly complete, forms an essential part of a meditative process that places the inquirer in harmony with the cosmic flux and facilitates intuitive understanding of the response. In contrast, a *Ling Ch'i Ching* trigraph is determined through a single toss of twelve disks on which are inscribed three sets of characters—"upper," "middle," and "lower"— four disks with each character. (Four dimes, nickels, and quarters can be substituted temporarily, with heads indicating the presence of the character and tails its absence, but a set of personalized disks should be created.) Because the mechanical act is so brief, personal practices that increase concentration and enhance intuitive receptiveness— such as nurturing a respectful attitude, burning incense, and geomantically orienting oneself in a secluded space or darkened room—assume even greater importance than when consulting the *I Ching*. In consonance with traditional methods, the following preliminary procedures are suggested but are by no means necessary:

Select a quiet place, or one at least minimally free of loud, disruptive noises. It need not be indoors, and the overall experience can be much enchanced by sitting in a powerful location, one in which the *ch'i* seems conducive. Obviously a shaded glen or quiet wood would be ideal; mountain vistas and sandy beaches, while energized, may prove too spectacular and therefore distracting. Consulting the Oracle late at night, in the silence of a darkened room, can also increase sensitivity if the struggles of the day can be shunted aside, while others may find that early morning, before the quests of the day intrude, proves more conducive.

The querent should face north, with an area for casting the disks immediately in front and the Oracle placed beyond that, toward the north. The burning of incense may prove beneficial; if used, the book can be circled through the incense several times whether concentrating on a particular question or just focusing attention. The twelve disks should be taken up in both hands, followed by a momentary pause, and then cast down on the grass, sand, a personally chosen sacred cloth, small rug, or similar soft material. The disks (or "chess" pieces) with inscribed faces showing are then arranged into their respective rows, and the resulting trigraph is immediately visible. The characters and their appropriate rows are as follows:

上   *shang* / upper   top row

中   *chung* / middle   middle row

下   *hsia* / lower   bottom row

Any disks with characters facing down can either be placed in their appropriate rows or set aside since they do not contribute to the trigraph's formation. (Note that the characters for top and bottom, upper and lower, can be distinguished because the small horizontal component extending from the main vertical line always runs to the right.)

The querent then proceeds to consult the Oracle by locating the trigraph within the text sequence and studying the response. A consultation Chart, appended at the back of this book following the glossary, organizes the trigraphs into five groups based on the top line. These groups are sequenced from one "upper" character showing through all four positions having the character present. The middle line can then be found by reading across the top of the appropriate group, and finally, the bottom line by reading down, yielding the appropriate number for the trigraph. Thereafter the Oracle can be consulted, and after pondering the result, a simple closing ceremony, such as again circling the book through the incense and storing away the disks and throwing cloth might prove psychologically satisfying.

The Disks

Instructions for creating the disks for a *Ling Ch'i Ching* casting—which may reflect the true tradition but are obviously later than the original core text—indicate that these disks should preferably be fashioned from wood cut from a tree that has been struck by lightning.

Obviously the lightning strike, being the essence of yang, is understood as empowering the wood (which is yin), making it receptive to the process of divination, just as persons struck by lightning acquired shamanistic powers in many tribal societies. Moreover, wood struck by lightning was thought to inherently possess special powers in warding off evil spirits and ghosts, both also falling into the category of yin. However, lacking such naturally empowered wood, the disks or chesspieces can be fashioned from three tree species: date, catalpa, and sandalwood. Furthermore, the disks should actually be cut on the first day (*chia-tzu*) in the sixty-day cycle still found in the readily available almanacs prepared according to the traditional Chinese lunar calendar. Every ten days thereafter, another step is performed: on the eleventh day, the characters should be written; on the twenty-first they should be carved out; on the thirty-first, filled in with bright red; on the forty-first, placed in their container; and on the fifty-first, an appropriate ceremony should be held. Thereafter they can be employed for divination, but castings should not be made on the six days in the sixty-day cycle designated by the heavenly stem *wu*.

Theory aside, common practice over the centuries and in all the sets seen employed in Asia today is to use wood with inscribed red characters. The choice of wood, being vegetative (just like the yarrow stalks used for the *I Ching*) is obviously significant. Wooden checkers would make an excellent choice, although any available uniform disks—even plastic poker chips or quarters, symbolic of the contemporary age—can perhaps suffice. To preserve the inherent receptivity of wood, it should never be lacquered or polished. Moreover, if you cut the disks from a readily available wooden dowel, such as 1⅜" or 1½" stock—approximately the modern equivalent to the size traditionally recommended—avoid making them too thick. Otherwise, the toss may prove indeterminate because one or more of the disks may remain standing on edge, with unknown implications other than perhaps that the time is incorrect or the inquiry inappropriate. A thickness of about 25 percent of the diameter is best using tree species of a softer wood. Care should be taken in the process, both to avoid injury and to ensure the proper degree of sincerity, and in the absence of a lunar calendar, initiated on a day felt to be empowered and auspicious.

On Consulting the Oracle

The texts in the Chinese divination tradition are essentially benign. They are not works that were or needed to be consulted because of evil being inflicted, illness being suffered, or fears of the pernicious activities of demons, witches, or other people. Questions of a divinatory—that is, fortunetelling—nature can be posed, such as "Is this an appropriate time to buy property?" Such questions are best framed in a general, rather than specific, sense. An example of an inappropriately specific query might be "Would this be a good stock to buy now?" (Even though the *Ling Ch'i Ching* was obviously employed in this fashion, in providing this translation we explicitly disclaim that the results thus obtained have any validity and advise against consulting the text for making important concrete decisions. However, the matter of belief is an individual one, and readers must determine the book's utility and validity within the framework of their own lives.) Employing the core text—the Oracle and the Verse—for oracular purposes, for clues to the contemporary situation and indications of the unfolding flux of events in the ancient way, with proper precautions, might prove illuminating and yield significant self-knowledge.

The responses are largely self-explanatory, and the querent should focus on the original core of the Oracles and Verses, and study the trigraphs that precede and follow the one obtained by the casting for further insights, as well as the glossary for historical and cultural explanations of many terms. Although the commentators provide well-founded explanations, their views are interpretations, removed by many centuries from the time of original composition and therefore affected by their own experiences and cultural mind-set, including Buddhism which was introduced and began to flourish only after the core material was completed. Contemplating the response, especially the Verse, with an open mind will often result in sudden understanding, in perceiving relevance to life's context. Furthermore, the environment of the original writer, the social world of imperial China, an agricultural society dominated by the contending views of Confucianism and Taoism, should be recalled when attempting to penetrate otherwise opaque statements. Their cosmic view was naturalistic; Heaven, while sometimes reactive, does not interfere in human life. Things inexorably continue in cycles and patterns because that is the nature of the world, not because it is being willed. The aim is to orient oneself with the flux, and harmonize with seasonal activity, so as to avoid frustrating struggles and to exploit opportune moments. Stated simply, it would be foolish to plant crops with the first frosts of fall or, as an ancient anecdote relates, to pull on the young rice shoots in spring with the hope of hurrying their growth. It was of course a male-dominated society, both in theory and practice, and therefore—despite much effort and consciousness to the contrary—not so different from today except in degree. However, female readers consulting the *Ling Ch'i Ching* would best avoid resentful, negative responses to male-tinged pronouncements and instead ponder the dynamics portrayed in the situation, the forces symbolically structured within the constrained mind-set of the *Ling Ch'i Ching*, for extractable paradigms.

LING CH'I CHING

TA T'UNG 大通

○ ○ ○ (上)
○ ○ ○ (中)
○ ○ ○ (下)

Great Penetration
The image of ascending and soaring
Pure yang gains command
Ch'ien (Heaven) ∘ Northwest

ORACLE

From the small to the great, nothing is endangered. From below, one ascends to the heights, subsequently attaining riches and prominence. It would be appropriate to embark on a distant journey. It would not be advantageous to lie in concealment or make secret plans.

VERSE

> Changing, the leopard completes its dazzled markings;
> Riding dragons, blessings arrive of themselves.
> Stark naked, one receives riches and honor;
> Every affair can again be renewed.

COMMENTARIES

YEN ∘ Desiring the great with the small, you can attain riches and prominence. If you dwell in the great and desire the small, there will be danger and destruction. Moreover, Heaven and Earth have already assumed their positions, while the Sage makes a triad with them. The great principles are in their primordial stages, the Original Source has been opened and a beginning forged. Thus it says, "from below one ascends to the heights." In establishing your merit and creating regulations, there is nothing in which you will not excel.

You cannot make secret plans; dark plots are inappropriate. It might be somewhat difficult to cure old maladies and hard to unite prospective parties in marriage because this trigraph is pure yang. It portends that the traveler will not yet return; the imprisoned will get out; and commercial activities will be profitable.

Ho ◦ Those serving in bureaucratic positions can expect promotions. It is appropriate to be conspicuous, inappropriate to be hidden. It is not appropriate for the ill to dwell in dark places; it would be auspicious for them to go out and escape them. "Mouths and tongues" (quarrels) will not prove harmful. Remain in residence and preserve the constant. Sending the army forth would be auspicious; engaging in battle, it will be victorious. The pregnant will give birth to a male. Agriculture, sericulture, fishing, and hunting will realize great harvests and lucky profits.

Ch'en ◦ The start of single *ch'i*, the beginning of the Three Talents of Heaven, Earth, and Man. Pure yang attains vigor, advancing, endlessly advancing, uniting in a body with Ch'ien (Heaven). Thus the Oracle speaks as it does, for the Original Source is penetrating.

Liu ◦ From the small to the great, yang is beginning to give life. When three people are of the same mind, it is appropriate for them to roam about together. "It is not advantageous to lie in concealment or make secret plans," for the Tao is luminous and clear.

In this trigraph the three positions are all yang. These young yang are just growing. Thus they create the image of "from the small attaining the great, from below ascending to the heights." When the querent obtains it, managing affairs, commencing a career, seeking fame, and searching for opportunities to profit will all be auspicious. Those involved in lawsuits ought to adhere to the Tao of justice and seek the straightforward. It is auspicious for travelers, but they will not yet return. You cannot engage in dark plots or crafty, secret affairs. The ill might grow worse; if they go outside to escape, it will be auspicious.

Sawyer ◦ The first trigraph echoes and correlates with Ch'ien, the first hexagram of the *I Ching*. However, while both are all yang, the nature of "Great Penetration" is purely youthful, spontaneous, and benign. Incipient yang is beginning to stir, to overflow and stimulate all things, nurturing growth and life's resurgence. While youthful yang, unbridled, may still hurdle into disaster, it lacks the destructive, vaguely dark potential of old yang. Yang, being light and fiery, ascends and soars. Thus it is the time for initiating plans, commencing action, and going forth, being visible and active rather than secretive and passive. However, those unsure of their course would best heed Ho's advice to "remain in residence and preserve the constant," emulating the practice of the ancient sages who constrained themselves during times of great seasonal instability and transformation.

2 CHIEN T'AI 漸 泰

Gradual Peace
The image of waiting for the time
Yin correctly obtains its position
Sun (Wind) ∘ Southeast

ORACLE

Dwell peacefully, arrange your enterprises, and manage your real-estate holdings, for then there will be gain, resulting in riches and honor as well. A salaried bureaucratic position will not yet be attained.

VERSE

> Marvelous things approach the gate door,
> Golden pheasants glitter in the sun.
> Yin and yang propitiously assist each other;
> Solitary, one will return astride a multihued, fabulous bird.

COMMENTARIES

YEN ∘ If you tranquilize your mind and settle your intentions in order to await the proper season and time, then all will be auspicious.

If you anxiously expect things, then you will not be in harmony. Moreover, yin is already in its correct position; the Tao of Earth is thereby realized. This is the image of human affairs, of dwelling in one's occupation. Seeking office, searching for material wealth, business enterprises, agriculture, and sericulture will all be equally auspicious. Marriage arrangements will at first be difficult, later easy. A traveler ought to arrive. Remain in residence, tranquil and peaceful. Official affairs will not prove successful. Those imprisoned in criminal matters, through great effort, will be released.

Ho ∘ A traveler coming from afar should arrive. The pregnant will give birth to a male. Those entangled in official affairs or criminal matters will be pardoned and escape. Illnesses will not be fatal. All affairs are auspicious.

CH'EN ∘ The positions of Heaven and Man are both yang; the Tao of Earth is pliant and beautiful. The yin in Earth's position has not yet attained the point of flourishing; above and below respond to each other.

LIU ∘ "If you dwell peacefully and manage your real-estate holdings"—this stems from the hard and soft in the trigraph having been obtained. If you do not wish for external things, you will receive good fortune in full.

In this trigraph two yang are in the top positions, while one yin occupies the bottom; the talents appropriate to all three positions are accordingly realized. Thus it conveys the image of becoming both rich and honored. It is appropriate to protect and preserve; you cannot engage in inexhaustible seeking. Only then will it be auspicious. Family affairs and marriage arrangements will be successful; official matters will not be disruptive. The traveler will return imminently. A sought-after office will be obtained, but you will not yet be entrusted with the management of affairs. Things heard about, apparently worrisome, will not prove troublesome. Illnesses, although not yet cured, might not be harmful.

SAWYER ∘ The two characters in this trigraph's title allude to the *I Ching,* where they are found as the names of hexagrams 53 and 11, respectively. The first character, translated as "gradual," describes the dynamics of subtle, ongoing increase, perhaps best imagized as being like water gradually accumulating in a bucket from a heavily dripping faucet. It clearly entails the feeling of continuity, of relentlessness. The second character in the title, translated as "peace" in consonance with the tenor of the trigraph, could equally well be rendered as "prosperity." Both meanings are clearly intended because it is the period of spring when yang's activity stimulates the growth of all things. A natural, tranquil order of developing prosperity thus results, and people obtaining this trigraph accordingly find themselves oriented in the midst of burgeoning growth. Thus virtually every activity proves auspicious, but since affairs have only just been initiated, care should be exercised to allow their growth to proceed naturally, in accord with the dynamics of life unfolding, rather than vigorously overstepping the constraints of seasonal evolution to forcefully pursue external things.

3 CHI CH'ING 吉慶

Auspicious Blessings
The image of wealth and prosperity
Pure yang attains its position
Ch'ien (Heaven) ∘ Northwest

ORACLE

Eminent and awesome, the family has gold and silk. All things are provided, affairs are well managed. Unsought, things are obtained.

VERSE

> Nobles congregate before the gate,
> The family frequently encounters the *ch'i* of multiple
>   happiness.
> Profits and emoluments naturally become wealth and honor,
> Throughout their lives all things are perfectly complete.

COMMENTARIES

YEN ◦ Since they have gold and silk it is unnecessary to seek them. Remaining in residence will be auspicious. The traveler will not yet return. Moreover, Heaven gives birth to the ten thousand things; its patterns fully flourish in them. Without being actively managed, they are naturally completed and ordered. This trigraph is pure yang; marital relations will not be harmonious. The criminally imprisoned will be found innocent. Agriculture and sericulture will both be profitable; all other affairs will be auspicious.

HO ◦ The traveler is about to arrive. The pregnant will give birth to a male. Commercial activities will be profitable. Legal entanglements will be pardoned. Attempts to arrest brigands will certainly result in their capture.

CH'EN ◦ All three positions are yang, but only the lowest one is flourishing. It is the image of fullness and substance in the Tao of Earth. Above and below are both free of any deficiency.

LIU ◦ "Eminent and awesome"—the trigraph is pure yang. "The family has gold and silk"—the Tao of Earth is glorious. "All things are provided, affairs are well managed"—their power flourishes and is strong. "Unsought, things are obtained"—fruit and vegetation are abundant.

In this trigraph there are three yang, and the bottom position is flourishing. The Tao of Earth produces things; thus gold and silk are overflowing, things and affairs are well managed. Flourishing yang has its root in the lower position, while young yang prospers at the top, like the base of a tree being vigorous and its fruit abundant. Thus it is the image of obtaining without seeking. When the querent obtains it, whatever affairs are undertaken will be auspicious. Real-estate transactions might be the most profitable. In warfare there will be achievement and great victory. Pursuing an escapee will certainly result in capture. Only if one is divining about lawsuits will there have to be expenditures before victory. Divining about illness would be somewhat inauspicious. It is not possible to successfully flee and lie in hiding.

SAWYER ◦ Like the first trigraph, all three lines are yang and therefore powerful and auspicious. More important, even though yin would be appropriate in the lowest position, the base is still envisioned as flourishing and thereby making all things possible. Since Earth, here strong, is fruitful of itself at the appropriate time, without human interference or Heaven's ongoing management, this trigraph presages the natural fruition of projects just now in hand. (Perhaps Liu's view is premature: the fruit has not yet appeared, rather than already burgeoning on the tree, for it is young yang, not great or old yang, that lies in the top position. In some editions Ch'en asserts that this is still a deficient position, just as suggested by the young yang in the position of Man. However, being in harmony with the ascendancy of yang should lead to extraordinary results and surpassing happiness, all without extreme exertion.)

4 *Fu Sheng* 富盛

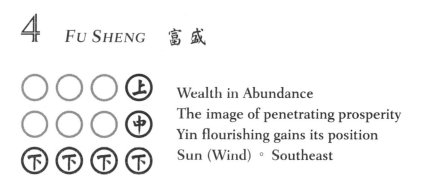

Wealth in Abundance
The image of penetrating prosperity
Yin flourishing gains its position
Sun (Wind) ∘ Southeast

Oracle

Wealth in abundance, the pinnacle of nobility. The Tao of Heaven reverts. Following the cycle, above and below ebb and flow with the time. Your descendants will be reckoned by myriads and millions.

Verse

> The light boat meets the waves as if flying along,
> Whatever is sought, the hundred affairs, attain their time.
> Moreover, sharing the road with the noble,
> Henceforth a hundred blessings follow of their own accord.

COMMENTARIES

YEN ∘ Those who dwell in wealth and honor, unforgetting of poverty and meanness, will leave their names to posterity. Conversely, those unable to be humble and retiring will inevitably be overturned. The traveler has been in a distant place for a long time and just started to return. Moreover, in changing from two yin in the second trigraph to four yin in the lowest here, the Tao of Earth is again complete. The pattern of riches and honor thereby realizes its extremity. Thus those who dwell in fullness will invariably become deficient, those who dwell on high will inevitably be endangered. Thus the Oracle says "reverts." If the ebb and flow, repleteness and vacuity are not contrary to the time, throughout the cycle you will invariably be able to preserve your body and keep your name intact, while the benefits will extend to your descendants.

Under this trigraph it would be appropriate to be humble and retiring. It will be difficult for the imprisoned to get out. The person now expected will be somewhat late. The traveler has not yet set out.

HO ∘ Illness will be cured but perhaps slowly. It would be appropriate to sacrifice to the spirits of Heaven and seek blessings. Holding a marriage ceremony would be auspicious. It is not appropriate to greedily accumulate material things. Those traveling far away should not advance any further. It would be appropriate to seek legal officials to resolve verbal disputes and official entanglements.

CH'EN ∘ Two yang in the upper positions, yin flourishing at the bottom; the Tao of Earth is full but unopposed by the top positions.

LIU ∘ "Wealth in abundance, the pinnacle of nobility"—the family's enterprises are successful. Follow the turning of above and below in order to preserve fullness. It would be appropriate for your descendants to avoid conflict.

In this trigraph two young yang are in the top positions, while old yang occupies the bottom. Upper and lower attain their positions. They have position, they have things, riches and honor flourish in the extreme—the image of the unsurpassable. Thus it is appropriate to follow the revolutions, accord with the time, and know the point of sufficiency. Those who are not reckless can preserve what has already been achieved, and their descendants will continue to conserve it without loss.

Divining about marriage arrangements would be auspicious. Seeking office, searching for wealth, and affairs that were hoped for have already all gained favorable results that cannot be exceeded. If the expected traveler stops, it will be auspicious. If the compromise previously sought in official affairs should be disavowed, there will be regret. Illnesses will soon be cured. Military attacks should not be recklessly undertaken: it would be appropriate to determine what is possible and stop, for then it will be auspicious. People being sought are not trustworthy.

Now when affairs have reached the pinnacle, they must revert. What had been auspicious will then be inauspicious; what had been inauspicious will then be auspicious.

SAWYER ○ This trigraph echoes fundamental themes found in the *I Ching* and the classic work of Taoism known as the *Tao Te Ching* in warning that all affairs—being inherently unstable—tend to revert to their opposites. The four disks upturned in the Tao of Earth symbolize old or mature yin. They represent strength and abundance, the fruitfulness that Earth can bestow. However, their time is limited; they will soon evolve to the young yang seen in the base of the next trigraph. Natural patterns are of course inescapable; however, care can be exercised to ensure that one doesn't hasten the process by reaching the pinnacle and then exceeding it! Better to exercise restraint and know the point of sufficiency, maintaining awareness and enjoying constraint, as these famous verses from the *Tao Te Ching* advise:

> To hold and overfill something is not as good as stopping;
> When something is forged and sharpened, it cannot be
>   preserved for long.
> When gold and jade fill a hall, no one is able to protect it.
> When the rich and honored are arrogant, they bring forth
>   calamity.
> Achievements complete, the person withdraws—this is the Tao
>   of Heaven.
>
> (chapter 9)

> Among misfortunes none exceed not knowing the point of
>   sufficiency;

Among calamities none exceed desiring gain.
Thus one who experiences the sufficiency of knowing
   sufficiency will always be content.

(chapter 46)

5   LE TAO   樂 道

○○○ 上
○○ 中 中   Tao of Pleasure
○○○ 下

Tao of Pleasure
The image of surprise and delight
Yang firm, yin pliant
Li (Fire) ○ True south

ORACLE

Externally firm, internally pliant, harmoniously uniting, complete in
oneself. Nourish your nature, preserve your destiny, and travel about
with the spirits.

VERSE

Two people, harmoniously united, experience the joy of
   happiness,
Whatever they seek, the affairs they plan, can be successful.
Even though a green snake momentarily causes turbulence,
In the end it will not harm their profit or fame.

COMMENTARIES

YEN ○ What is sought is perversely inappropriate. Cultivate virtue,
preserve yourself, that's all. For illnesses that have not yet been cured,
it would be appropriate to offer sacrifice, complaining about the problem, and seek blessings without worrying. The traveler is not yet returning. For bureaucratic officials, no advancement. Official affairs
will not be successful. It will be difficult for the imprisoned to get out.

Moreover, marriage arrangements will be auspicious; the pregnant will give birth to a male. The ill should pray for the intercession of the spirits.

HO ∘ Holding a marriage ceremony would be auspicious; the pregnant will give birth to a male. Commercial activities will be profitable. Military campaigns would be extremely auspicious. Moreover, yin dwells in yang's position, thus the exterior is firm. It would not be appropriate to forcefully go forward, but rather to conserve life, nurture your nature, and preserve your destiny. It is the image of self-nourishing.

CH'EN ∘ The upper and lower positions are both yang; in the middle the Tao of Man is dark and weak, unable to take action. It is the image of embracing the pliant and nourishing one's nature. But yin dwells in yang's position—both frightening and joyous!

LIU ∘ "Externally firm, internally pliant"—it is appropriate to join with others. By planning well and being cautious in affairs, you will be able to preserve yourself intact. "Traveling about with the spirits" likewise is not inauspicious.

In this trigraph a single yin dwells amidst two yang, thus creating "external firmness, inner pliancy." When yin occupies yang's position in the middle, it is not appropriate to be active. Thus you ought to harmoniously unite all around. If you are cautious about preserving and protecting yourself, it will be auspicious. If divining about illness, there seem to be evil emanations. Reverently seeking the intercession of the spirits would be auspicious. Lawsuits will not be successful. Marriage ceremonies and commercial activities are auspicious. If you send the army forth, they will not engage in battle. It will be difficult for the imprisoned to get out. In judging affairs, there will be many specious and deceptive claims. It would not be appropriate to concoct secret plans.

SAWYER ∘ In this trigraph the determining factor is perceived to be the inner weakness embodied within a strong exterior that results from pliant yin being sandwiched between two yang. Against a more ideal "inner strength—outer pliancy" paradigm, the dynamics emphasize the mismatch and a need to cultivate the interior. All three positions are in fact occupied by youthful manifestations, signifying energy that may be undisciplined, possibly echoing the dangers posed by youthful folly frequently described in the *I Ching*. At the same time, the prospects are not inauspicious; rather, the situation conveys an impression of surprising joy, of finding delight in associations with others that can simultaneously further one's own development. However, the core remains the relative need for self-cultivation and being cautious that this sort of forceful exterior will not inappropriately entangle the inner spirit before it has gained the requisite balance.

6 CHING PU 驚怖

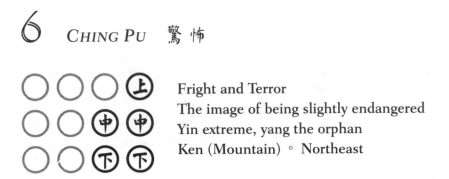

Fright and Terror
The image of being slightly endangered
Yin extreme, yang the orphan
Ken (Mountain) ∘ Northeast

ORACLE

A rooster crows at morning, mounting the roof and stretching his neck. The hens below the wall are frightened by a fox. Breaking off his crowing, the rooster comes to the rescue. He manages to avoid loss and being overturned.

VERSE

> In the darkness beware of falling into a pit.
> The rivers and seas give rise to wind and waves.
> Thinking back to times of happiness,
> I turn again to bitter labors.

COMMENTARIES

YEN ∘ All affairs, although troubled in the beginning, will end without further anxiety. In general, business enterprises and the hundred affairs will all at first be virtually ruined but later achieve success. The traveler will not yet return. Illnesses should be promptly treated. Moreover, the top line's response to yin at the bottom is at the beginning and is interfered with by yin in the middle, so the top and bottom cannot sustain each other. This results in being frightened. Although dwelling on high and treading in danger, in the end there will be regulation and strong control.

"Breaking off his crowing, he comes to the rescue; he manages to avoid misfortune and defeat"—the rooster belongs to yang, the hens to yin. As for chicken thieves, there are none like the fox. This trigraph signifies worry and fright. Official affairs will not be successful. Only if the imprisoned have some power will they be released.

Ho ∘ The distant traveler encounters brigands. Seeking office, marriage arrangements, and commercial activities will not be advantageous. Borrowing money and searching for profits will prove difficult. Whatever you seek, the results will be contrary to your inclinations. Agricultural crops will not be harvested. Every affair will at first be worrisome, later joyous.

Ch'en ∘ Yang rules security; yin rules danger. Two yin lie in the middle; the single yang at the top is insufficient to depend on. In addition there are two yin below.

Liu ∘ One male, two females, inevitably there will be conflict. Hard, robust yang is at the top; the soft is unable to encroach on it. Yin at the bottom accords with its movement and responds correctly, preserving without being overturned.

In this trigraph, young yang dwells in the honored position, while the two yin below both want to follow it. The top begins to respond but is interfered with in the middle. Thus it takes the image of the rooster mounting the roof while the hens below are frightened by the fox. Yet yang occupies the top position and acts as the ruler, while the yin in the middle is not yet flourishing. Thus they finally unite without being harmed or overturned.

As for any affairs divined about: by expending great effort, at first there will be danger, later security; at first worry, later happiness. The traveler is returning but has obstacles en route. If the army goes forth, it will be put in fear. In cases of illness, it would be appropriate to urgently consult a physician. Seeking office, marriage arrangements, and other hoped-for affairs are all facilitated by people. Accordingly, you must rely on some powerful personage. At first everything will be difficult, but later your objectives will be attained.

SAWYER ∘ The situation depicted by the Oracle is one of mortal danger for the hens, consonant with the trigraph's name, "Fright and Terror." If the querent identifies with the rooster, and thus the youthful power presented by yang in Heaven, a resolve to action will vanquish threats and wrest good results. However, the general tenor is more with the hens, and thus with the need for rescue, or at least assistance from a powerful figure. Depending on your sphere of action, this may be a political figure, financial executive, mentor, or even a dreaded superior. Among the commentators, Ho is particularly pessimistic (or perhaps realistic), while Yen and Liu emphasize the dictum that intense effort will win through.

This trigraph exemplifies the greater importance placed on the response between Heaven and Earth, for it emphasizes that the two yin between them "interfere with the responses," rather than also according with Heaven and uniting with Earth in a conjoined response. (Young yang and young yin are generally held to match or be responsive. In the *I Ching*'s conceptualization, submissive yin in the position of Man could be viewed as auspicious—signifying voluntary compliance with the will of Heaven—or inauspicious, being too weak and insubstantial. This illustrates the impossibility of accurately predicting oracle values simply from apparent dynamics because of the complexity of the framer's original vision.) Furthermore, while the base is weak—always a sign of instability—being young yin, it should have a submissive character, willingly yielding to yang's possibly inexperienced direction. It would be inappropriate to envision the trigraph as suggesting that domination by the ruler, or submitting to domination, would resolve the difficulties. The ruler's position is also symbolized as Heaven, and Heaven appropriately provides guidance and assistance to those maintaining the proper relationship with it.

7 NIEN FENG 年豐

○○○㊤
○○㊥㊥
○㊦㊦㊦

Year of Abundance
The image of agriculture being
    appropriate
Yin going, yang coming
Li (Fire) ∘ True south

ORACLE

The first month, at noon. The year star is in the Heavenly Mansion of Ta-liang. An eastern wind breaks the freeze. It is appropriate for agriculture and sericulture. At the end of the year an abundant harvest, happiness and pleasure overflowing.

VERSE

Repressive *ch'i* has fully melted away;
Spring comes, the myriad things are glorious.
Agriculture and sericulture are appropriate to your house;
Plowing and digging, take pleasure in vegetative life.

COMMENTARIES

YEN ∘ What you seek will be appropriate on the years, months, days, and hours [designated by the cyclic characters] *tzu wu mao yu*, for then it will be auspicious. However, the response will be slightly tardy. Apart from [initiating affairs on] these years, months, days, and hours, you will not be successful. If divining about agriculture and sericulture, there is nothing that will not be profitable. Moreover, as for the image of "yin going, yang coming," when the Great Year star is in the Heavenly Mansion called *yu*, it is referred to as Ta-liang for that year. The saying has it, "When the Great Year star is in *yu*, begging for broth one gets wine!" This speaks about the abundance.

Under this trigraph, agriculture and sericulture are auspicious. If inquiring about an official position, you will not yet be successful. However, holding office will be free from worries. Any illness will not entail suffering.

Ho ○ Traveling by either water or land; marriage arrangements; and joining with others are all highly auspicious. The traveler has been detained. The imprisoned will eventually get out.

CH'EN ○ In the upper two positions, yin at the top and yang in the middle respond to each other, while three yang are in Earth's position. It is the image of the Tao of Earth full and substantial.

LIU ○ Heaven and Man cooperate harmoniously; yin follows yang. Earth being abundant and overflowing, this trigraph is appropriate for agriculture and sericulture. Whenever the year is signified by *wu* or *yu*, the profits will be unstoppable.

In this trigraph, young yang is at the top and young yin occupies the middle. Accordingly, the positions of Heaven and Man are realized, while flourishing yang occupies the position of Earth. The upper is harmonious, the lower abundant and rich; therefore it is appropriate to agriculture and sericulture.

The "first month" in the Oracle refers to the beginning line. Taliang is the year star's designation when in the Heavenly Mansion of *yu*. The lower three yang in the trigraph's body are taken as the trigram *Li*, which is correlated with *wu*. The two yin in the middle are taken as the trigram *Tui*, which is correlated with *yu*. Whatever might be divined about will be as desired, and the response will be in the years, months, and days designated by *wu* and *yu*, or when the year star is in the Heavenly Mansion of *yu*.

SAWYER ○ This trigraph provides a glimpse into Chinese astrological thinking, for it correlates the auspiciousness of future undertakings with dates designated by certain characters within the Chinese calendrical system. In the traditional system, times and dates are indicated by the concurrent running of two cycles of characters, the Ten Heavenly Stems and the Twelve Earthly Branches. Beginning with the first entry in each series, they are consecutively paired until all ten stems have been employed; thereafter the heavenly cycle is repeated, and the Earthly Branches are eventually similarly recycled. This concurrent pairing of ten and twelve produces a sixty-term cycle that can enumerate days and years. (Double hours are counted by the Twelve Earthly Branches.) Meanwhile, each year had another rubric derived from the position of Jupiter, the year star, among the Heavenly Mansions; it is to this that "Ta-liang" refers. Accordingly, if the divination happens to have been performed on a day whose calendrical designation includes the Earthly Branch of *yu,* or between the hours of 5 P.M. and 7 P.M., it will be extremely auspicious. Alternatively viewed, only events that might be initiated on such a day (which recurs every sixty days) or within the appropriate year in the cycle of twelve will be auspicious. However, the trigraph's nature and its placement at spring's unfolding within the twenty-four calendrical periods of the agricultural or lunar year presages great success for agriculturally based enterprises.

8   *Hsiao Chieh*   小 戒

Slight Wariness
The image of cautious prevention
Yin flourishing conquers yang
Ken (Mountain) ◦ Northeast

Oracle

Misfortune arises from below. Be wary and cautious against youthful servants secretly plotting and subversively uniting, about to instigate some harmful action.

Verse

When the axe is lost, where will the firewood be?
The clan feels anxious about incendiary disaster.
Money and wealth will be lost in the end.
One must also guard against youthful servants.

COMMENTARIES

YEN ∘ Although yang has gained its position at the top, it is plotted against by a host of yin at the bottom. Thus it says "there are youthful servants secretly plotting, about to do harm." It would be appropriate to take precautions against those around you. Under this trigraph, the hundred affairs are all worrisome but will not result in great balefulness. Official affairs will certainly be successful. It will be difficult for the imprisoned to get out because yang is weak.

HO ∘ The traveler meets robbers. Those at home are anxious. Youthful servants cause harm; gathering together they argue. Affairs sought will not proceed expeditiously. Those suffering from illness may have been cursed by subordinates.

CH'EN ∘ Even though the top and middle two positions are mutually appropriate, the four yin below flourish excessively. The Tao of Man is already weak. It is the image of numerous menials encroaching on each other.

LIU ∘ Solitary yang at the top, its powers few and weak. Yin flourishes at the bottom: anxiety about servants.

In this trigraph a single yang occupies the top position, while a host of yin lie below. In the middle position is young yin; pliant and weak, it is unable to control the bottom, thus indicating that misfortune will arise from below. It is the image of taking precautions against youthful servants. Nothing divined about will be advantageous. This trigraph and the sixth one both have a single yang occupying the top position, but the Oracle is not the same. In the sixth one the lowest position is young yin. Accordingly, there is compliance with the intent of the upper, but obstruction in the middle. However, in this one, old yin's power below, unrestrained, cannot be governed by the middle. It is similar to a weak husband or a young wife controlling a household: willful slaves and ruthless maids will not follow the master's orders. The balefulness is clearly apparent.

SAWYER ∘ While the tone of the commentators seems strident, the danger portrayed by the trigraph is actually minimal. What is portended is not a bloody palace revolution or even local mutiny, but obstinacy, disobedience, willfulness, or perhaps even larceny and flight. Otherwise, the trigraph's name could not be the reasonably mild "Slight Wariness." The lesson, of course, should be extrapolated to contemporary hierarchical situations of every type. The danger is posed by subordinates, by anyone—whether contractually or otherwise—even temporarily in relationship with you.

9 TE CHIH 得志

Realizing Ambition
The image of self-sufficiency
Pure yang suffuses all the positions
Ch'ien (Heaven) ◦ Northwest

ORACLE

Conspicuously realizing one's ambitions, according with the time, material wealth comes and is ample for use. No lack of minions.

VERSE

When fate and time cohere,
Cloud dragons and wind tigers will follow.
Selflessly undertaking the responsibilities of official rank,
One's fame will reach the palaces of emperors and kings.

COMMENTARIES

YEN ◦ Ambitions and inclinations have already been realized, things are also ample for use. Furthermore, one has minions. Moreover, pure yang exerts authority; it is the image of realizing one's ambitions. If you focus your mind selflessly, material wealth will be fully ample for use. Han Fei-tzu says, "King Wen attacked Ch'ung. When he had reached the wastes of Huang-chu, the laces on his leather boot came untied. Looking to his left and right, they were all worthies; there was

45

no one who could be ordered to tie it. Thereupon he did it himself." This is the Tao of the highest civic principles held by the perfected and worthy.

H o ∘ Those serving in bureaucratic offices will be granted generous salaries. A traveler will arrive from afar. Illnesses should improve by themselves. The imprisoned will manage to get out. The pregnant will give birth to a male. Commercial activities will be profitable. It is the image of copiously obtaining whatever is sought.

C H ' E N ∘ Three yang in the middle: The image of the Tao of Man fully complete; the upper and lower positions do not destroy it.

L I U ∘ The Virtue of the Dragon exactly in the middle, perfectly according with the time. Upper and lower cooperatively follow, being adequate to take action.

In this trigraph, flourishing yang occupies the middle position, attaining its ambitions and realizing the time, while in the upper and lower positions young yang joins with it in the same mind. What worry is there that material goods will be insufficient for use or that minions will be lacking? When the querent obtains the trigraph, even without seeking there is nothing that will not be realized. It is a very auspicious trigraph!

S A W Y E R ∘ The trigraph's strength lies with the Tao of Man; therefore, human activities should all be promising and auspicious. Heaven, with a single yang, may be seen as offering appropriate guidance, while Earth, although somewhat inappropriate, is still sustaining. However, the Image and Verse emphasize the constraints of temporality: even the greatest talent, lacking opportunity, failing to accord with the time or meet the right moment, remains unrealized. Fortunately, this should not be the case when the querent obtains this trigraph.

10   *SHIH SUI*   事 遂

Affairs Proceeding
The image of imminent prosperity
Yin and yang mutually unite
Sun (Wind) ∘ Southeast

ORACLE

In the past, matters did not proceed as desired; now you will be able to follow your ambitions. The myriad affairs attain their patterns; intelligently and clearly take action.

VERSE

> Like the dust ever accumulating, he has long awaited the hour;
> In a darkened window, amid loneliness, who knows of him?
> When the moment evolves, those bearing swords look to each other;
> Gaining profits and attaining fame always have their time.

COMMENTARIES

YEN ∘ In beginning to realize your ambitions, it would be appropriate to take loyalty and uprightness as your foundation rather than make yourself the focus of affairs. The traveler is returning. Illnesses should be cured. Moreover, the Three Talents are all correct; yin and yang are mutually harmonious. The Tao of the perfected is therein able to create prosperity. A bureaucratic transfer would add to your longevity. Commercial activities will be profitable. The hundred affairs will all be auspicious.

HO ∘ Marriage arrangements will result in a harmonious union. Employing the army will yield victory. Agriculture and sericulture will be profitable. The impoverished will be enriched; the imprisoned will be released. Sought-after affairs will proceed as desired. The distant traveler will arrive. "Intelligently and clearly take action," for "the myriad affairs all attain their patterns."

CH'EN ∘ Three yang in the middle, the Tao of Man is already flourishing, while the upper and lower positions also respond to each other.

LIU ∘ "In the past, matters did not proceed as desired"—the pliant lies within (at the bottom). When yang flourishes and is manifested in exterior action, it is the time for opening prosperity. Correct and straight, unselfish, the Tao is thereby great.

In this trigraph the positions of the Three Talents are correct; yin and yang are mutually harmonious. The Tao of the perfected is now penetrating. It is not appropriate to secretly act for yourself but is instead appropriate to undertake upright, great, glorious, and clear affairs. When the querent obtains this trigraph, it is highly auspicious!

SAWYER ∘ As discussed in the introduction, according to the traditional theory evolved over the centuries to characterize the *Ling Ch'i Ching*'s dynamics, trigraphs with appropriate yin/yang components in each position should be auspicious. Accordingly, the eight trigraphs with yang in the positions of Heaven and Man (top and middle, respectively), and yin at the bottom, for Earth, should all portend prosperity, good fortune, and the smooth attainment of desires. While these eight—numbered 2, 4, 10, 12, 34, 36, 42, and 44—are in fact auspicious, others, such as number 11, which is all yang, greatly surpass them. This indicates that the various explanatory systems evolved to account for the trigraphs' prognosticatory value remain ad hoc rationalizations rather than comprehensive, predictive guides. Resort therefore must first be made to the Oracle and the Verse, and only secondarily to the postcreation commentaries that arose across the gulf of time.

11 TS'AI TA 才達

Talent Advancing
The image of tranquility and
    auspiciousness
A host of yang flourishing below
Ch'ien (Heaven) ∘ Northwest

ORACLE

Respectful and refined the many officers, excellent virtue glorious and bright. Seeing each other, happy and joyous, lasting pleasure without calamity.

VERSE

Nobles assist each other in the darkness,
Retirement and employment must be appropriate.
Do not sigh about the flower branches being few,
You must realize that the fruit will form later.

COMMENTARIES

YEN ∘ Yang numerous, dense, and heavy. Thus it speaks about many officers becoming prominent through their talents. There must be nobles assisting them; by the end of the year they will thereby gain strength, not last for only a season. Illnesses will be cured. The traveler will return. The hundred affairs will all be auspicious. If an officer wants to have an audience with the king or a duke to seek fame and praise, it would be an especially good time.

HO ∘ Those seeking bureaucratic offices will realize their ambitions. The traveler will arrive. Commercial activities, agriculture, and sericulture will be profitable. Holding a marriage ceremony would be

49

auspicious. Illnesses will be cured. Official affairs will not be success-ful. This trigraph is very auspicious.

CH'EN ∘ Three yang: the Tao of Man flourishes. One can be active. The Tao of Earth is also flourishing. Yang is replete and substantial; wherever you dwell will be peaceful.

LIU ∘ "Respectful and refined the many officers"—they are follow-ing the top line. "Seeing each other, happy and joyous"—they regard each other with respect.

In this trigraph a single yang is in correct position at the top, while the middle and lower positions are both triple yang. This is like the ruler having firm and clear virtue and numerous Worthies follow him. When ordinary people obtain this trigraph, it becomes the image of nobles and worthy friends providing assistance. The Oracle indicates that seeking office; having an audience with the noble; marriage; and commercial activities will all be auspicious. In employing the army you will gain Worthies. In seeking to implement affairs, you should obtain the assistance of others, for then it will be auspicious.

SAWYER ∘ The trigraph's name and image are strong and positive, yet the tenor of the Verse is somewhat equivocal, as if looking to darker times before talent can be appreciated and take center stage. Perhaps it reflects and thereby provides evidence of having been com-posed during the turbulent Wei-Chin period, when life expectancy was short and many great talents disdained or bemoaned the lack of official opportunity.

12 *Tzu Yu* 恣 遊

Unfettered Journeying
The image of taking pleasure
Yin and yang realize their positions
Sun (Wind) ◦ Southeast

ORACLE

Riding a dragon, driving thoroughbreds, roaming about the four quarters; joyously attaining one's desires, taking pleasure without bound.

VERSE

> Sitting alone on an upper floor reminiscing about old travels,
> The moon as bright as a day-lit river eastward flowing.
> This year an appointment that ought not to be missed.
> Hereafter, when we meet, laughter unceasing!

COMMENTARIES

YEN ◦ One does nothing but follow the heart's desires north, south, east, and west. There is no affair that will not be successful. The traveler will not yet arrive. Illnesses will be cured. The *I Ching* says, "At the appropriate time one rides six dragons in order to drive up to Heaven." It also says, "The mare is of the category of Earth; she travels the earth without bound."

HO ◦ The thief will be apprehended and any stolen goods also recovered. The pregnant will give birth to a male. Commercial activities will be profitable. If seeking marriage, the union will come of itself. Agriculture and sericulture will be as desired. The imprisoned will not have any anxiety. The hundred affairs will all reach completion.

CH'EN ∘ The upper and middle positions are both yang, while the lowest position has four yin. Yin and yang gain each other. Even more, the Tao of Man is complete and flourishing, thereby sufficient to drive the host of yin below it.

LIU ∘ "Riding a dragon, driving thoroughbreds"—those below obediently follow. "Roaming about the four quarters"—no one dares hinder me.

In this trigraph one yang dwells at the top, while yang in the middle and yin at the bottom are both appropriate. Three yang signify a dragon; four yin signify a thoroughbred mare. Each realizes its place and is thereby employed by me. It is appropriate to roam the four quarters and take pleasure without bound. When the querent obtains this trigraph, it will be highly appropriate to "advance and take." Only if inquiring about travelers will they not return but outside will similarly realize their desires.

SAWYER ∘ Heaven and Man both yang, the Earth appropriately yin. This is the image of an energetic, if youthful, ruler, enjoying the support of strong officials. Yin below, like the standard carriage team of four horses, responds to commands from above. Yet the image is not heavy but, rather, is one of freedom to travel and roam about, to "take pleasure without bound." However, "without bound" should be understood not as referring to going to the excess of debauchery, licentiousness, or oblivion, but to intense enjoyment without guilt. One should not be entangled by either the mundane worries of circumstances or any questioning of whether self-enjoyment is appropriate or undeserved!

Yen's *I Ching* quotations appear in the commentaries nominally attributed to Confucius for the first (Ch'ien, or Heaven, the Creative) and second (K'un, or Earth, the Receptive) hexagrams. Although the "six dragons" are normally understood as referring to the stages of life or the lines of the *I Ching* hexagrams, Yen cites them simply as images for "unfettered roaming." K'un's association of the mare with Earth strikingly dovetails with the trigraph's structure, not only evoking pastoral scenes of open country and unrestrained movement, but also imagizing their inherent relationship.

13 *Yu Huan* 憂患

Anxiety and Trouble
The image of an orphan standing alone
Two yang separated by yin
Li (Fire) ∘ True south

ORACLE

Upper single, lower orphaned, the perverse plot against them. Anxieties of the heart and belly cannot be quickly eliminated, but must await yang's arrival in spring. Then one will be free from constraints.

VERSE

Achieving success has not yet given the body peace,
Fright and anxiety are constantly in mind.
Many the times I've met danger and obstacles,
When will I encounter someone who understands my song?

COMMENTARIES

YEN ∘ One constantly harbors fear and terror, fearful of trouble and harm. Fortuitously gaining a noble's aid and protection, in the end there will be no calamity. Illnesses might be somewhat difficult to cure for two or three months. Moreover, the two yang positions are separated by doubled yin; they cannot aid and sustain each other. It is similar to a crafty minister stealing away the government's power by first reaching out to the menial people. This is the image of worry and trouble. The hundred affairs are only somewhat auspicious. The traveler is delayed by evil.

HO ∘ Real-estate transactions might not be profitable; brigands are plotting against your properties. The ill will slowly recover. The imprisoned will not yet get out. The management of affairs will be slow and obstructed. This trigraph is slightly baleful.

CH'EN ○ Four yin in the middle, the Tao of Man is at the extremity of emptiness and weakness. Upper and lower positions are slender yang, unable to sustain and assist.

LIU ○ "Upper single, lower orphaned"—yin flourishes in the middle. Petty individuals cause obstruction; the ruler's will does not penetrate. By adhering to uprightness and awaiting the time, one can preserve the end.

In this trigraph both the upper and lower positions are single yang, while petty individuals—the four yin occupying the middle—form friendships and cliques. This is the image of the upright Tao not penetrating. Affairs divined about will all be obstructed and disadvantageous. You should preserve yourself in uprightness in order to avoid disaster.

This trigraph is similar to the fifth trigraph ("Tao of Pleasure"), but this one signifies anxiety. The fifth one has young yin dwelling in the middle, according with yang's intent at the top. Thus it forms the image of harmoniously joining and self-sufficiency. In this trigraph, the four yin form cliques, combining their power. When the many flourish, eliminating them will be extremely difficult. Thus you must await the arrival of the yang months for help in eliminating the evil.

SAWYER ○ The strength of four or doubled yin overwhelms the youthful yang, making it impossible for correct principles to prevail. However, it is not simply the presence of old yin that causes difficulty and hardship, but the imbalance found in the trigraph. In terms of Heaven-Earth-Man, the human realm is beset by dissolution, licentiousness, perversity, and general disorder, making it difficult for projects to succeed, for people to be in harmony. Viewed as ruler-minister-people, the agents of government interfere with the sage's benign directions, acting selfishly and willfully. At best the bureaucracy is moribund; at worse it exploits the people. Fortunately, Earth/people and Heaven/ruler are yang, offering some prospects for optimism, particularly as their strength increases.

The Verse bemoans the poet's plight, for although some degree of success has been realized, the author still feels troubled and uneasy, lamenting the lack of official recognition. The last line echoes a common theme—that only someone who truly understands music will "know" the musician. Such encounters are a matter of chance; rarely attained, easily lost, they symbolize the loneliness of not being truly known and appreciated. China's ancient history abounds with tales about suddenly being recognized for one's worth, with ensuing dramatic consequences as the individual subsequently struggles valiantly to repay a mentor's confidence. Many assassins struck a mortal blow and thereby cast away their own lives to avenge the wrongs suffered by those who knew them. This trigraph conveys a sense of this situation, of waiting for the time and being impeded by difficulties mounted by common people.

14 SHEN TE 慎德

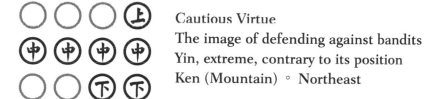

Cautious Virtue
The image of defending against bandits
Yin, extreme, contrary to its position
Ken (Mountain) ○ Northeast

ORACLE

Heaven and Earth extensive and expansive, petty individuals freely indulgent. Prohibitions and orders unimplemented, thieves watch my hut.

VERSE

Clusters of evil extend throughout the six quarters,
Sun and moon are obscured by wind-borne dust.
Even if you cultivate virtue and are henceforth introspective,
It will still be difficult to avoid disaster and failure.

COMMENTARIES

YEN ○ A host of yin just flourishing; solitary yang does not give birth. The Tao of the petty is waxing, the Tao of the perfected is waning. It is the moment of losing wealth and things. The family patriarch is troubled by illness; not until spring will he be cured.

Under this trigraph it would be highly appropriate to grasp the upright, but not appropriate to seek affairs. The traveler has not yet set a time to return. Pursuing thieves will not result in their apprehension.

Ho ∘ Illnesses may be difficult to cure; medication being taken has not yet proven fully beneficial. Official matters will prove onerous. Seeking wealth will produce but meager profits. Remain in residence, carefully guard against thieves and brigands. This trigraph is very baleful.

CH'EN ∘ Four yin are in the middle, two yin lie below; the single yang at the top cannot govern them. This is the season when the petty realize their desires.

LIU ∘ "Heaven and Earth extensive and expansive"—the laws and orders are lax. "Thieves watch my hut"—hidden, they cannot be seen. The perfected individual's sorrow is the petty individual's happiness.

This trigraph contains a host of yin and a single yang, with yin flourishing in the middle. At the bottom the foundation responds to the upper line but is obstructed by the middle, then reverting to conjoin with the middle. This is what causes the perfected individual's house to be occupied by thieves. The querent should guard against thieves and brigands and remain in residence. The management of holdings, commercial activities, seeking office, employing the military, and going out to travel—each and every affair is baleful. Only fleeing and secreting oneself in hiding will be auspicious.

SAWYER ∘ The image characterizes Heaven and Earth as extensive and expanding—terms that, while correctly rendered, also connote a lassitude and congeniality or generosity of spirit that might best be termed indulgence. Contrasted with the normal draconian laws and punishments found in traditional China, this ease, confronted by a host of yin representing the hordes of common people bent on their own venality, suggests indulgent tolerance for all forms of human behavior, as Liu suggests. Whether his interpretation has been inappropriately applied or not, both the Image and the Verse stress the precariousness of the present moment, the need to retrench, cultivate virtue, act inoffensively, and maintain a low profile to avoid disaster and loss. Fortunately, moments in which virtually everything goes awry are few—although everyone has experienced such days—and quickly pass, for all extremes are inherently unstable.

15   HSING LING   行 令

Implementing Orders
The image of destroying brigands
Yin dwells in the middle position
Li (Fire) ∘ True south

ORACLE

The ruler commands the army's officers to extirpate brigands, the wicked, and the evil. Bringing forth their weapons and brandishing halberds, many are those who follow.

VERSES

> Shooting deer is a moment's joy,
> But awaits reliance on the masses to be achieved.
> Heavenly peaches have already ripened,
> Looking up, one begins to enjoy their splendor.
>
> The deer runs off, a host races after him,
> Achievement and fame lie in the moment.
> The wicked and valiant now already known,
> Peace and harmony pervade the Four Seas.

COMMENTARIES

YEN ∘ It is appropriate to order others about and is also appropriate to have others command you. If you are totally self-reliant, everything will be defeated. Those suffering from illness may have been affected by ghosts; it would be appropriate to expel them. Travelers are free from discomfort but not yet returning. Urgently bringing them back would be auspicious. If inquiring about extirpating brigands and apprehending fugitives, victory is certain. Moreover, the trigraph indicates that within they act wickedly, and without they act evilly.

Under this trigraph it would be appropriate to conduct campaigns of rectification and apprehend fugitives; great victories will certainly result. Commercial activities will be profitable; seeking office will also produce results. Agriculture, sericulture, and marriage arrangements will all be auspicious.

Ho ∘ If the king is to eliminate evil, he must have those he can order about. Official matters will be resolved of themselves. The hundred affairs are free of baleful aspects.

Ch'en ∘ Four yin in the middle separate the yang lines; it is the time when brigands freely traverse the realm. But the three yang at the bottom are adequate to provide security for the masses. This is the image of having the army go forth to extirpate the guilty.

Liu ∘ Yin wickedly in the middle, wanting to separate the upright. The ruler commands that it be extirpated; the army's strength is flourished. "Bringing forth their weapons and brandishing halberds," they attack the wicked.

In this trigraph a single yang is correctly positioned at the top, while three yang are vigorously deployed at the bottom. Four yin dwell in the middle. Even though they want to be obstructive in the middle, the two yang lines unite their virtue. Yin's evilness has already been exposed; thus the trigraph forms the image of a ruler commanding the army's officers to extirpate the wicked and eliminate the evil. If divining about sending the army forth on campaign and apprehending fugitives, there will be great victories. If illnesses are treated, they should be cured. If you adhere to principle in your lawsuit, you will be victorious. The traveler is free from discomfort; any intervening obstacles can be penetrated. All affairs, whatever they may be, will be auspicious.

Sawyer ∘ Although this trigraph resembles the preceding one, being largely defined by the activity of four yin in the middle, the portended outcome differs radically. In "Implementing Orders" all difficulties can be resolved through the application of correct, if forceful, methods, whereas in the previous trigraph the sole recourse might be dwelling in quiet obscurity. Thus it is highly auspicious, provided only that effort is exerted and an upright path maintained. Although the problem of evil and perversity may be everlasting, at least momentary victory appears possible.

The Verses employ two images fraught with traditional meaning. Hunting deer was a royal prerogative in ancient times, mainly organized around the use of peasants to flush the animals for the ruler's pleasure. However, deer hunting also came to symbolize the furious pursuit of kingship itself by contending parties, nobles, and even discontented peasants in millenarian movements. Shooting the deer was thus a brief pleasure but was also a momentary impulse as the people arose to contend for kingship. "Heavenly peaches," mythical in nature and therefore never seen, were believed to confer almost unlimited longevity, to transport one to the tranquil, pleasurable realm of the immortals.

16   CHIANG SÜN   將損

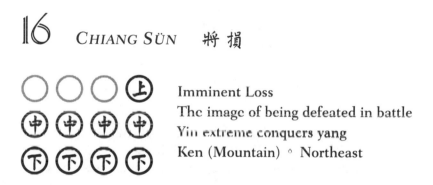

Imminent Loss
The image of being defeated in battle
Yin extreme conquers yang
Ken (Mountain) ∘ Northeast

ORACLE

Wolves and tigers howl and roar; incessant rain and floods of water. Fighting in battle will not yield victory. Weak soldiers and dispirited officers are insulted by invaders; numerous are the losses and deaths.

VERSES

> Shooting at pheasants, in the end difficult to obtain;
> Longing for the marvelous, yet not gaining wealth.

The efforts of seeking, the pursuit of hopes,
Footsteps that stir danger and disaster.

Power too slight to defend against enemy invaders,
Losses and thieves accumulating to disaster and danger.
Human affairs are all like this,
The time of Heaven is not yet conducive to impulses.

COMMENTARIES

YEN ∘ Conquering those, increasing these, neither in accord with proper principle. All affairs, whatever they may be, are extremely difficult. The traveler ought to return but suffers from fear and terror en route. It is not appropriate to extirpate brigands. Moreover yin *ch'i* is increasingly robust, while the Tao of the ruler diminishes daily. Wolves, tigers, and foreign invaders link up on all four sides. The enemy will be difficult to conquer.

HO ∘ Regional earls protecting the borders will inevitably suffer from robbers and brigands. Although you occupy the highlands, great floods will still be encountered. The ill may suffer some discomfort. The imprisoned are solidly incarcerated. Contesting lawsuits, employing the army, commercial activities, seeking office, agriculture and sericulture—none of the hundred affairs will be advantageous. This is the trigraph of an army suffering loss.

CH'EN ∘ Things associated with the category of yin greatly flourish. Wild animals, thieves, and brigands link up to harm the people. The single yang at the top, unable to govern them, will certainly be overturned and defeated.

LIU ∘ The wolf howls and water overflows; the Tao of yang is solitary. Great villains cooperate and unite; the danger cannot be withstood.
    In this trigraph a single yang is perched above an accumulation of yin. This it forms the image of "wolves and tigers howling and roaring; incessant rain and floods of water." As for affairs divined about, there aren't any that are not baleful. Employing the army is especially proscribed. Only if you are seeking rain during a severe drought will you certainly realize what is desired.

SAWYER ∘ This is another in the series of trigraphs dominated by the pernicious influences of excessive yin. Although yin, being the necessary complement to yang, is not inherently evil, when it multiples promiscuously and exceeds its relative appropriateness in nature's constantly evolving but balanced pattern, trouble and turmoil result. In "Imminent Loss" the prospects for dramatic, positive, corrective actions are extremely poor; therefore, the wise will shun involvement, knowing that even Virtue itself will not prevail. (In marked contrast to the purely Confucian view, throughout the *Ling Ch'i Ching* it is made painfully clear that even surpassing Virtue fails to cower the evil into submission, and that the good suffer equally with the bad. Of course, this realism never constitutes a license to stray from the path of goodness, for evil—apart from being morally condemned—invariably engenders further retribution.) The first stanza clearly depicts someone with keen desires, hoping to shoot pheasants and longing for marvelous, wonderful things, but lacking the skill and means to obtain them. Moreover, at this moment all such efforts may prove contrary to the time and entail the seeds of disaster. Footsteps, symbolic of the tracings of every act, stir up trouble, rather than falling softly into silent oblivion in a benign world.

17 SHEN HU 神護

Spiritual Protection
The image of availing oneself of the
   spirits
Yin dwells in yang's position
Tui (Metal) ∘ True west

ORACLE

T'ai-i commands the soldiers, Jade Woman by his side. Wu Hsien precedes them shaking a spirit-duster to clear away perversities.

VERSE

> Thin clouds obscure the moon's light,
> Opened blossoms half destroyed by rain.

Expelling evil, in the end one obtains blessings,
Quietly retiring to seek tranquility.

COMMENTARIES

YEN ∘ The family patriarch is ill; a female ghost is working an evil influence over him. It would be appropriate to expel her. All affairs, whatever they may be, are mostly dark. The traveler also suffers difficulty and has been unable to return.

Moreover, the most honored spirit in Heaven is T'ai-i. Jade Woman and Wu Hsien act as his assistants. Wu Hsien was a worthy minister in the Shang dynasty and probably took his attractive name. Under this trigraph, praying for the intercession of the spirits will result in blessings. The ill may be suffering from evil influences; it would be appropriate to expel them. Seeking office, hoping for things, commercial activities, and marriage arrangements would not be auspicious.

HO ∘ The traveler ought to arrive. Arguments will not prove harmful. Official affairs will, in the end, be free from misfortune. Through uniting with others you will gain their strength. It would be auspicious to seek blessings and the expulsion of calamity, for then whatever you do will be successful.

CH'EN ∘ Two, a fundamental yin number, on the contrary dwell in Heaven's position. This is the image of the spirits of Heaven. For the lower positions to respond—one yang in the middle, one at the bottom—they must obtain the blessings of the Heavenly spirits.

LIU ∘ "T'ai-i commands the soldiers; they clear away perversities." Yang arrives, yin is solitary; the unnatural cannot grow. In this trigraph, although yin dwells at the top, the two yang in the middle and bottom positions manage to form a friendship below. They have the power to eliminate the perverse through the accord of their wills, while the upper yin, contrary to expectation, is employed by me. Thus it results in the symbol of T'ai-i commanding the soldiers, and the image of Jade Woman by his side, with Wu Hsien preceding them shaking a spirit-duster. As for any affairs divined about, there will be doubt and difficulty, but in the end you will gain the assistance of friends and thereby be successful. If the sick pray to the heavenly spirits, they should be cured. The traveler will return. Fighting in battle will result in great victory.

SAWYER ∘ Young yin and young yang normally form a match; however, here the order is inverted, with yin dwelling in Heaven—the penultimate yang position! The lower positions both being yang, and therefore strong and active, create the possibility of bringing the ruler (the two yin) under sway, thus making progress. To attain this objective, cooperation and harmony must be realized, and actions sanctioned by the spirits. It certainly does not seem to be the time for solitary, heroic efforts. As the *I Ching* teaches, yin above tends to descend while yang below rises, so the possibility of dynamic, fruitful interaction exists.

18 *CHIANG PAI* 將敗

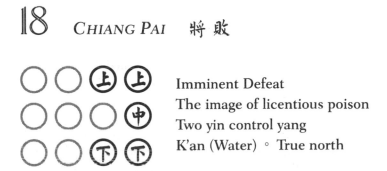

Imminent Defeat
The image of licentious poison
Two yin control yang
K'an (Water) ∘ True north

ORACLE

Two women and one male—above and below mutually incite each other. Yin *ch'i* mounts yang, thereupon using it until it is dissipated and vacuous.

VERSE

Solitary yang slender, a host of yin robbers;
Its strength already exhausted, it will never attain longevity.
Be cautious, be cautious—you should preserve yourself.

COMMENTARIES

YEN ∘ Male and female conquer each other. At first there is marriage, later separation. Although the traveler is returning, on the way thieves are encountered. Moreover, outside (the two yin in the upper and lower positions) is not Jade Woman, within (the single yang) is not T'ai-i. A single yang being controlled by two yin is the image of dissipation and vacuity. Illnesses might grow more serious (if not properly treated).

HO ∘ Whatever you seek will be useless; whatever you do will not be harmonious. The traveler will not yet return. Agriculture and sericulture will be disappointing. Official affairs will be difficult to resolve. Illnesses might grow serious (if not properly treated). The hundred affairs are very baleful.

CH'EN ∘ The Tao of Man is solitary and weak; above and below, two yin both want to advance on it. "Two women and one male"—the image of licentiousness and evil. Slender yang is not victorious.

LIU ∘ "Two women and one male"—yang is beguiled by yin. Raising up its essence, casting away its spirit, it indulges in licentiousness. "Thereupon using it until it is dissipated and vacuous"—yang continues to sink.

In this trigraph a single yang is beguiled by two yin. Yin and yang are all young and weak. They seek to unite, and yang unshaken is mounted by yin. It will certainly result in dissipation and vacuity. If one obtains this trigraph when divining about affairs, everything will be baleful.

SAWYER ∘ The great, overt fear of Confucian society was the disruptive potential of licentiousness. Although the prevailing moral order—which was sanctioned by government measures—constrained the individual and repressed impulses, it was essentially hypocritical and hardly in keeping with the original views and spirit of Confucius. One mark of wealth and rank was the number of wives and concubines, so the presence of two yin—two women—was not always thought by upper male-dominated society to be incapable of order. However, the basic principle that adversarial conflict, as well as moral dissolution, must result from two women with one man is clearly expressed herein, and throughout Chinese history and literature. The Taoists also taught that sexual excess depletes vital essence, and that the pleasures of the senses can cause the spirit to go mad. Interpreted in a modern context—whether for men or women—the principle of this trigraph is simply that balance is the ideal; romantic and sexual partners at any given time should be single, not multiple. Otherwise, pleasures will be illusory and entail stress, tension, distraction, and eventual misery. Extrapolated into the spiritual realm, the querent must avoid being seduced by multiple paths or projects, instead discovering a true match. Meanwhile, this trigraph presages that plans and activities will be frustrating and unproductive, at least for the moment.

19 LI LUAN 理亂

Ordering Turbulence
The image of repressing the wicked
Yin steals yang's position
Tui (Marsh) ◦ True west

ORACLE

In Heaven, yin ascends like the clouds; yang rises up from below. The perfected impose order on the turbulent; the petty fear correction.

VERSE

> Only after gold ore is smelted a hundred times is it completely pure;
> Only after the white jade was presented three times was its rarity first perceived.
> What is secreted away in a case is as yet uncoveted;
> Take pleasure in dwelling in retirement and resting in poverty.

COMMENTARIES

YEN ∘ "Yin steals yang's position," like the clouds rising up. Yang, flourishing below, is about to mount to the highest position (of rulership). By eliminating the contrary and prohibiting the brutal, the mass of perversities will diminish by themselves. A little correction, a great warning! This trigraph will be most outstanding for those who hold the great power of government and for high local officials. The hundred affairs will at first cause anxiety, later bring happiness.

HO ∘ Whatever is sought will not be obtained. Whatever is done will not be successful. Exercise the power of government, "impose order on the turbulent." The petty fear retribution. Illnesses may not yet be fully cured. Although the traveler will return, it will not be advantageous. There is slander.

CH'EN ∘ Two yin at the top, flourishing yang at the bottom, the image of intersecting prosperity. With three yang dwelling in Earth's position, the petty have no chance to indulge themselves in the world.

LIU ∘ "In Heaven, yin ascends like the clouds"—a dragon leaps in the abyss. The perverse are eliminated through uprightness just as if being suddenly inundated.

In this trigraph, although yin and yang have not gained their appropriate positions, the single yang dwelling in the middle coupled with the three yang at the bottom form the image of the perfected imposing order on the turbulent, constraining weakness through firmness. Effecting government and imposing order on the people, apprehending fugitives, and rectifying the rebellious—divination for all these is auspicious. Lawsuits will be victorious through uprightness. It is not appropriate to be yin and selfish. If a perfected individual obtains this trigraph, it will be very auspicious! For the petty individual it will be the opposite.

SAWYER ∘ As usual, Ho's interpretation strikes a more pessimistic tone than the others, who discern a successful outcome to the task of imposing order on the chaos wrought by miscreants and evil-doers. The Image, Oracle, and Commentaries repeatedly echo themes and phrases from the *I Ching*, particularly from the first hexagram for Heaven. However, the order of the lines in this trigraph, with yin in

Heaven above and yang below, suggests the hexagram for "Prosperity," as Ch'en has observed, because their tendency is to intersect—yin to descend and yang to rise. Thus the situation's dynamics appear highly auspicious, despite petty individuals posing difficulties in one's personal environment. (The Oracle does not mention murderers or brigands, but rather "the petty," the small-minded menial offenders encountered in life at every stage. Not invariably evil, though capable of wicked self-interest, they rob life of many joys.)

The Verse strikes a different theme—that even the greatest treasure or talent may go unrecognized until fully polished and appropriately presented to a discerning world. The second line alludes to an ancient story, a tragedy in which an ordinary man named Ho, finding a jade of great rarity, presumed to present it to a succession of rulers. The first two, failing to perceive its value, punished him by having his feet amputated, one after the other; only the third, realizing its potential, had the jade edged and polished until its true magnificence was revealed. Accordingly, in contemporary terms, one lesson might be that unless products are properly packaged, even the best will go unsold when cast before an undiscerning public. Similarly, one's talents, however great, are apparently undervalued at present; perhaps they need to be "polished"? Or perhaps it would be best to remain quiet and simply enjoy life?

20 WEI HUAN 未還

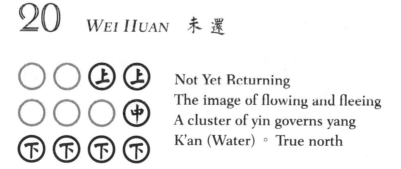

Not Yet Returning
The image of flowing and fleeing
A cluster of yin governs yang
K'an (Water) ∘ True north

ORACLE

Fields barren, the earth void. People move their dwellings to await fruitful years before returning to their old huts.

VERSE

> Mouths and tongues bring about turbulent confusion,
> Business affairs will certainly be harmed.
> If you seek the assistance of yin's power,
> Only then will you be spared misfortune and disaster.

COMMENTARIES

YEN ∘ In this trigraph, yin ascends, attaining its pinnacle. Yang is unable to control it. The fields are barren, the people have scattered. Only in prosperous years will they return. The ill will slowly recover. Agriculture and sericulture will not be profitable.

HO ∘ Those serving in bureaucratic positions will not receive their salaries. The traveler will not yet return. Agriculture and sericulture will not be profitable. Although this trigraph is not auspicious, it cannot harm people. Simply being content in poverty, preserving stillness, and praying for blessings will be auspicious in themselves.

CH'EN ∘ Two yin on top, four yin on the bottom, one yang solitary and weak. The Tao of Earth is void and impaired. It forms the image of baleful years, of turning and moving away.

LIU ∘ "Fields barren, the earth void"—they cannot be relied on. Petty individuals have different desires; in the end they do not remain together. I preserve the upright and wait, being certain to protect my place.

In this trigraph yang has sunk into yin, but in the lower position yin flourishes. Thus it implies that "the fields are barren and the earth void." It is the image of people fleeing and scattering. But the lower yin is already old and doesn't seek to unite with others. The petty attain their wishes. What is already extreme must decline, and the young yin at the top reverts and joins with the Tao of Man. Thus in the end the people return to their old huts.

In any affair divined about, there will certainly be obstacles. If you preserve stillness and await the time, then it will be auspicious.

SAWYER ∘ In concluding this sequence of four trigraphs characterized by two yin in Heaven's position, "Not Yet Returning" depicts a situation that has virtually reached the extreme but not yet gone beyond. Accordingly, although circumstances may cry out for a return to more balanced, positive conditions, the moment has not yet arrived. Strictly speaking, four yin in Earth's position should theoretically be extremely auspicious, fully in accord with Earth, suggesting a bountiful maturity in vegetative life. However, because of the absence of the active principle in Heaven, the negative aspects of a plethora of yin tend to dominate. Therefore one of the two most dire and threatening of human nightmares arises—famine with all its attendant miseries. Although modern society is essentially insulated from the rhythms of nature except for such inconveniences as rain and snow, hunger's specter continues unabated in Africa and drought may yet threaten the world's tenuous food supply in any given year, with humanity's survival tenuously depending on singular events as simple as a volcanic explosion or mutating virus. No need for drama or a drifting meteor; many are the mundane ways to perish. Accordingly, as the commentators observe, it is hardly a time to be active and energetic. A pause until the cycle brings about more conducive conditions is generally indicated for all affairs.

21 CHIEH T'AN 戒貪

Guarding against Greed
The image of spirit dissipated
Two yin contrary to their positions
Chen (Thunder) ∘ True east

ORACLE

Burying gold and hiding jade away, boasting about one's nobility. Accumulated ghosts cannot be extirpated; the spirits will not send down blessings.

VERSE

Presuming on riches, thereby forgetting the foundation;
Surpassing greed, in the end the middle is lost.

Heaven will not assist a deceptive heart,
The Tao of the spirits is not selfish achievement.

COMMENTARIES

YEN ∘ Yang, which dwells at the bottom, is put into difficult straits by yin. Thus the Oracle speaks about "burying gold and hiding jade away." Yet when people boast about their own nobility, the spirits will not assist them. The ill have been affected by ghosts; it would be appropriate to quickly pray for the intercession of the spirits. In official matters, if you seek out an influential person, they will be successfully concluded.

HO ∘ Coveting wealth while occupying official position will invariably bring about disaster and censure. Even though one has wealth and precious things, there will inevitably be anxiety about brigands and thieves. Perhaps the ill will not yet be cured. The traveler will not yet return. It will be difficult for the imprisoned to get out. Agriculture and sericulture will not produce harvests. Sending the army forth would not be advantageous. "Being in the grasp of ghosts" speaks about the balefulness of the situation. Under this trigraph it would be appropriate to correct transgressions and cultivate virtue and thereby be spared.

CH'EN ∘ Yang dwells in the Earth's position, signifying wealth from gold and jade. In responding to the two yin in the middle line, it suggests greed without end. Furthermore, the position of Heaven, also being yin, is unable to bestow blessings. The Tao of Heaven is cracked and overflowing; ghosts and spirits bring about harm and licentiousness.

LIU ∘ "Burying gold and hiding jade away"—yang is at the bottom. The Tao of ghosts prevails above; blessings cannot be bestowed.

In this trigraph a solitary yang is repressed beneath two yin in the middle, unable to take action. Moreover, the two yin at the top are pliant and weak, without any standing. Thus there are no blessings, only anxiety. The querent should guard against greed.

SAWYER ∘ The *Tao Te Ching* and *I Ching* both remark about the imminent danger that greed and the excessive possession of goods and wealth may produce. Confucianism also officially disdained riches and property accumulated through commercial rather than governmental or agricultural activities. The prevalent popular attitude, even after the introduction of Buddhism (which strongly advocated casting out desires) of course believed that being rich far surpasses being poor, and that more wealth is preferable to less. Chuang-tzu perhaps best resolved the complex question of riches and their pursuit with an underlying philosophical perspective that emphasized while such activities make people go mad, human nature entails an inherent inclination to desiring wealth and comfort. The problem stems from greed and its excesses, not the basic tendency.

In this particular trigraph the subjects clearly enjoy a degree of success; difficulties arise through their boasting and grasping. Not only do the spirits reject such behavior, one's own spirit is wasted and irrecoverably expended in the fevered pursuit of material possessions. In short, to have desires, despite Taoist warnings to the contrary, is not problematic; to be stimulated and motivated by desire is inherent and necessary to action and human achievement. Only when desire assumes a power of its own, when it compels and obsesses beyond all bounds, does it portend disaster. Then even the ill-boding spirits, who of course are also psychic symbols of transgressive action, are attracted and may cause illness. (It should be noted that unlike many ancient cultures, Chinese medicine did not generally attribute illnesses to the effects of spirits, but it did recognize a limited category of complaints that included strong emotional experiences, such as fright and anger, and contact with spirits or ghosts.)

22 AN T'AI 安泰

Resting in Tranquility
The image of vibrant gardens
Pure yin, unmoving
K'un (Earth) ∘ Southwest

ORACLE

The year bountiful, the month prosperous. The land and fields open and expansive. Peace like Mount T'ai. In the end, neither misfortune nor calamity.

VERSE

> A strip of land on the central plains,
> In the depths of spring rain and dew are frequent.
> Employ Heaven, rely on the advantages of Earth,
> Be content in your occupation, take pleasure in peace and
>   harmony.

COMMENTARIES

YEN ∘ Broaden the rice fields, open the dry plots to await the year's completion. Employ Heaven, divide Earth—"in the end, there will be neither misfortune nor calamity." Peace and stability will be like Mount T'ai. Remaining in residence would be auspicious. Agriculture and sericulture will yield great harvests. The ill will not suffer. The traveler will not yet return.

HO ∘ You will occupy an official position and receive a salary. Wealth and silk will come of themselves. If the army is sent forth, it will gain territory. The pregnant will give birth to a male. For those of scholarly attainment, this trigraph will be highly auspicious and advantageous.

CH'EN ∘ All three positions are yin, but they have not attained the extremity of flourishing. It is the image of neither one-sided victory nor mutual conquest. It is the pattern of according with pleasure and accepting blessings. When compared with the trigraph having a single yang in the upper, middle, and lower positions, in both cases they are initial yin and initial yang, pure harmony without conquest. Thus they are both auspicious.

LIU ∘ "The year bountiful, the month prosperous"—the will of the masses (indicated by the young yin in all three positions) is united. Being pliant and submissive, it is advantageous and auspicious. The blessings will be inexhaustible. "Peace like Mount T'ai"—there will be a beginning and an end.

In this trigraph all three positions are yin, gaining centrality and uprightness. This is the image of dwelling peacefully and occupying the submissive, of not directing desires outside. Thus it is auspicious without any balefulness. Divining about family matters, agriculture and sericulture, occupying bureaucratic office, commercial enterprises, and other major affairs will all be auspicious. Engaging in battle to rectify the evil will gain territory. Even without extensive treatment, illnesses may improve somewhat. Public suits will be free from censure. The traveler will not yet return.

SAWYER ∘ The general auspiciousness of this trigraph, being all yin and therefore unbalanced and extreme, is remarkable and hardly to be expected. In contrast, the sixty-fourth trigraph, consisting of all mature yin lines, portends every sort of misfortune. However, apparently because the three positions are young, and therefore compliant, yin, harmony and auspiciousness are indicated by "Resting in Tranquility." (The character translated as "tranquility," previously encountered, might also be rendered as "prosperity." While the trigraph indicates general good fortune and a bountiful harvest, the peace and security imagized by China's famous Mount T'ai tilts the balance in favor of "tranquility" rather than "prosperity." The meanings, of course, always echo and overlap, rather than being mutually exclusive.)

23   CH'ANG CHI   昌吉

Glorious Auspiciousness
The image of blessings arising
Yin and yang purely auspicious
Chen (Thunder) ∘ True east

ORACLE

One receives Heaven's blessings just like the sun ascending. The youthful serve in office, their ranks and emoluments just rising.

VERSE

Fate extending to where the winds and clouds conjoin,
A person relying on the glory of the sun and moon.
Felicitous smoke floats in the treasure pavilion,
A bright moon shines on the golden bed.

COMMENTARIES

YEN ∘ Remaining in residence and seeking wealth are auspicious. The traveler will not yet return. It would be auspicious for the ill to sacrifice and seek the intercession of the spirits. Moreover, flourishing yang stirs and moves like the sun ascending. This approaches being purely auspicious. It is appropriate to go out to travel. It is not appropriate to dwell in retirement or skulk in caves. It will be difficult for commercial enterprises, youthful servants, and slaves to accord with one's wishes. All other affairs will be extremely auspicious!

HO ∘ Whatever you do, no matter how distant or high, will inevitably accord with your ambitions. The ill may at first suffer some discomfort. If the army is sent forth, it will gain victory. It is appropriate to seek out the beneficial influence of the stars and planets; then your plans will follow your desires. However, in all affairs it would not be appropriate to secretly seek your own interest.

CH'EN ∘ Yin above, yang below, the image of prosperity interacting. In the Tao of Earth, yang is flourishing, while in the top position, two yin act as the spirits of Heaven, mutually responding and uniting with Earth's flourishing yang. This is the image of blessings and prosperity at their fullest.

LIU ∘ Yang flourishes, the lower rises, the firm curbs the pliant. Advance in virtue, cultivate your occupation, and receive the blessings of Heaven.

In this trigraph, two yin dwell at the top, flourishing yang lies at the bottom. It is the image of advancing and moving upward like the sun ascending. Divining about seeking office and bureaucratic advancement will be highly auspicious.

SAWYER ∘ The tenor and significance of the trigraph are set by the presence of mature yang in the position of Earth, envisioned as the sun about to ascend through the formerly darkened sky of night, symbolized by the yin lines directly above. Accordingly, the moment for initiating actions, just like the breaking of day, has arrived. Moreover, they should probably be of a resolute, incremental nature, ongoing and increasing, like the sun inexorably mounting to the heights, rather than impulsive, momentary, and hesitant.

24 HENG T'UNG 亨通

Success Penetrating
The image of abundant wealth
Pure yin gains the positions
K'un (Earth) ∘ Southwest

ORACLE

Riches like the spring in a well that, although used, is not exhausted. Whatever is being sought will comply with one's desires. Happiness and pleasure will be unbroken.

VERSE

At the first clearing of the early morning rain, the sun glistens
    on the jade green rivulet;
Layer by layer the autumnal colors on the woodman's cottage.
Yellow gold inexhaustible, the family abundantly rich,
Why must they trouble in such petty ways about silk clothes?

COMMENTARIES

YEN ∘ In the *I Ching* the hexagram K'un generously sustains all things, its virtue uniting with them unbounded. Here the three positions are all yin; thus they do not conquer each other. The myriad things are all auspicious. Remaining in residence, there will be affairs to joyously celebrate. The traveler is already returning. "Riches like the spring in a well that, although used, is not exhausted"—whatever one seeks will be obtained; happiness and joy will be without comparison. The ill may at first experience difficulty but will recover later.

HO ∘ Those serving in bureaucratic offices will be shifted to higher positions. Managing productive activities will bring increasing riches.

Agriculture and sericulture will have double the normal harvests. Auspicious and felicitous, happiness and pleasure! The ill may recover largely by themselves. The imprisoned will manage to get out. Marriage arrangements will result in an advantageous union. This trigraph is highly auspicious!

CH'EN ∘ The three positions are all yin and the bottom is flourishing—resources for accumulating riches and honor. Using them, they will prove inexhaustible, just like the extensiveness of a spring.

LIU ∘ "Riches like the spring in a well"—one harvests the profits of Earth. The pliant accords with movement upward; whatever one seeks, everything will comply. In the lower position of this trigraph, yin is flourishing but does not go contrary to or conquer the lines above. Thus it creates the image of fertile lands. The two yin at the top, pliant and acommodating, do not wantonly move but rest in their advantage. This is why it is auspicious. Whatever affair the querent undertakes will be highly auspicious.

SAWYER ∘ Although this trigraph consists solely of yin lines, it portends great success and the unfettered realization of desires. Its power derives from the presence of mature yin in the position of Earth at the bottom, symbolizing things coming to fruition and being bountiful. Since there is no discord with the lines above, even though extremes should normally indicate instability, the prospects are dazzling!

25 *Yu Hsi* 憂喜

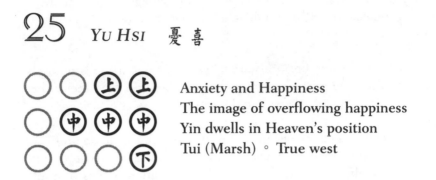

Anxiety and Happiness
The image of overflowing happiness
Yin dwells in Heaven's position
Tui (Marsh) ∘ True west

ORACLE

The heart has matters that worry it; anxious, I am unable to sleep. Although I fear trouble and disaster, on the contrary, good fortune arrives. Great blessings, happiness and joy. It will be greatly advantageous for me!

VERSE

> Who knew that I would become established as if ascending to Heaven,
> Now that I'm old my troubles are many; at night I'm unable to sleep.
> Suddenly I see the splendor of spring's colors in my old familiar garden,
> Fluttering about, the butterflies and bees fight over fragrant beauty.

COMMENTARIES

YEN ∘ Although there will be worry in the beginning, in the end there will be happiness. Moreover, "yin dwells in Heaven's position"—not something that can be relied on. Thus although there will be anxiety, with the three yang in the middle uniting to control it, the upper yin cannot bring about harm. Thus this trigraph indicates minor worries at first, later great auspiciousness. Therefore, no calamity.

Ho ∘ Disputes will not be successful. The traveler ought to arrive. Marriage arrangements and commercial enterprises will at first be difficult, later easy. The ill may at first suffer some discomfort, but will recover later. Official affairs will in the beginning be worrisome, later auspicious. Things lost will be sought with difficulty.

CH'EN ∘ Three yang dwelling in the middle, the basis of the Tao of Man flourishes. At the top there are two yin that mutually respond to the single yang in the bottom position. The middle does not interpenetrate with the upper and lower; thus at first there will be worries, and later, when the three yang flourish, the two yin will be unable to separate them. In the end one ought to obtain one's ambitions.

LIU ∘ Because yin has displaced yang from its position at the top, it is not appropriate. One is anxious over impending misfortune but obtains good fortune because the middle is firm.

In this trigraph, yin dwells at the top and yang dwells below; they have not gained their proper places. However, a single yang lies in the lower position and flourishing yang occupies the middle, while the yin at the top is weak and unable to control the firm yang lines. Even though there are doubts at the beginning, in the end one will attain good fortune and felicity. All affairs will at first be worrisome, at the conclusion auspicious. The worries will prove empty, the auspiciousness substantial.

SAWYER ∘ Chinese tradition is replete with stories warning against being complacent, stressing the need to contemplate potential disaster, especially during prosperous times. No doubt their overarching perspective reflects the violent heritage of the Warring States period (from which many famous anecdotes and illustrative incidents derive) and the ephemeral nature of an agricultural society in which a single drought could reduce the populace to misery and starvation. However, anyone steeped in such a tradition—or troubled by the inexhaustible worries of contemporary daily life—can only rejoice over this trigraph's portents because all anxieties will apparently prove unfounded. Joy and success are in the offing, not failure and sorrow.

26 P'ING AN 平 安

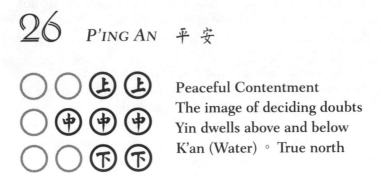

Peaceful Contentment
The image of deciding doubts
Yin dwells above and below
K'an (Water) ◦ True north

ORACLE

Above and below both settled, the mind does not give birth to perversity. Contented, it has no worries. Do not believe rumors.

VERSE

> A pair of swallows return to the southern states,
> Seeking out the families Wang and Hsieh.
> Amid the carved halls of spring light serene,
> They entrust their lives to fate.

COMMENTARIES

YEN ◦ The mind being correct is itself auspicious. "Do not believe rumors." The traveler will arrive. The imprisoned will get out. Even though in this trigraph the upper and lower positions are both yin, triple yang dwells in the middle. Although at first there might be anxiety and error, since each of the two yin positions is settled, there will be no regret. The hundred affairs will proceed as desired. At first there will be anxiety, later good fortune. Serving the ruler and forming alliances would be especially good.

HO ◦ If taking a wife, you will obtain a beautiful woman. The traveler is on the road. The pregnant will give birth to a male. The ill may have seen a ghost or other abnormality, but they will not suffer. Official entanglements will dissipate. There will be good harvests from agriculture and sericulture. Sending the army forth on campaign, commercial enterprises, and the hundred affairs will all be auspicious and advantageous.

CH'EN ○ The Tao of Man is just flourishing, while the two yin in the upper and lower positions respond to each other. Triple yang is yet by itself able to control them.

LIU ○ The upper and lower positions are both pliant, taking the middle as their ruler. The middle is firm and correct, unbending, what the masses will join with.

In this trigraph, triple yang dwells in the middle while the upper and lower are both yin. Being young yin that are not yet flourishing, they are neither obstinate nor contentious, but harmonious and inclined to unity. Yang is firm and flourishing; yin is unable to conquer it. Thus it creates the image of upper and lower both being settled. There is auspiciousness without balefulness.

SAWYER ○ The trigraph's auspiciousness derives from the presence of mature yang in the Tao of Man. Since it is unopposed by the other positions, even though they are both yin and, moreover, inappropriate to the position of Heaven, no obstacles are raised to tranquil freedom and happiness. The Verse expressively captures the mood with the serene image of spring light falling in the carved hall.

27 *PI O* 辟惡

○ ○ 上 上
○ 中 中 中
○ 下 下 下

Expelling Evil
The image of awesome Virtue
Yin weak, yang strong
Tui (Marsh) ∘ True west

ORACLE

The masses of people, loving their ruler, expel trouble and eliminate misfortune. The fierce dog does not bite. The myriad affairs will certainly be fruitful.

VERSE

A dragon spews water; it's the moment of spring,
Withered grass and dry trees are completely renewed.
Happily I have found an old man who speaks with me,
Henceforth my impoverished path becomes enriched.

COMMENTARIES

YEN ∘ Affairs will all be auspicious because they will gain the help of others. The traveler is returning. Working to gain material wealth and remaining at home will be equally auspicious. Moreover, even though yin dwells at the top, it is not in the correct position. The clusters of yang, fully flourishing, are able to "eliminate trouble and misfortune since the masses all love the ruler."

This trigraph and the previous two trigraphs all have yin stealthily occupying yang's position in Heaven. The virtue of yang in them suffers no deficiency. If you cultivate it, it will be auspicious. Whatever has been causing anxiety will be free from suffering.

Ho ∘ Dukes, marquesses, and regional lords will certainly obtain good assistants. In marrying and bringing a woman into the family, one will definitely gain a good wife. The ill should be cured. The imprisoned will get out through the assistance of others. Engaging in battle will result in victory. The pregnant will give birth to a male. Commercial enterprises will be profitable.

CH'EN ∘ The Tao of Man is already flourishing; the Tao of Earth is similarly flourishing. It is like having awesomeness that is fearsome, that expels perversity and eliminates evil. Although there are two yin at the top, they are unable to cause harm.

LIU ∘ Being humble and illustrious at the top is what the masses love. With a cluster of worthies aiding and assisting, the ruler is preserved unharmed.

In this trigraph, yin dwells in the top position but does not grasp Heaven's power. A cluster of yang lies below, firm and correct without perversity. The fierce dog not only doesn't bite but, on the contrary, "expels trouble and eliminates misfortune on the ruler's behalf." With regard to affairs divined about: through gaining the assistance of the masses, they will be successful.

SAWYER ∘ "Expelling Evil" integrates two significant themes of great import in contemporary life: the assistance of others, which is necessary to contend with the manifold evils and perversities constantly assaulting the individual, and the critical role of advisors or mentors. The commentators make the former quite clear; this trigraph explicitly advises relying on associates and the massed help of others. However, the role of the aged advisor, the Sage who has attained both worldly and transcendent wisdom, is imagized only in the Verse, which suggests that the moment for rebirth has arrived. This implies that affairs, perhaps having lain fallow or withered over time, are about to be revived, just like all the vegetative life that has passed through the drying effects of winter. The subject of the poem will begin to prosper after the necessary wisdom is imparted; only then will opportunities arise, will success be achieved. Therefore, advice, wise counsel, and experienced teachings should be sought out before undertaking new projects or recommitting to a fruitless course.

28 *Ta Huo* 大獲

Great Harvest
The image of profitable things
Yang in the middle controls yin
K'an (Water) ○ True north

ORACLE

Han's great black dog pursues a rabbit; running along, it hardly stretches its legs. The rabbit, being bitten at, is in front; the pursuer is behind. Repeatedly the dog catches it; once seized, it is unable to run off.

VERSE

> The ways of the world have no brambles,
> Hereafter human hearts should not sigh.
> In seeking fame and pursuing profits,
> Bitter efforts will ensure your livelihood.

COMMENTARIES

YEN ○ Three yang occupy the middle, capable of controlling a cluster of menials just like a fierce dog biting a rabbit. Once seized, it cannot run off. This speaks about gaining an objective in no time at all. All affairs are beforehand small, later great. This trigraph is highly appropriate to apprehending those who have fled or stolen off. Seeking wealth will also yield abundant results. Hunting will obtain great catches. For the ill, this trigraph might not be particularly advantageous.

HO ○ Remaining in residence would be auspicious. The traveler will be late. The ill might suffer some distress. The imprisoned will encounter obstacles. It will be difficult to resolve official affairs. Campaign armies will return empty-handed.

CH'EN ∘ In the Tao of Man, yang is flourishing; in the Tao of Earth, yin is flourishing. Yin and yang mutually respond to each other and, moreover, accumulate in abundance.

LIU ∘ Three yang in the middle: the Tao of firmness is flourishing. The petty embrace the pliant and are unable to compete with the firm. Even though they want to jump up on the rafters like robbers in the end they obey its mandate.

In this trigraph, although three yang occupy a position between two yin, young yin is at the top and old yin dwells below. The old and young have different desires and are controlled by yang, unable to combine together. Thus this creates the image of Han's great black dog pursuing a rabbit. When the querent obtains this trigraph, it will be very auspicious for apprehending fugitives and rectifying brigands. Seeking wealth, searching for profits, and marriage arrangements will all be auspicious. There are obstacles to going out to travel. The imprisoned will find it difficult to escape their entanglements. The ill might be in some danger. If one remains in residence and maintains an attitude of sincerity, there will be no calamity. In divining about affairs, those in which objectives are sought will be successful. However, it will be difficult to resolve official matters or extirpate entanglements.

SAWYER ∘ This trigraph is probably the most textually corrupt among the entire 125, several variations being given for almost every line by the different editions. However, the trigraph's auspiciousness remains obvious, as well as the main theme that the rapid pursuit of prey—an analogy for elusive objectives—will easily produce great results. Less promising would be any desire to escape from burdens and entanglements, including those weighing on the spirit or inflicted by ghosts. One edition adds a few intriguing lines to Ho's commentary: "Hereafter you should cast aside unimportant matters. Going forth, why must you trouble yourself with bitter labors? Only drop your line in the lake's depths, for you will certainly catch a leviathan."

29   SHUAI WEI   衰微

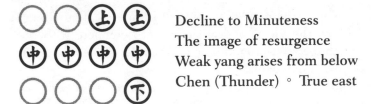

Decline to Minuteness
The image of resurgence
Weak yang arises from below
Chen (Thunder) ∘ True east

ORACLE

Sages and Worthies successively continue their teachings. The minute again resurges like melon vines stretching and extending, gradually arising and ascending.

VERSE

> I dreamt I entered the path to Mount T'ien-t'ai,
> Ascending the mountain, the moonlight so clear and bright!
> How extraordinary, the distinctive spring colors.
> Again I see the glory of old flowers.

COMMENTARIES

YEN ∘ Affairs, which have all been at odds with each other, again cohere. What is being sought will certainly be obtained; the hundred affairs will comply with your desires. Moreover, although yang is minute and weak, its intent is fixed on the upright. From below it ascends on high like the creeping melon vines stretching and extending upward. If you focus on your affairs, you will realize the growth of the minute and the continuance of the severed. This trigraph presages that those serving in bureaucratic offices will be promoted and transferred. Praying for beneficence and blessings as well as seeking posterity will be auspicious.

HO ∘ There will be success in literary endeavors. The traveler will arrive. There will be great harvests in agriculture and sericulture. Commercial activities will be profitable. A wife taken in marriage will prove worthy and beautiful. Those serving in bureaucratic offices will ascend and advance. Whatever you seek will comply with your desires. The ill might suffer some discomfort; it would be appropriate for them to sleep deeply. Beseeching the spirits would be auspicious. Any lost articles divined about will not be found.

CH'EN ∘ Four yin are in the middle, the image of decline and weakness. A single yang being at the bottom, an excellent root still exists. The two yin at the top respond to the single yang at the bottom. It is the image of Heaven protecting a good person.

LIU ∘ Yin flourishes in the middle; extreme, it will inevitably decline. "Melon vines stretching and extending"—yang will again come forth. Gradually it ascends upward; the upright Tao is returning.

In this trigraph, since young yang dwells below a cluster of yin, the orphan's danger is extreme. However, young yin is at the top, old yin dwells in the middle; their wills do not cohere. When the petty reach the pinnacle of flourishing, they inevitably become obstinate and turn against themselves. Yet young yang is just rising below. The four yin daily decline; young yang daily advances like "the melon vines stretching and extending," ascending upward. It is an omen that signifies the revitalization of what was in decline and the expulsion of turbulence. All affairs that might be divined about will be auspicious.

SAWYER ∘ While the commentators have succinctly explained the basic theme of the minute—the slender, weak, and subtle—resurging as the cycle of yin and yang once again enters the phase of yang ascending and therefore yin diminishing, the Verse strikes a somewhat different, ethereal tone. Rather than a vision of unimpeded growth, like melon vines stretching out across the ground, soon to be heavily laden with fruit, the poem weaves the image of a dream world, a magical land of escape. In traditional Chinese culture, stories abound about people venturing into deep woods or ascending various mountains—especially Mount T'ien-t'ai and Mount T'ai Shan—to encounter exotic persons or strange plants that waft them into another existence. Finally surfeited or piqued by curiosity, they return to their native places only to discover a world much changed, perhaps even unrecognizable, due to the long passage of time. For them their stay was brief; in reality it amounted to years or decades. Generally they are never able to rediscover the sacred path and must sadly remain in a strange world to which they no longer belong. Many poems, Taoist or not, draw on this allegorical experience of a delightful, heavenly world to express dissatisfaction and longing, as did the writer of these verses. The person mentioned in the Verse, probably burdened by the cares of many years, has focused on the plight signified by the "decline to minuteness" rather than embracing any prospects for resurgence and would simply prefer to opt out rather than rejoin the struggle, however auspicious it might appear.

30 *Pi Tsai* 避災

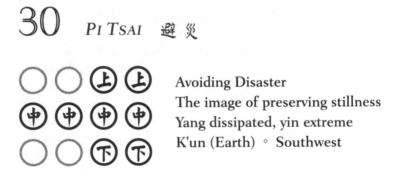

Avoiding Disaster
The image of preserving stillness
Yang dissipated, yin extreme
K'un (Earth) ∘ Southwest

Oracle

Summer is going, autumn coming; cold frosts cause disaster. Birds and beasts, their fur glossy; grasses and trees reduced to their roots.

Verses

> Recklessly acting, one encounters Earth's mesh,
> Carelessly commencing, one enters Heaven's net.
> Carefully proceeding in a cautious manner is paramount,
> Through escape, you can begin to preserve harmony.
>
> Heaven and Earth just turning barren and cold,
> Henceforth the myriad things are harmed.
> Fierce wolves occupy the important roads,
> Worthy officials now hide in obscurity.

COMMENTARIES

YEN ∘ In the spring, every affair will begin to accord with your mind. Remaining in residence would be auspicious. The traveler will not yet return. Moreover, in summer, one goes forth; in autumn, one stores away. "Yang dissipated, yin extreme"—therefore, the fur of birds and beasts is glossy, the grasses wither, and the color of the trees declines. It is the season for the perfected to dwell quietly, not a time to concentrate on advancing. This trigraph is somewhat inauspicious.

HO ∘ Those serving in bureaucratic offices will encounter perversity; brigands and the disciples of evil will harm them. The ill may be endangered or miserable. Sending the army forth on campaign would not be advantageous. It will be difficult to resolve legal entanglements. The traveler is not yet coming. In the matter of one's livelihood, you might lose what you have. There will be disputes, brigands, robbers, conflict, and fighting.

CH'EN ∘ It is the time when yin flourishes. The Tao of Man is in decline and weak; it is not appropriate to take action. Misfortune and change are about to arise.

LIU ∘ "Summer is going, autumn coming"—yin *ch'i* is flourishing. "Grasses and trees are reduced to their roots"—quietly preserve uprightness.

In this trigraph a cluster of yin wields authority. Old yin dwells in the middle; it is the time when the Tao of the perfected is blocked. The querent ought to retire, store things away, and preserve stillness. It is not appropriate to seek to advance. Whatever affairs are divined about, the results sought after will not be realized. The ill might experience some misery.

SAWYER ∘ The generally inauspicious nature of this trigraph illustrates the startling effects even an apparently minor change in a trigraph's lines can produce. All three positions are yin, just as in trigraph 22, "Resting in Tranquility," but the latter portends great success and tranquility. Clearly the presence of mature yin in the Tao of Man bodes ill, indicating that petty individuals have gained control, obstructing the Tao of order and justice, while the other two positions, being young yin and therefore compliant, simply accord with them. Furthermore, the previous trigraph, "Decline to Minuteness," while having an inauspicious-sounding name, bodes well because of the presence of the single yang at the bottom, in contrast to this one with young yin occupying the position of Earth. The active principle of even a solitary yang line amidst a setting of overwhelming yin can still presage growth and progress. Accordingly, this trigraph imagizes the onset of autumn, the time for withering and withdrawal, preparing for winter and complete stillness. However, since two of the positions have yet to mature to become old yin, it is not yet the season to completely cease all activities, but rather a time for caution and self-preservation amidst a troubled, perverse world. The Verses thus convey the trigraph's message exceedingly well.

31 *Fa Meng* 發 蒙

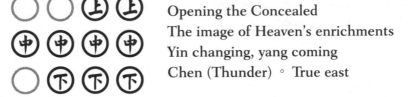

Opening the Concealed
The image of Heaven's enrichments
Yin changing, yang coming
Chen (Thunder) ∘ True east

Oracle

Yin extreme changes to yang. Torpid insects awaken and stretch. Great amnesty to All under Heaven. Bells and drums resound in ordered array.

Verses

> Yin extreme has just encountered tranquility,
> The door to the torpid insects begins to open.
> The three yang should exercise authority,
> Fame and profit will come together.

Through Heaven's gate the sun's rays gleam, the multihued
  clouds then part;
Abundant blessings generously descend, overspreading the nine
  wild regions.
The myriad things at once spiritually transformed;
All living beings dance about, drunken from golden cups.

COMMENTARIES

YEN ∘ Yin changing to yang startles the swarms of torpid insects,
just like striking bells and drums. Great leniency is granted to all those
imprisoned in darkness. This is a trigraph for obeying mandates and
establishing control. If inquiring about official advancement, it is
highly auspicious. Marriage arrangements would not be appropriate,
because in this trigraph, yin and yang are mutually injurious and not
in harmony.

HO ∘ Overbounding beneficence descends, bestowing abundant
benefits on the myriad things. The entangled will be released. Those
serving in bureaucratic offices will be transferred to higher positions.
The hundred affairs will be successful. One's livelihood will increase
tenfold.

CH'EN ∘ In the *Ling Ch'i Ching* as well as the *I Ching*, the previous
and subsequent trigraphs are based on each other and are mutually
productive. In the previous trigraph, yin is at the extreme; in this one,
two yin have changed to become three yang dwelling in Earth's position. It is the image of turbulence becoming extreme and then being
reordered.

LIU ∘ "Yin extreme changes to yang"—the firm comes within at the
bottom. "Torpid insects awaken and stretch"—thunder comes out
from the Earth. "Bells and drums resound in ordered array"—it is the
sound of virtue overarching.
  This trigraph employs three yang to curb the extreme flourishing of
yin, just like the sound of thunder inciting the torpid. It is the time
when the Tao of the perfected increases. Whatever affairs are divined
about will be auspicious. Employ the time to bespread civil virtue.

SAWYER ∘ In one edition, Ho quotes a sentence from Sun-tzu's *Art
of War* to explain the meaning of *t'ang t'ang*, translated in the Oracle

as "resound in ordered array." While the doubled character for "hall" (*t'ang*) is without doubt being used onomatopoetically, suggesting the unified beating of the drums and ringing of the bells—something like "thud thud," "boom boom," or "thump thump"—it also entails a sense of order and majesty. Thus Ho's citation from the "Military Combat" chapter of the *Art of War*: "Do not intercept well-ordered flags; do not attack well-regulated formations," where *t'ang t'ang* is translated as "well-regulated." While Ho's intent is simply to gloss the meaning of the phrase, it is worth noting that divination and military activities were closely intertwined in China from early antiquity, when the Shang dynasty employed plastromancy (divination by using turtle plastrons) to determine the auspiciousness of undertaking military campaigns and engagements. This tradition continued through the Warring States period, being more frequently witnessed early rather than late. Eventually there was a reaction to using "dead shells and bones, dried grass and stalks" to interpret events in which two parties would participate and one would invariably suffer defeat. However, a parallel tradition continued throughout the period and was clearly significant in the minds of both commanders and soldiers.

32   Ping Huan   病 患

Troubled by Illness
The image of plans impoverished
Yin extreme, becoming licentious
K'un (Earth) ∘ Southwest

ORACLE

Yin licentious; minor illness. He falls rigid, suffused with sadness. He looks upward expectantly toward Heaven, then bends low, bowing his head.

VERSE

> Alas, my fate is difficult, the time contrary,
> Disaster arrives, my body grows weary.

Supreme Heaven sustains me not,
Sadly, I am ill and endangered.

COMMENTARIES

YEN ∘ Whatever is sought will not be obtained. The traveler has difficulties. Moreover, as for yin being the cause of illness, its licentiousness is only gradually arising, so it will not reach the pinnacle. Therefore the Oracle says "minor illness." Yet "he falls stiff; he looks expectantly toward Heaven"—he doesn't see any rescuer. Thus he "bows his head and bends low"—nothing but melancholy thoughts. Under this trigraph the hundred affairs are all baleful. It is only appropriate to be cautious and secretive.

HO ∘ Illnesses should be treated quickly. The imprisoned will be judged guilty. The traveler is in difficulty, unable to advance. This trigraph is not auspicious.

CH'EN ∘ In the Tao of Man, yin is weak; in the Tao of Earth, yin is extreme. It is the image of being "troubled by illness," of poverty and difficulty. Even though there are heavenly spirits above, they are unable to effect a rescue.

LIU ∘ Yin flourishing, gradually immersing into licentiousness, signifying grief, sorrow, and distress. "He falls stiff; he looks expectantly toward Heaven"—his melancholy turns extreme.

In this trigraph, two old yin lines are impoverished below, while a single young yin is perched above. Thus it creates baleful omens. If inquiring about illness, medical treatment should be sought quickly. Those entangled in prison will not get out. The besieged will lack rescue. All affairs whatsoever are baleful.

SAWYER ∘ This trigraph is not simply all yin but is also dominated by old yin as well. Even though the associated trigraph is Earth, the commentators stress the feelings of weakness, darkness, and submersion that result from this plethora of yin. Affairs will be characterized by sinking and being bogged down, for yang's energy is completely absent. Earth itself lacks activity, while the Realm of Man is equally depressed. In such times, withdrawal and inactivity are the only options while awaiting a change in the moment. Fortunately, such extremes pass quickly; only moderate patience should be required.

33 MING YANG 明陽

Bright Yang
The image of slight auspiciousness
A cluster of yang gains authority
Ch'ien (Heaven) ∘ Northwest

ORACLE

The time for holding bureaucratic office has arrived; emoluments will be granted within the year. Force yourself to concentrate on affairs, being cautious not to lose them.

VERSE

An east wind blows, throwing open the nine great thoroughfares;
Harmonious *ch'i* returns, coming from below the sun.
Hereafter every affair will be joyous;
Riding the clouds, at once I ascend to the top of Jade Terrace.

COMMENTARIES

YEN ∘ "The time for holding bureaucratic office has arrived"—wherever one goes to assume a post will be auspicious. Good fortune and blessings will arrive in turn. It would be appropriate to be cautious about it; do not become remiss and idle. The ill will slowly recover. Although the traveler is returning, obstacles will be encountered en route. Moreover, this trigraph has cast out the accumulated yin of the preceding all-yin trigraph and is driving a cluster of yang. Doubly bright, it scintillates gloriously. Citing the *I Ching*, which advises one to "observe the brilliance of the state," the Oracle speaks about seeking position. The hundred affairs will be prosperous. It is similarly a time when external affairs can be hastened and advanced. Marriage arrangements and seeking official positions will be particularly auspicious.

Ho ∘ For everything that is sought, it would be appropriate to choose a good time. The ill should pray for the intercession of the spirits. The traveler might return shortly. If the imprisoned seek out someone with legal authority, they can escape punishment.

Ch'en ∘ Flourishing yang at the top shines down on the land below. The Tao of Man and the Tao of Earth are both single yang. There is advancement without retreat; it is advantageous for thoroughly penetrating.

Liu ∘ Yang brilliant, in the correct position, the Tao is greatly pervasive. It is the time for the perfected to hold office and take action.

In this trigraph, three yang dwell in the correct position at the top, while the middle and bottom are both young yang that are just ascending. The Tao of yang is pervasively penetrating; yin's perversity is being driven out. This should be the time for holding bureaucratic office and implementing the Tao. Affairs divined about will be highly appropriate; the moment for advancing cannot be lost. Affairs in general are auspicious; only secretly furthering selfish interests would not be appropriate.

Sawyer ∘ This trigraph is best understood in conjunction with the preceding one entitled "Troubled by Illness." Yang's resurgence in comparison with the overwhelming yin found in "Troubled by Illness" bodes well for externally directed actions, particularly those germane to structured organizations and extensive bureaucracies. The Tao of Heaven, being mature and vibrant, provides guidance and blessings that the lower positions, strong but not overbearing, can capitalize on through adding their own energy. The Verse raises the image of all the roads in the realm having been opened; therefore, the moment's potential appears virtually unlimited. Not only should joy be experienced, but the possibility of ascending even to the realm of the immortals is glimpsed.

34   *T'IEN YU* 天佑

Assistance of Heaven
The image of special prominence
Yin and yang mutually appropriate
Sun (Wind) ∘ Southeast

ORACLE

Climbing high, peering out far, above I see the Milky Way. The divine, exalted Jade Woman bestows a spiritual talisman on me. It forever grants that it will be difficult for age to affect me and thus preserves my body.

VERSES

> Although the rarities before my seat are expensive,
> I must still await a buyer to sell them.
> Fate is bringing prosperity and profit,
> I will not trouble myself with planning ordinary affairs.

> She being a beautiful person,
> The perfected man seeks her.
> Admirable virtue true,
> She confers blessings on me.
> Forever preserving the true,
> Do not lose her counsel.

COMMENTARIES

YEN ∘ It is the image of obtaining assistance. Affairs proceed from women. Remaining in residence would be auspicious and profitable. Official duties will lead to a glorious transfer. Scholarly endeavors will be extremely successful. The traveler is not yet returning; some rare object has certainly been found. The ill will recover largely by themselves.

Moreover, the position of Earth is already correct. Heaven and Man unite their Virtue just like ascending on high and seeing the six quarters. Furthermore, the bottom position responds to them. The man of yin has obtained his mate. The spiritual talisman to be given to me can be eagerly seen. One who attains a hundred years' longevity may sit even in the emperor's presence. This is a trigraph for the noble. Yin and yang gain their appropriate positions without conquering or harming each other. The hundred affairs will all be auspicious.

Ho ∘ Officeholders will be transferred to higher positions. If one takes a wife, he will obtain a beautiful woman. The route is open for the traveler. The ill will get well. Seeking out a high minister for official matters would be auspicious. Agriculture, sericulture, and commercial enterprises will all be auspicious. The pregnant will give birth to a male.

Ch'en ∘ In the Tao of Man and the Tao of Earth, yin and yang are mutually responsive. The three yang in Heaven radiate down on the Earth below.

Liu ∘ "Climbing high, peering out far"—one is in a high place. "The Jade Woman gives me a talisman"—yin associates with me. The middle is correct and responsive, the Tao of Man gains the "Assistance of Heaven."

In this trigraph a single yang lies in the middle; above is the ruler from which it receives firmness and brilliance, below a responsive mate of young yin. The trigraph's auspiciousness is without equal.

Sawyer ∘ This is the first of three generally auspicious trigraphs that derive their signification from the presence of mature yang in the position of Heaven. In each case the central theme is rendered as spiritual power, with the Tao of Man, being young yang, thus able to actively comply with Heaven's direction and receive its blessings. Throughout this series, yin's presence at the bottom modifies the image and expectations somewhat, but overall the appropriateness of the top two yang positions dominates. In the "Assistance of Heaven" all three positions are perfectly correct, with yang occupying the positions of Heaven and Man, and yin dwelling in Earth. The Verses convey a more this-worldly interpretation, while the Oracle drifts into the realm of Taoist seekings and thoughts of near immortality.

35 *Tsun Kuei* 尊貴

Respected and Honored
The image of spiritual assistance
Yang bright above and below
Ch'ien (Heaven) ∘ Northwest

ORACLE

Bright Virtue exceedingly glorious, longevity unbounded. The seven stars of the Dipper protect me. There will be a transfer to a generously renumerated position. Great good fortune for generations.

VERSE

> Before the carriage no ravines or obstacles,
> The boat floats easily down the river.
> Rain and dew descend from Heaven,
> The outer courtyard is again renewed.

COMMENTARIES

YEN ∘ What is being sought will certainly be obtained. The traveler is returning. Moreover, since the top and bottom are both yang, interior and exterior illuminate each other. This trigraph would not be appropriate for the ordinary person but is one for the respected and honored. It would be desirable to gain an audience with the ruler, to face north and serve him.

HO ∘ Those serving in bureaucratic offices will be transferred and promoted. Scholarly activities will produce achievements. Sending the army forth on campaign will gain territory; the army will not suffer loss or harm. It would be appropriate for the ill to seek the intercession of the spirits. Whether taking a wife or husband, they will prove compatible. Commercial activities will be profitable. The traveler is already returning. Agriculture and sericulture are auspicious. Official affairs will dissipate. This trigraph is highly auspicious.

CH'EN ∘ The Tao of Man is already correct; in the Tao of Earth, yang is flourishing. The three yang at the top radiate down on the Earth below. It is the image of riches, honor, and longevity, and thus is titled "Respected and Honored." It would be advantageous to gain an audience with the noble.

LIU ∘ "Bright Virtue exceedingly glorious"—the Tao of yang is luminous. "The Dipper preserves me"—yin's evil is dissipated. According to this trigraph, in seeking office and planning affairs, you will obtain the strength of a noble person. If plotting a funeral mound, you will certainly obtain auspicious ground. Those remaining in residence will receive assistance; those traveling will find companions. Although this is a trigraph for the nobility, an ordinary person obtaining it will also be extraordinarily happy.

SAWYER ∘ This is another of the all-yang trigraphs, one surprisingly held to be auspicious because of the mutually illuminating relationship of mature yang in the top and bottom positions. In contrast, conventional theory holds that yin appropriately dwelling in the bottom position should basically be auspicious. However, yang's active power even in the realm of Earth, yin's domain, portends achievement and success, as seen in other trigraphs as well. The Verse imagizes the unfettered future course presently unfolding, coupling the much-favored boat analogy with the natural renewal of all things as Heaven moisturizes them. Moreover, the Oracle indicates that the querent will enjoy the protective influence of the powerful stars in the Big Dipper, thus facilitating progress in officialdom and establishing the family's position for generations to come.

36 *I TAO* 宜禱

Praying for Intercession
The image of heavenly bestowal
Accumulated yin conquers yang
Sun (Wind) ∘ Southeast

ORACLE

When a number of unnatural oddities are seen, it becomes essential to engage shamans and wizards to pray for the intercession of the spirits and seek good fortune. The dissipation of disaster and mitigation of misfortune, gaining tranquility in great and minor affairs, will stem from the power of Heavenly and Earthly spirits.

VERSES

When sorrow appears, truly it is the basis for harm,
When anxiety comes, guard against it in the darkness.
Only when you again encounter winter's cold or summer's
  heat,
Will you manage to dispel calamity and disaster.

Disasters and oddities stir grief within;
A cluster of yin looks to overcome yang.
But by beseeching Heaven to grant its protection,
Old and young gain peace and repose.

COMMENTARIES

YEN ∘ This trigraph definitely emphasizes the experience of seeing unnatural oddities. In the beginning, affairs will not accord with your intentions, but later everything will comply with your desires. The traveler ought to return, but beforehand there will certainly be worry. Remaining in residence would be auspicious. Moreover, the accumulated yin in the bottom position, opposing the extreme of yang at the top, is like dwelling correctly at home yet seeing unnatural oddities. What are termed shamans and wizards respond to the top position. It is appropriate to pray for the intercession of the spirits, for they can dissipate disaster and mitigate trouble. Isn't this the power of spirits? The hundred affairs will be somewhat auspicious.

Ho ∘ Possibly there will be disaster and evil. It would be appropriate to cultivate good fortune through prayer. Perhaps there will be bickering, arguments, legal disputes, evil, and hardship. Or perhaps evil dreams of unnatural oddities, in which case beforehand there will be disaster, afterward good fortune. At first, matters will be difficult, in the end easy. The auspicious and baleful will be equally half; it will only be appropriate to cautiously pray. For the ill to sacrifice to the spirit of Heaven would be auspicious. Marriage arrangements will eventually result in union because the interior and exterior are mutually responsive.

CH'EN ∘ A single yang in the middle, the Tao of Man is solitary and weak. Heaven has three yang, Earth four yin; they mutually illuminate and respond to each other. This is the image of the spirits of Heaven and Earth manifesting themselves.

LIU ∘ "A number of unnatural oddities are seen"—the mind has something about which it is doubtful. If the family has an old ghost, their power will be inadequate to control it. If they announce it to the bright spirits, they will be preserved without suffering any loss.

In this trigraph, accumulated yin lies in the interior, while the upper position is flourishing yang; therefore the middle position is spoken of as the ruler. When the querent obtains it, the household has had the experience of seeing unnatural oddities. It would be appropriate to pray about them. For illness and legal disputes, it would also be appropriate to pray for the intercession of the spirits. All affairs will be worrisome beforehand, afterward auspicious.

SAWYER ∘ In this trigraph, the fourth in the series with mature yang in Heaven's position and young yang in Man's position, the overwhelmingly pernicious influence of mature yin at the bottom generates the unsettled nature of the momentary situation. Clusters of yin, whether simply four yin in one line or two lines of two or more yin, are frequently interpreted as representing petty individuals at their worst, the embodiment of willful chaos and unconstrained disorder. Accordingly, although Heaven is here strong and active, and has the energetic response of the youthful yang in the middle, assistance is needed. The single yang can derive power from Heaven, but complications arise because Heaven and Earth are also locked into a mutually responsive situation. However, as the Verses indicate, the main danger is not the experience of seeing unnatural oddities (such as horrible apparitions, grotesque figures, and goblins), but in allowing them to cause emotional harm. Liu has perhaps provided the most succinct psychological explanation—the mind is troubled and unsettled, unsure of its course. Prayer and other ritual activities help to settle such unease and restore the confidence to proceed. Thus, affairs are troublesome at first but should eventually prove manageable. However, it is hardly the time to undertake major projects involving risks that would preclude the confidence necessary to succeed.

37   SUNG HUO   送貨

Sending Goods
The image of abundant profit
Yin obtains external yang
Li (Fire) ∘ True south

ORACLE

A guest who comes from the south bestows excellent materials, precious goods, wondrous curios, golden bowls, and jade cups.

VERSE

> In the golden valley a profusion of flowers just opening;
> Clusters of immortals gather ethereally round the jeweled
>   terrace,

Pouring out gold bowls, emptying out jade cups, startling
  mortal eyes;
Balmy spring days in succession have I been drunken.

COMMENTARIES

YEN ∘ This trigraph portends that visitors will come to bestow
things. Remaining in residence will be auspicious. The traveler is returning, having obtained treasures and rich things. Moreover, with
yin occupying the middle and responding to exterior yang, isn't it appropriate that friends come from afar? The south is yang's position,
thus the Oracle states "coming from the south." "Precious goods" and
"marvelous amusements" are valuables of the nobility. "Golden
bowls" and "jade cups" are the utensils for a superlative banquet.

HO ∘ Marriage will be auspicious for both parties. What is being
sought will be obtained. The ill will be cured. Commercial activities
will be profitable. Official affairs will dissipate. The traveler will return. Obtaining this trigraph is highly auspicious.

CH'EN ∘ One and two respond to each other, while a single yang
dwells in the Earth. It is the image of possessing in abundance. Three
yang are at the top; yang's brightness radiates down.

LIU ∘ "A guest . . . comes from the south"—the firm and the pliant
respond to each other. "Golden bowls and jade cups"—they are employed to show respect.
    In this trigraph, young yin dwells in the middle, a solitary yang
associates with it from below, while flourishing yang obtains its position at the top. Yin, pliant and submissive, responds to exterior yang;
thus one will certainly obtain wondrous goods coming from the south.
As for the phrase "coming from the south," the upper three yang are
associated with the trigram *Li,* which is the southern region. As for
the "golden bowls and jade cups," the single yang at the bottom is
associated with the trigram *Ch'ien,* which is the image of gold and
jade. It is the image of "golden bowls and jade cups." At the beginning
it responds to the top and forms a mate with the middle. This is receiving what a guest bestows. For the querent, seeking wealth and
marriage arrangements will be most auspicious; the hundred affairs
are all very auspicious.

SAWYER ◦ This is of course a marvelous trigraph: without effort (beyond one's basic character and virtue), powerful individuals send valuable gifts and wondrous presents. Accordingly, profit-making activities should prove enormously promising without extreme exertion. The Verse suggests the mesmerizing quality of the realm of the immortals, where gold and jade are found in such profusion as to be commonplace but still dazzling to human eyes.

The commentators incorporate a number of allusions to the trigrams and hexagrams of the *I Ching* to explicate the trigraph's extended meaning. Complex explanations of this sort can readily be constructed, as may those explaining every statement in the Oracle and Image in terms of the yin/yang character of the individual lines. However, the passages remain intelligible without extensive annotation, though parallel consultation of the *I Ching* might prove illuminating from time to time. Yen's reference to friends coming fro..ι afar echoes a famous statement in the *Analects* of Confucius in which he notes such visits by friends as one of life's pleasures, while the golden valley of the verse's first line may refer to an ancient location famous for the splendor of its garden. (This Oracle is quoted in the biography of one Chiang Mi who was forced to commit suicide for offending the throne late in the fifth century CE, thereby suggesting that the *Ling Ch'i Ching* existed in core form by that time.)

38 WU NAN 無 難

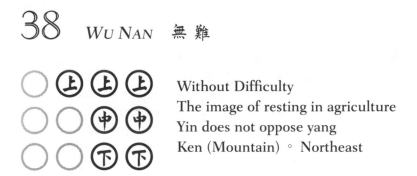

Without Difficulty
The image of resting in agriculture
Yin does not oppose yang
Ken (Mountain) ◦ Northeast

ORACLE

The land peaceful and tranquil, without hardship or difficulty. It is highly appropriate to engage in sowing the fields and is advantageous to travel about.

VERSE

Above the vast sea, clouds part to reveal an expansive
thoroughfare,
The multihued phoenix carries a proclamation to the edges of
Heaven.
The common people take pleasure in their occupations, settled
and secure.
Officials advance, their achievements and fame praised
throughout the realm.

COMMENTARIES

YEN ∘ The lowest position does not oppose the top, thus it says that "the land is peaceful and tranquil." Scattering seeds is thus auspicious. Commercial activities will also be profitable. Those serving in bureaucratic offices will advance. If inquiring about illness, there will not be any calamity. The traveler is peaceful and secure and sooner or later will return. Marriage arrangements will lead to union. Remaining in residence would be auspicious.

HO ∘ Whatever is sought will follow one's desires. Illness should easily be cured. Official matters will be untroubling. The hundred affairs will be peaceful and prosperous. This is a highly auspicious trigraph.

CH'EN ∘ The middle and lower positions are both yin, but they have not yet reached the extreme. The Tao of Earth is pure and beautiful, while the three yang at the top radiate down on it. Yin and yang are harmonious and joyful; it is the image of abundant harvest.

LIU ∘ "The land peaceful and tranquil"—the pliant dwells in an inferior position. "Without hardship or difficulty"—the mind has no doubts. When above and below are free from opposition, what will not be appropriate?

In this trigraph, firm yang is at the top, while the middle and bottom are both cooperatively submissive. Thus "the land is peaceful and tranquil, without hardship or difficulty." Accordingly, movement and rest, advancing and withdrawing will not encounter any obstacles. Every affair inquired about will be auspicious.

SAWYER ∘ Mature yang in the position of Heaven powers the moment because the two lower lines, both young yin, are submissive and compliant. Furthermore, yin dwells appropriately in the position of Earth; the trigraph's only weakness might be the Tao of Man. Perhaps this is why the name is less positive than the tenor of the commentary, designated as "Without Difficulty" rather than "Great Advancement" or "Magnificent Prosperity." For an agricultural society, the explanation of the Image and its echo in the Oracle, stressing the stability and productivity of agriculture, is unsurpassable. Moreover, it implies that any projects "seeded" now will have excellent prospects for success. It is not just the land that is plowed and exploited, but the entire realm as well, explaining the advantage of "going forth and returning"—translated as "travel about"—at the end of the Oracle. The Verse paints a glorious picture of the world opening up, with the human realm being anchored by a stable agricultural population whose vital efforts underpin the economic system as well as nourish the people and thereby sustain the very possibility of life.

39 KUNG HO 恭和

Respectful Harmony
The image of harmonious peace
Yin and yang continue submissive
Li (Fire) ∘ True south

ORACLE

Above, the correct and straightforward; below, people offer their services. The household is harmoniously in accord. The great and small unite their strength. No one contravenes your will. Whatever is sought will be obtained.

VERSE

> The *ch'i* of happiness fills the household,
> Within the family no stumbling or faltering.

Wherever the noble cast a sympathetic eye,
Henceforth becomes smooth sailing.

COMMENTARIES

YEN ○ Yin dwells in the middle position; it is the image of "continuing submissiveness." Thus the Oracle states that "below, people offer their services." This trigraph succeeds in uniting the clusters of strength below. Whatever is sought will be realized.

HO ○ Marriage arrangements will be auspicious; husband and wife will unite harmoniously. Remaining in residence will prove tranquil and secure. The traveler is about to return. Business enterprises, agriculture, and sericulture will all be profitable. The pregnant will give birth to a male. Official matters will be free from suffering. Sending the army forth would be highly advantageous. The hundred affairs are very auspicious.

CH'EN ○ The Tao of Man is pliant and submissive. Three yang above and below invariably presage fullness and repleteness. It is the image of the Tao of the family just flourishing.

LIU ○ Yang is firm above, "correct and straightforward." The robust and submissive sustain each other—"below, people offer their services. The household is harmoniously in accord." There is nothing sought that will not be obtained.

Under this trigraph, holding bureaucratic office, managing family affairs, mobilizing the army, governing professional matters, marriage arrangements, and commercial activities, not one of them will lack profit. Whatever is sought will in all cases be obtained. It is a highly auspicious trigraph.

SAWYER ○ In stating "yin and yang continue submissive," the image for this trigraph emphasizes the compliance of the two lower positions with the will and direction of the mature yang in Heaven's position. For the authors, it epitomizes the fundamental structural unit of Chinese society, the extended family with the patriarch being virtuous and correct, and all other members submissive in accepting and performing their respective duties. Although surprisingly unexpressed, the family is also the model for the state, and the trigraph thus entails connotations of the great accomplishments possible for a united people under a strong, benevolent ruler. Generally speaking, it should be particularly relevant to organized efforts, and especially promising for querents who exercise power over others, however limited such power might seem.

40 *WEI K'E* 違剋

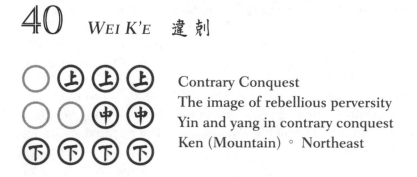

Contrary Conquest
The image of rebellious perversity
Yin and yang in contrary conquest
Ken (Mountain) ∘ Northeast

ORACLE

Lower does not follow upper, interior does not control exterior. Upper and lower in contrary conquest, rules and regulations in chaos and defeat.

VERSE

> Happening on mountains you must avoid danger,
> Encountering rivers, embrace concern.
> On the day you return to your native village,
> You will certainly learn about the two-tailed ox.

COMMENTARIES

YEN ∘ The Tao of yin is incessantly growing; yang is unable to constrain it. For this reason it is perversely transcendent. Thus the Oracle says "chaos and defeat." The ill might suffer some distress; doctors and medicine may not yet be fully effective. If the army goes out on campaign, it will be defeated and destroyed. The traveler is not yet returning. Under this trigraph the hundred affairs will all be baleful.

Ho ∘ Whatever is sought will not be obtained; whatever is undertaken will not be successful. Unless caution be exercised, one might see one's family separated and scattered, one's properties squandered away. The ill may be somewhat troubled and in distress; medical treatment may not yet prove fully effective. If the army goes out on campaign, it will not be victorious. The distant traveler will meet with disaster and not return. Official affairs will become more entangled. It will be difficult for the imprisoned to get out; it is as if they had entered death's gate. Ordinary affairs are all inauspicious. It would not be appropriate to change or move. Only if this trigraph is obtained in the first month of the year will it be auspicious; at all other times it will be baleful.

CH'EN ∘ The Tao of Man is pliant and soft, unable to control the cluster of menials below. The top position has three yang, while in the middle and lower positions yin flourishes.

LIU ∘ "Lower does not follow upper"—yin is exceedingly active. "Upper and lower in contrary conquest"—they encroach on each other. "Laws and regulations in chaos and defeat"—in the end they cannot be victorious.

In this trigraph, upper and lower conquer each other, while the pliant dwells in the middle. It is unable to govern the cluster of menials (represented by the bottom line) and is also unable to correctly follow the top position. Its power must lead to chaos and defeat. For the inquirer, then, the hundred affairs will all be baleful.

SAWYER ∘ As this is one of the *Ling Ch'i Ching*'s truly baleful trigraphs, it vigorously admonishes the querent to be extremely cautious because the moment is clearly unstable and perversity tends to dominate. However, avoiding exposure to risk by not undertaking anything new or aggressive, the time should pass without incident. Accordingly, it would not be an opportune moment to indulge in visibly dangerous activities such as skydiving or mountain climbing. While these are of course extreme examples, certainly the trigraph's implied injunction can be extrapolated appropriately. Nevertheless, it should be remembered that dwelling in correctness and applying rational thought to matters, as the Confucians advise, remain paramount in any situation. If inquiring about an illness, the trigraph would seem to suggest that maximum attention should be paid to the underlying problem and medical resources fully exploited.

41 CHEN SHOU 貞壽

Perfected Longevity
The image of concealed Virtue
Pure yang responds in three positions
Ch'ien (Heaven) ∘ Northwest

ORACLE

The Four Luminaries of Mount Shang nourished their nature and practiced the Tao. Breathing Original *Ch'i,* they attained the point of not aging.

VERSE

>With bracken for greens and pine for a meal, I break off the
>   world's dust;
>White clouds, flowing waters for ten thousand springtimes.
>The vermilion summons of the imperial realm suits me not;
>Completing my nature, preserving my mind, I nourish a
>   solitary purity.

COMMENTARIES

YEN ∘ Even though this trigraph is purely yang, the lower position acts as the subject. It is almost the image of excellence in concealment. Through voluntary retirement one can nourish pristine purity; the myriad affairs will thereby be secure and truly auspicious. Only marriage would not be advantageous because this trigraph is purely yang.

HO ∘ Those serving in bureaucratic offices will be transferred to higher positions. In agriculture and sericulture it would be appropriate to act early. The traveler will arrive. Official affairs will be resolved. The ill should recover largely by themselves. Commercial activities and remaining in residence will both be profitable. The hundred affairs will be prosperous and successful. It is an omen of great auspiciousness.

CH'EN ∘ Three yang dwell in both the upper and middle positions and respond to each other. A single yang lies below, unable to advance upward. It is the image of a Worthy in an inferior position who does not do anything but only dwells in concealment, nourishing longevity.

LIU ∘ "Four Luminaries of Mount Shang"—brightness dwelling in gloom. "Breathing Original *Ch'i*"—they can freely wander about.

In this trigraph, heavy yang dwells in each of the upper two positions. It is the time when civilization shines brightly throughout the realm, while a solitary yang dwells below. Only the Four Luminaries of Mount Shang could act appropriately. When the querent obtains this trigraph, it would be appropriate to dwell in tranquility and be upright so as to enjoy the blessings of health and peace. It would not be appropriate to go forth and seek things from others.

SAWYER ∘ The varying perspectives and temperaments of the four main commentators become visible in this rather startling trigraph. Heaven and Man are both strong, being mature yang, and therefore fundamentally auspicious. Heaven provides guidance and radiates down; people respond vigorously, putting affairs in order and nurturing prosperity and civilization. The realm of Earth, also being yang, is subject to ambivalent interpretations throughout the *Ling Ch'i Ching*, sometimes being seen as good—energy in the Earth—sometimes as inappropriate because Earth should be inherently yin. Widely viewed, this trigraph should be very auspicious, certainly more so than, for example, certain all-yin trigraphs that paradoxically portend excellence in affairs. Yen and Ho strike this tone, but Ch'en sees the superior man cut off—although voluntarily—from the sudden resurgence of civilization, nourishing his original nature in some mountain realm untroubled by the cares of the world. Confucianism would suggest that superior men should serve when the Tao prevails in the world, when a good ruler brings order and nourishes the people, and retire when darkness dominates. The Four Luminaries of Mount Shang in fact were originally men who had retired during the bloody chaos that reigned as the Ch'in was overthrown by the eventual founders of the Han dynasty and remained in unsullied purity after the Han's inception and the restoration of order. Although, according to the historical records, they deigned to interfere in worldly affairs once more, they essentially eschewed the political world. From a Taoist perspective they pursued the ultimate goal, purity and longevity, and attained it, being known for their great age and the whiteness of their eyebrows (hence their name). But Liu suggests the problematic aspect of such voluntary withdrawal: psychologically, it may cause regret except for recluses characterized by the most steadfast resolve. The Verse, however, paints an image of this idealized tranquil life contrasted with the dross of civilization and its entangling ways. Perhaps the trigraph depicts the frustration experienced when even the untainted find their way limited during an enlightened age, and correctly points to a more satisfying course.

42   Kang Chang   剛長

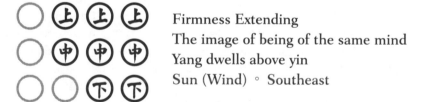

Firmness Extending
The image of being of the same mind
Yang dwells above yin
Sun (Wind) ∘ Southeast

Oracle

Two men of the same mind, acting as exterior and interior. Dwelling together in one state, they are like lips and teeth.

Verse

> Two intents cast their lot together,
> The seasons of Heaven again change to be open.

The time is coming when the myriad affairs will proceed
   smoothly,
At this moment do nothing hurried or bumptious.

COMMENTARIES

YEN ∘ Under this trigraph, what you obtain will inevitably be
through others; what you lose will also be through others, not yourself. Moreover, two yang dwell together above a single yin. Although
yin has no power, and thus yang spreads forth, they do not conquer
each other. Thus it speaks about "two men of the same mind." Remaining in residence and other affairs will be auspicious. Serving in
bureaucratic office will be especially excellent. Marriage arrangements may suffer minor calamities. Illnesses will slowly be cured.
Planning on behalf of others will be successful. The traveler will not
yet return; however, word will definitely come.

HO ∘ Ruler and ministers form a united body; friends share the
same intent. Commercial activities will be profitable. The pregnant
will give birth to a male. Agriculture and sericulture will be somewhat
auspicious. In official affairs, someone will manage to rescue you.
Even though the ill apparently suffer from evil influences, it would be
appropriate to seek medical treatment. This trigraph does not presage
any misfortune, only great auspiciousness.

CH'EN ∘ Two yang in the upper part, a single yin below, above and
below are of the same mind. But when a single yin interacts with two
yang, inevitably there will be gains and losses. Profit lies in harmoniously joining with others.

LIU ∘ "Two people of the same mind"—resulting from the two
heavy, firm positions. Pliant, submissive yin dwells in an inferior position; it does not cause harm anywhere. "Like lips and teeth"—the wall
of hedges is made more solid.
   In this trigraph a single yin dwells beneath doubled yang, pliant and
submissive without any contrary movement to conquest. Two yang
above, of the same mind, implement affairs. Together they create the
image of exterior and interior, of dwelling in a single state. Lips and
teeth are mutually reliant, neither can be lacking. If inquiring about
affairs such as between ruler and minister, elder and younger brother,

husband and wife, or friends, there is none that will not be auspicious and profitable. It is not appropriate to wantonly guess or have doubts. Remaining in residence and commercial activities will be outstanding. Neither listen to nor believe rumors. Sowing seeds will produce a great abundance. Sericulture and wheat will have good harvests. The pregnant will give birth to a male. Official affairs will be favorable as there is an omen that others will provide assistance. It would be appropriate for the ill to receive medical treatment and to pray for the intercession of the spirits to preserve them. Marriage arrangements will result in a harmonious union and pairing with a beautiful mate. Divination about travelers indicates that they will not yet return, but word of them will arrive. Under this trigraph a desire to plan affairs, remain in residence, or undertake business activities would in every case be highly auspicious.

SAWYER ∘ The theme of close association receives extensive treatment in traditional Chinese thought, for it is perceived as not only providing the basis for superlative achievement in the world, but also the joys that friendship with others of like mind and true understanding may bring. Consequently, it appears to be the time for working in common with others rather than undertaking individual, even heroic efforts. That this trigraph is entitled "Firmness Extending" (or "Firmness Growing") rather than the previous one, in which the lower position is also youthful yang and therefore the principle of growth, merits nothing.

43 CH'IANG SHENG 強盛

Strongly Flourishing
The image of being sustained by the
　masses
Three yang at the pinnacle of flourishing
Ch'ien (Heaven) ∘ Northwest

ORACLE

The masses flourish and are moreover strong, already having become rich and prosperous. If they are employed to establish achievements, no one will be able to withstand them.

VERSE

> Having crossed a dangerous bridge, the hundred affairs are
> 　settled,
> Why overly trouble yourself about hardship and difficulty?
> The flood dragons gain their desire, flourishing the clouds and
> 　rain,
> Once you ascend to the celestial realm, nothing is ordinary!

COMMENTARIES

YEN ∘ In this trigraph, each of the three positions has three yang. This can be termed the pinnacle of flourishing. Thus no one can obstruct the establishment of achievements and implementing of affairs. In all matters, straightforward unselfish ways will be appropriate. If you are cautious not to follow perverse ways, it will be auspicious.

HO ∘ This trigraph presages a period of good fortune! The pregnant will give birth to a male. The traveler will return shortly. Business enterprises will be profitable. Sericulture and agriculture will produce double the usual harvest. Hunting and fishing will have good results. Guarding the frontiers will result in internal security and tranquility. Remaining in residence will be secure and stable. Illnesses will be cured. Official affairs will be dismissed. Commercial activities will be profitable. Moving would be auspicious. Mobilizing the army will garner a victory. The many affairs are highly auspicious; only marriage arrangements will not be advantageous.

CH'EN ∘ In all three positions, yang is at its extremity. This presages riches, strength, and power without the slightest interference by yin's weakness.

LIU ∘ Three yang with the same Virtue, flourishing and strong. Establishing achievements and implementing affairs, who is able to oppose them?

In this trigraph the three positions are all yang—firm, robust, flourishing, and great, the pinnacle of riches and prosperity. Thus it is appropriate to establish achievements and implement affairs. When the querent obtains this trigraph, it will be highly appropriate to actively exploit it. Employing the army on campaign would be especially auspicious. Only if inquiring about marriage arrangements will it not be advantageous, because the trigraph is pure yang.

SAWYER ∘ This is of course the ultimate yang trigraph, with strong, mature, fully flourishing yang in each position. Remarkably, it presages achievement and success rather than conflict among the Three Talents of Heaven, Earth, and Man. Perhaps the only danger is allowing such energy and the resulting enthusiasm to lead to the total abandonment of reasonable constraints, to venturing beyond the realm of possibility, for it must be remembered that the pinnacle is unstable and imminently subject to inescapable reversion.

44 CHIA LI 佳麗

Surpassing Beauty
The image of being appropriately yin
Yin's position gains command
Sun (Wind) ∘ Southeast

ORACLE

Within the lavender chamber of green-latticed windows, there are superlative women with countenances whose beauty arouses. They are like irises and orchids wafting forth their fragrance.

VERSES

A branch of flower blossoms beautiful and fragrant,
Their clear perfume, effusive and delightful, penetrates the
    orchid chamber,
Blown by the wind to end by becoming a smile.
Well should I ask at how many feasts I have heretofore been
    drunken.

Gathering medicinal herbs along a Heavenly Terrace, I turned
    and was enthralled,
Peach blossoms and flowing waters wafted me to a liaison with
    beauty.
In the spring wind the birds sang out full of emotion,
I told that Liu fellow not to return home.

COMMENTARIES

YEN ∘ Yin's position has arisen and prospers; affairs proceed from women. Illnesses will be cured largely by themselves. Whatever is sought will be obtained. Moreover, pure yin at the bottom responds to Heaven and Man above. Its disposition is that of a rare fragrance, like that of irises and orchids. The hundred affairs will all prosper. The traveler will return. Marriage arrangements will be especially excellent. The myriad affairs will all be auspicious. The ill will be at peace. All men incline to affection.

Ho ∘ This is a trigraph of nobility within. If inquiring about marriage arrangements, the noble will succeed, the lowly will not. This is a yin trigraph; inquiring about yang affairs would not be advantageous. If planning a lawsuit, you will encounter someone of power and nobility. For nuns and practitioners of the Tao, it is auspicious. Whether dwelling at home or going out, there will be the felicity of wealth and profit. The myriad affairs will all prosper.

Ch'en ∘ The Tao of Man is rich and flourishing, and has flourishing yin below it to mutually respond. This is the image of an extremely well-favored consort within a rich and noble family.

Liu ∘ The doubly firm are above; the Tao of yang is glorious. The cluster of yin lying below, receiving their influence, creates the image of superlative women. Your descendants will certainly be numerous.

In this trigraph, even though yin is flourishing, it dwells in the lowest position. The Tao of yang is glorious and bright above; the pliant dares not oppose it but subsequently acts to respond correctly. This trigraph presages that the hundred affairs will all proceed easily. The traveler will return. Marriage arrangements will be highly auspicious. Forming relationships would be especially excellent. Those suffering from acute illnesses should not die.

Sawyer ∘ This trigraph envisions the interaction of mature yang in the upper two positions with mature yin in the realm of Earth as signifying the attractive beauty and inherent power of women within the closely confined and structured traditional family. Although their strength fundamentally derives from their enthralling beauty— leading to the images in the two Verses, including the analogy of being drunken at a feast of beauty—it remains undeniably potent. Furthermore, throughout the commentaries the concept of "nobility within" plays on two meanings: high-ranking, noble women within powerful families, exerting great influence while yet dwelling in the inner apartments; and inner nobility of character or soul, more clearly identified with the nuns and monks Ho mentions in passing. Certainly this trigraph could be entitled "Women's Power" or "Empowering Women," for according to it, women will clearly control the course of events. Moreover, in ancient China, especially before the rise of Confucianism and the imposition of extreme strictures on contact between the sexes, the wives of famous kings and rulers often exercised great power, even personally commanding their own military forces, as did the daughter of China's first famous strategist, the T'ai Kung. The Oracle in fact employs the T'ai Kung's surname (Chiang) and that of the powerful founding family of the Chou dynasty (Chi) to refer to the women cloistered in the inner apartments. Although the two words evolved to eventually designate "consorts" and "concubines," vestiges of the original connotations seem appropriate here, leading to the translation of "superlative women" rather than "elegant concubines." For women, this is the paradigm trigraph of power.

45   *TE LU*   得祿

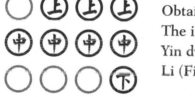

Obtaining Blessings
The image of rising fortune
Yin dwells below yang
Li (Fire) ◦ True south

ORACLE

Ruler and subject, exchanging positions, are about to give rise to great profits. Post horses run throughout the day; people attain unbridled freedom.

VERSE

> Like a boat crossing a great river,
> Or in a drought expectantly watching for frost and rain.

The four seas united as a single family,
The enlightened ruler obtains excellent support.

COMMENTARIES

YEN ∘ Moving would be auspicious; going out will be advantageous. What is being sought will certainly be obtained. The traveler is not yet returning; a letter will precede him. Illness seems to be related to locale; therefore, it would be appropriate for the ill to go out and avoid the cause, and to have someone sacrifice for them. Then it will be auspicious. Moreover, a single yang lies below, a cluster of yin dwells above it. Thus the Oracle states "exchanging positions, they are about to give rise to great profits." Achievements rely on people to be completed. Thus it says "run throughout the day." Under this trigraph, all affairs will at first be disharmonious, later fortunate; at first difficult, later easy.

HO ∘ Bureaucratic office holders will be transferred to excellent positions. Every affair will be auspicious. Travelers on both water and land will return. Your livelihood will yield ten times the usual profits. The pregnant will give birth to a male. If taking a wife, you will obtain a superlative mate.

CH'EN ∘ Yin flourishes in the position of Man, while a single yang lies below. It is the image of positions exchanged. Yet the three yang and four yin respond to each other; the human realm obtains the assistance of Heaven.

LIU ∘ "Ruler and minister exchange positions"—yin mounts on yang. "Post horses in unbridled freedom"—they have lost their control.

In this trigraph, four yin dwell in the middle and a single yang dwells below. This is what is meant by ruler and minister exchanging their positions. Yet how much more a single yang is mounted by the four yin! The three yang, firm and robust, occupy the outside unable to look after the ruler and, on the contrary, join with the cluster of yin and scheme to give rise to great profits. "Post horses run throughout the day," giving vent to their desires and acting on their own—extreme balefulness!

This trigraph and trigraph 15 are exact inversions of each other, with the fifteenth having one yang at the top and three yang at the bottom. By comparing them one can know the author's intent.

SAWYER ∘ This trigraph is the first in the series of four with mature yang in the position of Heaven and mature yin occupying the realm of Man. The former should be powerful and auspicious; the latter, being considered willful, should signify perversity and disorder in the human realm. However, there is an additional dimension because these two, both being mature, respond to each other in a dynamic, if not exactly congenial, fashion. Almost by default, the tenor of these trigraphs should thus be determined by the position of Earth, although in each case they portend some turbulence before order can prevail. The commentators embrace somewhat different interpretations for this trigraph's auspiciousness, with Yen, Ho, and Ch'en largely focusing on the Oracle's pronouncement about great profits, and Liu, troubled by implied problems, understanding the flurried activity of the post horses and the freedom of the people associated with them as portents of rising disorder and licentiousness. The reader must choose between these interpretations, although the Oracle clearly indicates a potential for great profit, and the Verse employs a voyage as an analogy for the state's condition, apparently just unified and beginning to prosper.

46 NING CHIH 疑滯

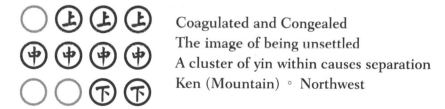

Coagulated and Congealed
The image of being unsettled
A cluster of yin within causes separation
Ken (Mountain) ∘ Northwest

ORACLE

My thoughts have plans but fear they cannot be implemented. Advancing and retreating are hesitant, not knowing what to do.

VERSE

> Advancing and retreating, affairs difficult to complete,
> Worry and doubt turn to impediments.
> If you want to know when you will enjoy prosperous days,
> Just wait until spring of another year.

COMMENTARIES

YEN ∘ In everything, whenever advancing and retreating are indecisive, affairs will not be concentrated. When affairs are not concentrated, they will not be successful. Moreover, yin dwelling in the lowest position responds to yang above. It wants to take action but is separated by the cluster of yin within the trigraph. Thus there is hesitation. However, if you strengthen yourself, in the end, business enterprises will have results. According to this trigraph the hundred affairs will lack a beginning but will have an ending.

HO ∘ What is sought will not be obtained; what is undertaken will not be completed. One's means of livelihood will not be profitable. Those serving in bureaucratic offices will retire. Travelers will be confused. It will be difficult for official affairs to be successful. The ill may be somewhat troubled. This is the image of being confused.

CH'EN ∘ In the Tao of Man, yin is at its pinnacle and wants to respond to the three yang above, but below there are two yin chaining and controlling it. Neither advancing nor retreating is possible.

LIU ∘ "My thoughts have plans"—the response lies below. "Fear they cannot be implemented"—petty individuals present obstacles. "Advancing and retreating are hesitant"—they cannot be managed.

In this trigraph, yin, dwelling in the lowest position, responds to yang above but is obstructed by the four yin in the middle. The top position initially wants to respond to it but is pulled by the four yin in the middle. Therefore, there is doubt and an inability to be decisive; worry and misfortune are born. Affairs inquired about will be confused and incomplete. Illnesses will wax and wane. The hundred affairs will not be advantageous.

SAWYER ∘ This is the second in the series of trigraphs with mature yang in the position of Heaven and mature yin in the realm of Man and should therefore be read in conjunction with the preceding and following trigraphs to understand the somewhat contradictory indications and dynamics. In particular, Yen and Ch'en exemplify the different perspectives that can be simultaneously imposed on the same configuration. The former stresses the separation and interference caused by the four yin in the middle; the latter attributes the difficulties to the presence and activity of young yin in the position of Earth. Fortunately the Oracle and Verse are both clear and consistent in depicting the adverse consequences of indecision. Moreover, the great T'ai Kung, traditionally considered China's first strategist, reputedly said: "Of the many harms that can beset an army, vacillation is the greatest. Of disasters that can befall an army, none surpasses doubt." Clearly, doubt and indecision doom even the simplest activities to mediocre results, and this trigraph should be viewed as an admonition to be decisive and resolute.

47   *O Hsiao*   惡 消

Evil Dissipated
The image of auspiciousness prevailing
A cluster of yang conquers yin
Li (Fire) ∘ True south

ORACLE

The sun comes forth from the eastern quarter, brilliant and fiery. In the middle [of the trigraph] there are evil emanations, but on the contrary they are scorched and consumed. Clusters of yang destroy yin; disaster is avoided, trouble eliminated.

VERSES

Wanting to advance, yet irresolute,
The mind endangered, affairs unthreatened.

At the side of the river a finger beckons,
Fame and profit achieved, a glorious return home.

Although a cluster of yin darkly flourish,
The Heavenly sun already unfolds its brightness.
A great opening, a new transformation,
Heaven and Earth hereafter peaceful.

COMMENTARIES

YEN ∘ In the middle yin flourishes; thus it says "evil emanations." The interior and exterior are pure yang, so the emanations "are scorched and consumed." All affairs will at first be obstinate, afterward harmonious.

HO ∘ Official affairs will not be successful; other people will provide assistance. The imprisoned will extricate themselves. The ill may at first be somewhat distressed but will afterward be cured. The traveler will soon arrive. Commercial activities, seeking office, and the hundred affairs will initially not accord with one's wishes but will later obtain very auspicious results.

CH'EN ∘ In the Tao of Man, yin is flourishing, but the strong yang above and below are both able to control it. It is the image of perverse sycophants fearing the upright. They will retire and disperse of their own volition.

LIU ∘ "Fiery and brilliant"—upper and lower are bright. "Evil emanations" are defeated and diminished, unable to take form. The cluster of yin is destroyed; the Tao of Man prevails.
   In this trigraph, two firm yang attack a single, extremely flourishing yin. At first, although they must exert force, in the end they will certainly be successful. Whatever affairs are divined about will be auspicious. Although there is danger, there will not be calamity. Divining about secretive or selfish affairs would not be advantageous.

SAWYER ∘ This trigraph discerns auspiciousness in vanquishing evils about to take form and thus represents a hopeful paradigm for contemporary existence. Clearly, myriad perversities are constantly unfolding about us; avoiding injury and reasonably prevailing within the parameters and context of individual life comprises a much sought-after but often unattainable goal. However, the present situation presages success.

48 SHANG CHENG 上正

Uprightness Above
The image of sagely administration
Yang encounters yin's control
Ken (Mountain) ∘ Northeast

ORACLE

Above, there is a worthy ruler; below, there are deceitful ministers. The sun and moon shine brightly, unseen through the dark dust.

VERSE

> Only the valiant are firm,
> Only the wise are enlightened.
> If one person grasps uprightness,
> A cluster of perversities will not arise.
> Making virtue your center,
> Gloriously preserve your purity.

COMMENTARIES

YEN ∘ Three yang at the top, the image of a worthy ruler. The sun and moon, although bright, do not illuminate the dark dust. Holding high office and remaining in residence would be auspicious. Arguments will not be successful. Marriage arrangements will result in gaining an excellent mate. The ill will not suffer.

HO ∘ Although yang at the top is bright, the masses of yin obscure its shining. Even though the sun and moon are radiant, dark dust still arises. Under this trigraph, there will be much regret. Only after seeking out lower magistrates will official affairs be remitted. The condition of the ill might vary; in some cases, only with the beginning of spring will they fully recover. The traveler is not yet returning. Seeking bureaucratic office will be especially difficult. Divining about marriage arrangements is auspicious because yin and yang are responsive. The hundred affairs are somewhat auspicious but will yield happiness with the coming of spring.

CH'EN ○ The three yang at the top and four yin in the middle respond to each other. It is the image of ruler and ministers cooperating harmoniously. Moreover, yin and yang each are at the pinnacle of flourishing. However, amidst the accumulated yin, there is the glory of yang—a single candle over the land. The Tao of the ruler has no deficiency.

LIU ○ Yang, firm, is in the correct position; there is a worthy ruler. Accumulated yin lies below like dark dust. This obstruction has not yet been broken through; the will cannot extend itself.

In this trigraph, firm yang dwells in the position of Heaven, while the middle and lower positions, perverse and pernicious, jointly obscure it. The ruler lacks ministers and is therefore unable to implement his will. The inquirer will have numerous causes for regret. Marriage arrangements will meet with a response. In this trigraph the auspicious and baleful are equal halves.

SAWYER ○ The visual impact of this trigraph is unsettling, being heavily weighed down with a plethora of yin. Although yin in itself is not inimical, a preponderance of menials in the Realms of both Man and Earth bodes little good. The Oracle interprets the image as the sun shining on the dark dust below, unable to penetrate it. (While the image has validity in itself, dust also symbolizes the world of toil and travail, of people and misery.) Ch'en's essentially Confucian optimistic view to the contrary, the mere existence of sagely administration does not guarantee that the forces of good will not be overwhelmed by the images of night. However, there is a potential for illumination, as well as some hope for an imminent transformation, because the two mature yin positions should soon revert to yang and engender a more promising time. Meanwhile, great care should be exercised in all affairs, and wisdom should be fully exercised in ferreting out activities or projects with appropriate potential due to their inherent harmonization of yin and yang.

49 *Ku P'in* 孤貧

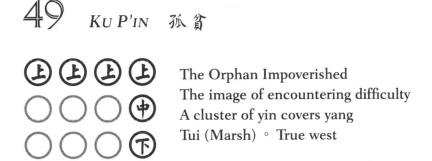

The Orphan Impoverished
The image of encountering difficulty
A cluster of yin covers yang
Tui (Marsh) ∘ True west

ORACLE

Going out from the warmth, entering the cold, with a thin jacket and unlined clothes. Departing from my beloved mother, I suffer from this unexpected misery.

VERSE

> Yang's harmony lacks expansive development,
> Coldly falling, it does not complete the spring.
> Truly like dreams on Shaman Mountain,
> Uselessly grievous and sorrowful.

COMMENTARIES

YEN ∘ Two single yang lie below, covered over by the cluster of yin. It is as if departing from what one loves and encountering a strong enemy.

Under this trigraph, it would be highly appropriate to preserve the old; it would not be appropriate to change one's actions. The distant traveler is not yet returning. Illness might grow slightly more severe. It is the image of departure and separation. If one obtains it in the second month, it is auspicious; in all other months, baleful.

HO ∘ Those serving in bureaucratic offices will lack advancement. Making a living will be unprofitable. It will be like dwelling in a solitary place, in poverty and distress, keeping a deathwatch. It will be difficult for the imprisoned to get out. It might be somewhat difficult to cure illnesses. Whatever is done will not accord with your wishes. Marriage arrangements will have neither beginning nor end. With regard to the hundred affairs, it would be appropriate to cautiously preserve yourself. At the beginning of the year, there will be energy.

CH'EN ∘ The Tao of Man is solitary and weak; the Tao of Earth is also thin. The four yin at the top lack the illuminating harmony of yang. Yin and yang do not respond to each other.

LIU ∘ "A thin jacket and unlined clothes"—one is lowly and alone. Yin flourishing at the top covers yang below; there is no one with whom to be a companion.

In this trigraph a single yang occupies a position beneath flourishing yin but does not respond to it, like an orphaned child. Yet the four yin that perversely dwell at the top are like a widow looking at her fatherless child. Her distress is extreme. If divining about illness, there might be some danger or a brief crisis. The traveler is overwhelmed with difficulty. Those serving in bureaucratic offices will meet with obstinacy and difficulty. Business affairs will not proceed as expected. An army on campaign will encounter hardship and obstacles. All affairs whatsoever are baleful.

SAWYER ∘ This trigraph, the first in the series of four with mature yin in the position of Heaven and a single, immature yang in the Realm of Man, lacks the resources to overcome the pernicious effects of petty individuals dominating on high. Thus, although the two youthful yang at the bottom are energetic and rising, they can only collide with the clouds and darkness above. However, while this depressing trigraph portends ill, imagized as separation and solitariness, there is still energy in the two lower positions and (contrary to the commentators), therefore, prospects for relief and success once the moment evolves. In particular, while illnesses should certainly not be neglected, the prediction is for temporary difficulty, not long-lasting suffering. This suggests that the orphan—a paradigm for voyaging into new worlds—while obviously depressed and perhaps still compelled to preserve old ways until becoming properly oriented and establishing a foothold, will eventually win through.

50 CH'IEN LUNG 潛龍

Submerged Dragon
The image of waiting for the time
A single yang controls yin
K'an (Water) ◦ True north

ORACLE

Emperor Shun personally plowed the fields around Mount Li. The land was enriched, the years abundant. His harvests multiplied ten and a thousand times.

VERSES

> Fate has brought the time for prosperity and enjoyment,
> The sorrowful heart has already cast out its sadness.
> Fully sustaining advancement and use,
> Every affair joyously pursued.
>
> Plowing and digging should accord with plans,
> Achievement and fame have their own time.
> A firm intent capable of enduring,
> Apart from the Sages, who can do it?

COMMENTARIES

YEN ◦ Any affairs that begin in the third or fourth months and end in the eighth or ninth months will be auspicious. Moreover, personally doing the plowing in a hidden place and thereby receiving abundant harvests, apart from Emperor Shun, who could have done it?

This trigraph is identical with the judgment for the "first nine" (lowest line) of the hexagram *Ch'ien* (Heaven) in the *I Ching*. Therefore, one should preserve oneself and dwell in seclusion in order to internally cultivate the Virtue of a ruler. No matter whether an affair is large or small, by relying on the Tao it will become feasible. However, business affairs will be difficult. Illness apparently stems from where the person resides; by the end of autumn it should be cured.

Ho ∘ Agriculture and sericulture will be appropriate. Whatever is sought will be obtained. Commercial enterprises will be profitable. Remaining in residence will prove rich and profitable. The traveler is returning. The pregnant will give birth to a male. Marriage arrangements will result in mutual union. The hundred affairs are all auspicious.

CH'EN ∘ One yang dwells in the position of Man; two yin dwell in the position of Earth. Yin and yang thus gain each other. The four yin in Heaven present the image of clouds and rain.

LIU ∘ The accumulated yin at the top are impoverished and no longer entangling. Virtue flourishes and responds, dwelling below in the position of Man. When the time comes to arise, no one will be able to constrain it.

In this trigraph, even though a single yang occupies a position amidst a cluster of yin, the yin at the top have reached the pinnacle of flourishing, their Tao is already impoverished. Young yin at the bottom makes a companion with the single yang in the middle. Although the four yin above don't look on solicitously, yin at the bottom is responsive. Thus one gets the image of Shun plowing around Mount Li. Even though he was not loved by his mother and father, his Mysterious Virtue in the end became manifest.

SAWYER ∘ While this trigraph is fundamentally auspicious, it depicts worth unrecognized, talent about to undergo a period of travail before emerging glorious and triumphant. Emperor Shun was not only unloved by his parents, his family made repeated attempts to kill him, such as by burying him alive in an unfinished well they had ordered him to dig. However, Shun successfully anticipated every evil act, preserved his life and his body (as was incumbent on a filial son), and never wavered in his service and devotion to his parents. Although the story of Shun's trials may well be interpreted as a paradigm about parental abuse and neglect, attention would best be directed toward his ultimate transcendence. Clearly a period of effort, even one of bitter incubation, is invariably necessary before one's true abilities can be perceived by the world. In Shun's case he became one of the three great legendary Sage Emperors; similar attainments are implied for the querent once his achievements are realized.

51 *I YU* 益友

Beneficial Friends
The image of going somewhere
Yang below transforms yin
Tui (Marsh) ∘ True west

ORACLE

There is a guest, Wang Sun, who comes to knock on my door. He speaks to me about good fortune and felicity. If I go out, I will be favored from above.

VERSE

> The time arrives, affairs plotted and planned will all be
>   completed;
> If you want Heaven's beneficence to descend, sincerity must
>   first precede it.
> Formerly, affairs never followed ordinary desires;
> Today, encountering the ruler, they begin to accord with one's
>   heart.

COMMENTARIES

YEN ∘ There are people calling each other; now one can go out. Some will be called yet not go, and it will not be auspicious. The

Oracle states that it is appropriate to go forth. However, a traveler summoned while away should return home. Moreover, responding to the outside from inside, intentions are not directed inward but to going out. This is because in this trigraph the middle position assists. How will the noble guests coming to knock on the door be limited to Wang Sun? Under this trigraph the time for marriage arrangements has arrived. Seeking from others would be especially excellent.

Ho ∘ Performing the duties of bureaucratic office will yield recognized achievements. Agriculture and sericulture are auspicious. Illnesses will be cured. Official affairs will dissipate. The traveler will return. In seeking bureaucratic office, if you have an audience with the noble, you will certainly be appointed to a position. The hundred affairs will accord with one's desires and be highly auspicious.

CH'EN ∘ Three yang dwell in the position of Earth; it is the image of Worthies below. They mutually respond with the four yin above and the single yang which, being of the same category, can draw it forward to ascend together.

LIU ∘ "Wang Sun knocks on the door"—response is to the outside. "Going out, one will be favored from above"—there will certainly be assistance.

In this trigraph, impoverished yin lies above while flourishing yang lies at the bottom. Yin, extreme, has an intention to seek out yang and thus creates the image of someone coming to knock on the door (symbolized by the bottom position). Wang Sun was an extremely rich and honored man. The middle position, young yang, does not contend with the bottom position, but assists it. Thus going out will certainly be felicitous. As for affairs divined about, it will be appropriate to advance; assistance from the noble will certainly be obtained. The ill should meet with an excellent physician. If the army is employed, there will be those who respond. Each and every affair is auspicious.

SAWYER ∘ This marvelous trigraph continues the theme of talent not yet manifest initiated with the preceding trigraph, the first in this series of four, portending that the moment has arrived when the world will beckon and the querent will soar forth. However, this recognition is premised on initiative being directed outwardly, being realized in activity and achievement in the world at large rather than in seclusion or the pursuit of individual commercial affairs. One need only discern an opportunity and maintain a readiness to capitalize on it to become successful, assuming of course that skills have been properly honed and effort appropriately exerted.

52 CHIEN CHANG 奸長

Wickedness Excelling
The image of numerous difficulties
Clusters of yin control yang
K'an (Water) ∘ True north

ORACLE

Cut off and separated, dwelling apart, again and again there are numerous obstacles. No affair is advantageous; whatever is done will not advance.

VERSE

> Tarrying for months, lingering for years, still unable to return
>   home,
> When it's time for affairs to be completed, thoughts turn
>   against them.
> Long ago I dispelled all anxiety over poverty brought by
>   contrary fate,
> I exhort you not to hate the weak affections of our age.

COMMENTARIES

YEN ∘ A single yang dwells in the middle, unable to relieve the situation by itself. Clusters of yin consort together; again and again one suffers harm. Whatever affairs are undertaken will not proceed as desired, but on the contrary, you will experience fear and fright because a single yang cannot relieve the situation by itself. Even though you withdraw and secrete yourself in a silent place, it will be difficult to completely preserve yourself all alone. Moreover, you must adhere to the old; do not yet change or make new plans. This is the image of everything being baleful.

HO ∘ Whether by water or land, the traveler will be overturned, destroyed, and defeated. It might be somewhat difficult to recover from illness at this time. The imprisoned will not get out. Commercial activities will not be profitable. Those holding office should request leave. This trigraph is very baleful!

CH'EN ∘ A single yang, solitary and weak, occupies the space between clusters of yin above and below without responding to them. It is the image of sinking into a pit. The Tao of the petty man excels; the wicked and perverse arise together. One's native place is not peaceful.

LIU ∘ "Cut off and separated, dwelling apart"—distress beyond comparison. When one is already solitary and moreover young, how can he initiate anything?
   In this trigraph a solitary yang is sinking amidst accumulated yin. It cannot bestir itself to arise. The hundred affairs, whatever they might be, are all baleful.

SAWYER ∘ Even the commentators are somewhat reticent about characterizing the nature of this trigraph, perhaps overawed by the powerful yin clusters ominously dominating both Heaven and Earth. The lone figure of a solitary yang crouching between two looming perversities clearly portends a battle against great odds, whatever one's projects or ambitions. Therefore, intensively conserving resources while remaining steadfast and temporarily awaiting a more propitious moment appears inevitable. However, there is no reason to be disheartened, because the inherent tendencies of the phase dynamics ensures a swift transformation to more auspicious times.

53   Shen Chu   神 助

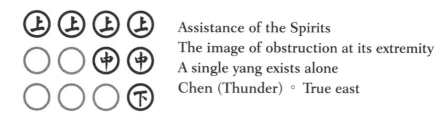

Assistance of the Spirits
The image of obstruction at its extremity
A single yang exists alone
Chen (Thunder) ○ True east

Oracle

Four ghosts and two shamans bow their heads toward each other. The spirits of Heaven descend, releasing the entangled and freeing the imprisoned. Misfortune dispelled, injury restored, one truly obtains the blessings of Heaven.

Verses

> Heavenly rain bespreading interminably,
> The virtue of the vast waters enriched anew.
> Dried roots reviving from distress and stagnation,
> In a single day all revitalized.
>
> Essential spirit affects Heaven and Earth,
> Yin *ch'i* dissolves away of itself.
> Alone, relying on sustaining strength,
> All realize achievement though the Great Transformation.

Commentaries

Yen ○ The myriad affairs are all resolved. Doubled yin lies in Heaven; ghostly *ch'i* is changing. A single yang survives alone, eliminating misfortune and mitigating disaster. Apart from the spirits of Heaven, who can respond to this? The hundred affairs will at first be baleful, later auspicious.

HO ∘ Jointly undertaking activities with others will be auspicious. Marriage arrangements will result in harmony and union. The imprisoned will be released. The ill will be cured. The traveler will return shortly. The pregnant will give birth to a male. Harvests in sericulture and grain will be meager. Enmities will be resolved by themselves. Seeking office and searching for wealth will at first be worrisome, later auspicious.

CH'EN ∘ Four yin lie at the top, ghosts and spirits confused together. Two yin are in the middle with a single yang below, responding between themselves. Evidently when a single yang dwells in the position of Earth, it signifies an excellent root and presages unbroken vitality. The spirits of Heaven send down good fortune.

LIU ∘ "Four ghosts and two shamans"—yin, flourishing, is active above. "The spirits of Heaven send down good fortune"—distress has attained its extremity and is turning to prosperity.

In this trigraph, yin is flourishing at the top, the image of ghosts and spirits. Young yin dwells in the middle; it is the image of things of the same category consorting with each other, of shamans. Even though the single yang, minute, is unable to rouse itself, when young males and young females seek each other, they will certainly come together. Thus the middle yin pray for intercession above, for the descent of good fortune and the elimination of calamity. When this happens, the yin flourishing above are not ghosts, but the spirits of Heaven. It is the image of prosperity coming when obstruction has reached its extremity. As for affairs divined about, entrust them to the strength of others. At first there will be distress, later good fortune.

SAWYER ∘ Despite the somewhat ominous appearance of the four yin in the position of Heaven, this trigraph portends an end to obstruction and an escape from the entanglements that presently frustrate one's freedom or constrain one's activities. The trigraph's auspiciousness derives from envisioning the middle position, two yin, as symbolizing two shamans beseeching the aid of the heavenly spirits, thereby understanding the four heavenly yin as spiritual powers rather than ghosts, as Liu has noted. When Heaven becomes active, what can withstand it, who will not receive its blessings? Thus the image conveyed by the first stanza, stressing the revitalization of stagnant affairs, the resurrection of everything formerly withered and dried. The trigraph also explicitly echoes the eleventh and twelfth hexagrams in the *I Ching,* which should be consulted for further illumination.

54   CHIEH SSU   解 杞

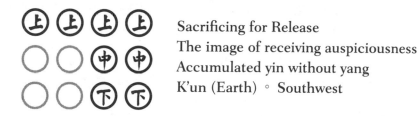

Sacrificing for Release
The image of receiving auspiciousness
Accumulated yin without yang
K'un (Earth) ∘ Southwest

ORACLE

Around funeral mounds and high hillocks ghosts and spirits roam. It would be appropriate to pray and sacrifice to them, for then one can be untroubled.

VERSES

> It's unnecessary to discuss poverty or success,
> Instead, worry about acute illness.
> But soon hidden virtue will be rewarded,
> Heavenly forces will yield profound achievements.

> When one's fate already dwells in straits and difficulty,
> It's unnecessary to sigh about the road being impoverished.
> Ancestral beneficence must be rewarded,
> Spiritual radiance will then become pervasive.

COMMENTARIES

YEN ∘ "Accumulated yin without yang," the image of precipitous peaks and high funeral mounds. The Tao of ghosts and spirits is flourishing. Only by sacrificing with a sincere heart will one manage to be untroubled.

Ho ∘ If things promised to the spirits have not yet been given, it would be auspicious to give them now. Possibly a supernatural entity has been seen; it would be appropriate to pray and offer sacrifice. Ghosts and spirits around mounds and hills are auspicious. Illness stems from a supine corpse in an old grave, causing disaster. It would be appropriate to excise it. The pregnant will give birth to a female. Travelers, outside, encounter those who secretly obstruct them. In the summer they will return by themselves. Bureaucratic advancement, seeking wealth, being troubled by illness, and official affairs will all at first be difficult, later auspicious. Other affairs will be neither particularly auspicious nor inauspicious.

CH'EN ∘ Accumulated yin is at the top while the middle and lower positions are also both yin. This is the image of ghostly *ch'i* being full and complete. Yang *ch'i* is already severed; the Tao of Man lacks rescue. It would be appropriate to urgently offer sacrifice.

LIU ∘ "Around funeral mounds and high hillocks"—ghostly *ch'i* is flourishing. "It would be appropriate to urgently offer sacrifice"— submissively accept your fate.

In this trigraph, four yin are at the top, while the middle and lower are both young yin, without yang. Thus it creates the image of funeral mounds and high hillocks. Only by sincerely and compliantly making an offering can one thereby avoid disaster. The querent should neither conflict nor contend with others. Ordinary affairs, if pliantly followed and properly and straightforwardly managed, will be auspicious.

SAWYER ∘ This trigraph draws the querent deeply into the world of ghosts and spirits, two entities found roaming about the many realms of traditional Chinese thought. While the main background is an ancient, common belief in ancestral spirits and their paramount role in the family's heritage, every sort of ghost and demon abounds. In theory, educated Confucians maintain a respectful, although largely skeptical attitude, even toward the ancestral spirits, but still fulfill their duty by sincerely sacrificing to them on a regular basis. Ghosts can be coerced into assuming nonharmful roles by integrating them into various bureaucratic hierarchies and thereby bringing them under the dominion of local officials, but unpropitiated spirits and vengeful specters possess more disruptive energy and may pose somewhat intractable problems. Naturally there is nothing unusual about seeing such entities in graveyards and about old battlefields, but not elsewhere. Thus, if they are suddenly witnessed, the individual should quickly act to minimize the potential harm by making a symbolic offering. However, readers who do not believe in ghosts may understand the entire trigraph allegorically, as a battle between restless psychic energy or malevolent exterior forces and oneself, with ritualized actions offering a path to reintegration and order. In this regard, "Sacrificing for Release" should be read in conjunction with the preceding trigraph, which becomes auspicious through the shamanistic activity of the two yin in the middle, stimulated by the young yang below them.

55   *I Tsai*   抑災

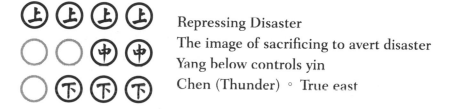

Repressing Disaster
The image of sacrificing to avert disaster
Yang below controls yin
Chen (Thunder) ∘ True east

ORACLE

Metal's essence is about to arise. Trust to Yüan Shih, for with his left hand he will repress it, and then you will gain rest and respite.

VERSES

> The leopard, ever changing, hides for years in the fog,
> One day the great *p'eng* bird soars straight up to Heaven.
> If you manage to gain the strength of men in the western quarter,
> Glory and honor will naturally follow in that year.

In fierce winds one will know unbending grass,
In the tumult of revolution recognize loyal ministers.
Relying on this to rectify sustaining strength,
The things of Heaven and Earth will be renewed.

COMMENTARIES

YEN ∘ Metal lies in the west, the position of young yin. It presages the affairs of halberds and soldiers, of killing and harming. Yüan Shih was a great man while the left constitutes yang. The Oracle says that yin *ch'i* is about to move and create harm, but a great man assists, repressing it with his left hand. The harm is thus dissipated; yang is able to control yin. Under this trigraph, what is troublesome will not become truly chaotic.

HO ∘ Under this trigraph, going forth to assume office or expectantly planning will at first be worrisome, later happy. Any matters that obtain the assistance of the great will be auspicious; all affairs that obtain the assistance of the perfected will be changed from disaster to good fortune. Preserving current activities will be auspicious and advantageous. Look for someone with power, for then serious official matters will be remitted. You must be equally defensive and cautious; then the hundred affairs will continue to be uneventful.

CH'EN ∘ Four at the top, two in the middle: yin *ch'i* descends from Heaven above. It is the image of soldiers and weapons about to arise. The three yang below can settle the masses and mutually respond with the four yin at the top, thereby gaining Heaven's blessings.

LIU ∘ Young yin in the middle moves upward, the essence of metal arising. When the three yang control it, one gains rest and respite.

In this trigraph, exhausted yin dwells at the top and young yin in the middle. The two create the image of the trigram *Tui*; thus the Oracle says "the essence of metal." The three yang below respond to the four yin above. Young yin is not able to participate in affairs. The left is yang. In all affairs, whenever the great assist, at first there will be caution, later happiness.

SAWYER ∘ The presence of mature yang in the realm of Earth should prove sufficient to control the otherwise overwhelming influence of mature yin at the top that is, in addition, supported by youthful, active yin in the middle. The commentators could have equally well emphasized the potential interaction between Heaven and Earth in this situation, both being mature and therefore tending to enmity, although less exuberantly than the mutual responsiveness of their youthful counterparts. (Such a reversal of the normal positions of yang in Heaven and yin in Earth is actually very auspicious in the *I Ching*.) However, they instead emphasize the image of metal, which they are forced, through some contortions, to drive from the trigraph because of the Oracle's statement. Actually, discord and contradiction characterize the explanations for this trigraph, and one of the important traditional editions even entitles it "Laughing Last." The Image, "sacrificing to avert disaster," is ignored, and the associated trigram, Chen, is not Tui, to which Liu refers. The trigraph's direction, true east, normally coupled with yang rising in prelude to peaking in the summer, of course stands in relative but complementary opposition to autumn, associated with metal in the west, when yin's activity is increasing. Consequently, active dynamics abound here, and the querent should perhaps focus on the idea that external threats, including potentially violent ones posed by persons or events of the yin category, may be successfully thwarted and repressed with the assistance of powerful individuals. The first Verse suggests that talent and character are about to soar, just like Chuang-tzu's great bird, for they have been cultivated and perfected, and the moment is drawing near.

56 Ch'i Heng 祈亨

Praying for Success
The image of being appropriate to pray
for intercession
Yin extreme above and below
K'un (Earth) ∘ True west

ORACLE

Offering sacrifice and praying in the ancestral temple, the baleful is diminished and misfortune prevented. Good fortune comes to fill the gate; calamity is expelled a myriad miles.

VERSES

A table without one leg, truly hard to stabilize,
A ceremonial tripod with two feet, standing ought to be difficult.
What is hoped for, what is sought, will in the end waste strength.
It's critical to pray for good fortune and mitigate harm and
　destruction.

With filial piety one moves Heaven,
With sincerity one moves the spirits.
May the spirits come and enjoy, may they come and be moved,
Then good fortune and wealth will extend to posterity.

COMMENTARIES

YEN ∘ A cluster of yin at the top, the image of an ancestral temple. Official affairs will dissipate. The ill will recover. Dreaming deeply, things are turned upside down. It all affairs it would be appropriate to offer sacrifice in the ancestral temple and seek good fortune. If one prays to the spirits, it will be auspicious.

Ho ∘ If you see a supernatural oddity—and for all other affairs as well—offering sacrifice in the ancestral temple to seek good fortune would be auspicious. The pregnant will give birth to a female. The household should be extremely cautious about flaming candles.

Ch'en ∘ The ghosts of Heaven and Man interact and assemble; the Tao of Man is dark (yin) and weak. This is the image of ghostly *ch'i* giving birth to illness. Even though you seek release through sacrifice and prayer, afterward there will certainly be disaster.

Liu ∘ "Sacrifices and praying in the ancestral temple"—these are what the spirits rely on. Sincerely supporting them will lead to good fortune and no calamity.

In this trigraph, above and below are both four yin. The upper forms the ancestral temple; the lower creates funeral mounds. The two of them together with the young yin dwelling in the middle position are like making an offering to the spirits and ghosts. If the sacrifice is respectfully and properly offered, without neglecting the rites, then one will receive good fortune and avoid calamity. For the querent this trigraph is auspicious.

Sawyer ∘ The main theme envisioned for many of the trigraphs that couple four yin in the position of Heaven with a second yin line is the need to ritually seek the intercession of the spirits and thereby mitigate potential disaster. Accordingly, this trigraph should be read in conjunction with those in this series of four, as well as in comparison with others defined by mature yin at the top. As discussed in the glossary, performing a sacrifice can be understood as simply making a symbolic offering of fruit or wine to the spirits—a common practice today throughout Asia—or even just burning incense as part of a personal prayer ceremony. While the traditional Chinese world view accepted the efficacy of such acts, contemporary belief need only focus on the ritual and psychological value if one eschews religious beliefs or one's convictions proscribe such activities. The first Verse perhaps provides the best image for the present moment—instability due to a lack of critical support. Accordingly, apart from any spiritual orientation, the querent should ponder whether the foundation for activities and life practices is sufficiently substantial and then impose appropriate measures of cultivation and self-discipline. (Ch'en expresses an unusually pessimistic view here.)

57 Ts'UNG HSIN 從心

Following One's Desires
The image of returning to prosperity
A mass of yang honors yin
Tui (Marsh) ∘ True west

ORACLE

Dark clouds lie above, no slanderers below. The hundred affairs proceed freely; all succeed in returning to correctness.

VERSES

Questing for fame and profit are constant affairs,
How could they be like unchanging plans?
When the time comes and fortune excels,
It is unnecessary to expend any effort.

The spirit's image dwells in an honored place,
Human mind complies with the time,
Naturally returning to the upright Tao,
Like relying on the masses for support.

COMMENTARIES

YEN ∘ Affairs all follow the mind's inclinations and gain the assistance of other people. Moreover, yin dwells in the upper position, being honored by the mass of yang. Disaster departs, good fortune comes. Affairs proceed from offering sacrifice.

Under this trigraph, offering sacrifice in the ancestral temple would be highly auspicious. The clan will be secure and tranquil, being forever preserved without calamity.

Ho ∘ The pregnant will give birth to a male. The traveler will return shortly. Arguments will not result in suffering. As for the ill, it would be appropriate to offer sacrifice and seek good fortune through prayer; thereafter, they will recover. Agricultural and sericultural harvests will be especially auspicious and profitable. It would be appropriate to undertake matters in autumn.

Ch'en ∘ A cluster of yin is at the top, while the Tao of Man is strong and flourishing. Yin and yang gain each other. Moreover, a single yang is at the bottom. The positions they occupy are all settled.

Liu ∘ "Dark clouds lie above"—yin ascends above. "No slanderers below"—the Tao of yang is pervasive.

In this trigraph, four yin are at the top, while the bottom two positions are both yang. Thus it creates the image of dark clouds. The three in the middle and the single one below each appropriately occupy their positions. Yang firm, without yin—there are no slanderers. Thus it creates the image of "the hundred affairs proceeding freely." For the querent, the hundred affairs will all be auspicious. The traveler is about to return.

Sawyer ∘ This trigraph, the first in the series of four with mature yin in the position of Heaven and mature yang active in the realm of Man, largely derives its implications from the dynamic interaction of Heaven and Man. Moreover, youthful yang in the position of Earth, although theoretically inappropriate because Earth is the paradigm embodiment of yin, signifies energy and ability. Therefore, as the Verses indicate, good fortune should be enjoyed in the immediate future.

58 TE SHIH 得失

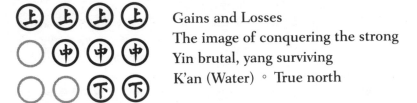

Gains and Losses
The image of conquering the strong
Yin brutal, yang surviving
K'an (Water) ∘ True north

ORACLE

I have lost valuable pearls, which are now in the Milky Way. I never thought it to be a place where thieves and brigands, the secret doers of evil, reside. I rely on the Mysterious Dark Bird to pursue them for me. When the winds still and the waves quiet, I return again to my cottage.

VERSES

Relaxing the eyebrows, opening the eyes, gold is exposed;
Stirred by the rivers and mountains, my old hut clearly recalled.
Fishing in the midst of the river, no fish yet caught,
At the end of the line I suddenly see a bright pearl.

Although the old man at the border lost his horse,
Do disaster and good fortune proceed from men?
When one realizes the Tao, many respond to assist,
The front courtyard will again be renewed.

COMMENTARIES

YEN ∘ At first all affairs will be repressed; later they will certainly follow your desires. If you attain things through other people, it will not take long. All affairs are like this. Moreover, even though yin is at the top, yang has gained its position. Although yin might act as a brigand to brutally steal my rare treasures, by relying on yang for preservation, in the end we will exterminate the perversely evil, just like the Mysterious Dark Bird driving off predatory creatures. "When the winds still and the waves quiet, I return again to my old cottage." This trigraph indicates that events will at first be baleful, later auspicious. If you go forth, you will at first be impoverished, later successful.

Ho ∘ At first repression, later success—the myriad affairs will all be like this. Agriculture and sericulture will be profitable. The pregnant will give birth to a male. It is a very auspicious trigraph.

CH'EN ∘ The upper and lower positions, both yin, overwhelm the yang in the middle. However, the position of Man is strong and flourishing, and they cannot harm it. Moreover the upper and middle respond to each other, so what is lost can be gained. It is adequate for controlling a strong enemy.

LIU ∘ "I have lost valuable pearls"—yin above has stolen them. In this trigraph the four yin are exhausted at the top, while two yin are growing below. Thus it creates the image of losing my valuable pearls and the place where the thieves secretly dwell. Yet the three yang in the middle are companions with the upper yin, while the young yin, pliant and weak, is not able to oppose them. In the end they do not bring about harm. For the querent, at first events will be obstructed, later successful. By relying on the assistance of others, you will obtain good fortune.

SAWYER ∘ This trigraph characterizes a situation in which losses have occurred but, through the intercession of others (symbolized by the Mysterious Dark Bird of Heaven), have excellent prospects for being recouped. The first Verse, whose initial two lines are somewhat enigmatic, dramatizes this sudden reversal of ill fortune by the image of an otherwise discouraged fisherman suddenly obtaining not just a good fish, but a valuable pearl. However, the second Verse succinctly captures the trigraph's essence by opening with an illusion to an extremely well-known story from the ancient *Huai Nan-tzu*: "Now misfortune and good fortune are constantly turning and reversing, mutually producing each other, but their changes are difficult to discern. Once among the men who lived near the passes along the upper border, there was one who excelled in the metaphysical arts. Without any cause his son's horse fled into barbarian territory. People all tried to console him, but his father, the adept, said: 'How do we know that this won't be a blessing?' After several months his horse returned, accompanied by several outstanding barbarian mounts. People all congratulated him, but his father said, 'How do we know that this cannot become misfortune?' The family was rich with excellent horses. His son, who liked to ride, fell and broke his leg. People all consoled him, but his father said, 'How do you know this won't turn out to be a blessing?' After a year the barbarians invaded the border in great force. All the strong males were drafted for combat. Among the men living near the border, nine out of ten perished. Only the father and son alone, on account of the son's lameness, were preserved. Thus good fortune becoming misfortune, and misfortune becoming good fortune, are inexhaustible transformations too profound to be fathomed."

59 *Chiu Chu* 救助

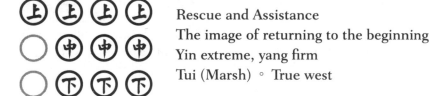

Rescue and Assistance
The image of returning to the beginning
Yin extreme, yang firm
Tui (Marsh) ∘ True west

ORACLE

The Master of Fate descends, checking and investigating his record books. He calculates that fate is not yet exhausted, that the deceased unexpectedly is without guilt, and then orders the legendary doctor Pien Ch'üeh to open the jade vessel and present a medicine pill. Then the deceased returns to life.

VERSES

> That felicitous affairs descend from Heaven is easily known,
> Achievement and fame have their time.

The worried man's eyebrows relax, the drunken man awakens,
Once the sun shines forth it illuminates a myriad miles.

Human life, whether long or short, with the time transforms,
Disaster and good fortune come forth, fate makes them so.
If you manage to cultivate yourself and preserve the Great Tao,
By following the precepts, even in the worldly realm you will
    encounter spiritual immortals.

COMMENTARIES

YEN ∘ The ill ought to take medicinal pills. What is sought will be obtained. The traveler is returning.

HO ∘ The Master of Fate is a spirit of Heaven. A cluster of yin are at the top; a mass of yang dwell in the middle. Even though they have gained their appropriate places, on the contrary they create obstacles. If one, without guilt, has sunk into unreasonable misfortune, Heaven will order Pien Ch'üeh to rescue him. Misfortune will thus be expelled.

Under this trigraph, through misfortune one will attain good fortune. The ill might suffer some distress but will not die. As for legal entanglements, the judge has the documents confused. Later they will be put in order, and the difficulty will dissipate by itself. Under this trigraph, the hundred affairs will at first be baleful, later auspicious. In official affairs one will gain the strength of a noble person.

CH'EN ∘ In the middle and lower two positions yang excessively flourishes. When it is excessive, it creates disaster. The four yin above are able to mutually respond with these three yang. Insofar as the pliant moderates the firm, yang does not reach the point of being oppressive.

LIU ∘ Yang is obscured by yin; there is no great guilt. The double firm moving upward in the end cannot be contaminated.

In this trigraph the middle and lower are pure yang, while four yin are at the top. Thus it creates the image of the guiltless being distressed. Yet yang is just flourishing. Even though it momentarily suffers repression, in the end it will not reach the point of sinking into nonexistence. How much the more so when yin's extremity must decline just when the Tao of yang is flourishing and ought to obtain the assistance of the spirits of Heaven. Affairs divined about will at first be distressed, later successful. Through disaster one will obtain good fortune. Although the ill may feel exhausted, they will not die. Employing the army is dangerous but will yield victory. In all affairs there will at first be worry, later joy.

SAWYER ○ In terms of single dynamics, the cluster of mature yin at the top should normally tend to sink down, while the two mature yang positions below strongly ascend. Contrary to the enmity that should supposedly exist between manifestations of mature or old yin and yang, this might produce a productive interaction because they are all near the point of exhaustion rather than immersed in youthful growth. Evolution and success should result, although not until the condition of the moment, which might be likened to a state of metaphysical death, is cast off, yielding revitalization. The Oracle focuses on the theme of resurrection, presaging an allegorical passage out of a depressed or suspended state, to be negotiated through the assistance of a magical elixir, the pill of life. The possibilities for the querent are thus limited only by one's imagination in discerning stagnation and surging forward to explore new life possibilities.

60 TA T'UNG 大同

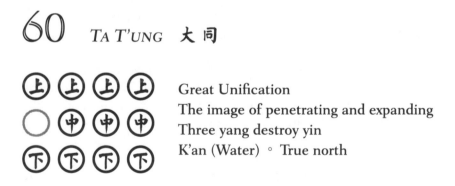

Great Unification
The image of penetrating and expanding
Three yang destroy yin
K'an (Water) ○ True north

ORACLE

The Milky Way level and smooth, extending in five directions, penetrating to six. I travel in its midst, mounting the clouds and riding dragons.

VERSES

The clouds disperse, the moon hangs in emptiness,
Right on the cusp of Aries and Taurus.
A stretched bow just aimed at its target,
An arrow decides future success.

His position honored, his Virtue flourishing,
The four barbarians all submit.
When the perfected bring order to chaos,
The petty are then unfortunate.

COMMENTARIES

YEN ∘ Three yang dwell in the middle, the position of honor and abundant virtue. I then am yang. The Milky Way penetrates everywhere. "Mounting the clouds and riding dragons," I command the six directions just like the fifth line in the *I Ching* hexagram titled Ch'ien. When ordinary people encounter this trigraph, they will not be victorious but, on the contrary, incur calamity. Acting as the ruler's assistant in a well-ordered era also will be free from calamity. Whatever is sought will accord with one's thoughts. Whatever official affairs might be causing consternation will be dissipated. The ill will recover. The traveler is about to return. Commercial enterprises will result in great gains. Marriage arrangements will result in a harmonious union. This trigraph presages great auspiciousness.

HO ∘ The sun comes out from the eastern quarter, shining on my northern corner. The illumination of its excess radiance extends to the dark valleys. It is said that at the winter solstice, marked by the response of the first yellow pipe, yang *ch'i* begins to nourish (all things), gradually proceeding toward great harmony. The six quarters hum and sing; the hundred affairs follow one's heart. Whatever is done is auspicious. The myriad affairs will produce happiness.

CH'EN ∘ Three yang in the middle, the Tao of Man fully flourishes. The four yin above and below both respond to it. Heaven associates with it; Earth associates with it—this is termed the "Great Unification."

LIU ∘ "The Milky Way level and smooth"—the pliant does not conquer the firm. "Mounting the clouds and riding dragons"—my position is precisely in the middle.

In this trigraph the upper and lower are old yin, unable to act, while the three yang dwelling in the middle are firm, bright, flourishing, and great. There is nowhere that one cannot go. Thus it forms the image of "the Milky Way level and smooth, extending in five directions, penetrating to six." When the querent obtains it, it will be possible to rectify neighboring states, give peace to the common people, eliminate the injurious, and expel the brutal. There is nothing that cannot be done.

SAWYER ∘ In some texts this trigraph is called "Great Penetration" or "Great Harmony" rather than "Great Unification." (The original Chinese title, Ta T'ung, is colloquially translated as "Universal Harmony" and has entered the modern language as a famous company name as well.) As the dynamics of the trigraph are well explicated by the commentators, attention can be drawn to the great auspiciousness of the Oracle, which promises free, unfettered roaming throughout the universe in control of great power. Clearly this is an auspicious moment, one vividly imagized by the first Verse in depicting the moon hanging in a clearing sky with an arrow below winging its way to a midnight target.

61 CH'EN I 沈翳

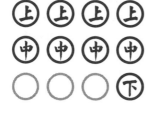

Sinking and Obscured
The image of minimal existence
A cluster of yin covers yang
Chen (Thunder) ∘ True east

ORACLE

On and on, merely seeing and breathing, without any *ch'i* or strength. Raising my face, I call on Heaven; bowing my head, I prostrate myself on the ground. What I seek is not realized; what I see is not obtained.

VERSES

> Old methods will bring about good fortune,
> Contention will inevitably result in punishment.
> With a tranquil heart, return to preserving and waiting,
> Do not envy the glory of others.

> Advancing one's steps, frequently tripping and stumbling,
> Contentious striving brings disaster and danger.
> For the rest of one's life there are only sighs,
> In poverty and distress, affairs are difficult to perform.

COMMENTARIES

YEN ∘ There is only a single yang mired in the position of Earth below; clusters of yin obscure it. "Bowing my head and prostrating myself on the ground," how much longer have I to live? This trigraph is very baleful. Illnesses might grow somewhat more severe. Agriculture and sericulture will be hopeless. Whatever is sought in business will prove unprofitable. The distant traveler will encounter thieves.

Ho ∘ Affairs will all fall outside the realm of what is known. You can sigh about them, that's all. In holding official office, managing personal affairs, being involved in arguments, and disputing over right and wrong, it will be extremely difficult to redress grievances. You ought only to cautiously preserve yourself, rest, and withdraw; otherwise, by going away a thousand miles, disaster can be avoided. It will be difficult to resolve official entanglements. It might be somewhat difficult for the ill to recover. Commercial activities will suffer the loss of their capital. Distant travel will result in disaster. Whatever plans might be initiated will not be advantageous; whatever is done will not be profitable. You ought to cultivate Heaven's blessings by offering sacrifice.

CH'EN ∘ In the upper and middle two positions, yin flourishes excessively. What is excessive creates disaster. A single yang lies below, barely able to breathe.

LIU ∘ "On and on, merely seeing and breathing"—thus one is "mired below." "Bowing my head I prostrate myself on the ground"—poverty-stricken, there is no one to turn to.

In this trigraph a single yang is obscured beneath doubled yin, the image of extreme distress. It presages that the ill might face a crisis; engaging in battle will result in defeat; those imprisoned will find it difficult to get out; and lawsuits will not be victorious. All affairs will be baleful.

SAWYER ∘ This is the first in the series of four trigraphs with mature yin appearing in the upper two positions, thereby dominating the dynamics and prognostication. The solitary, youthful yang—sorely repressed in the position of Earth—is virtually the image of anyone confronting a formidable, established system, any neophyte seeking to venture into a new arena. The moment, although certain to improve, is overwhelmingly dark and inauspicious. Caution is therefore advised, self-preservation stressed.

62 YIN CHANG 陰長

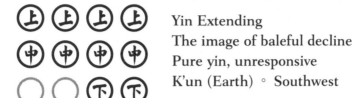

Yin Extending
The image of baleful decline
Pure yin, unresponsive
K'un (Earth) ∘ Southwest

ORACLE

Heavy yin lies above; ghostly *ch'i* floats and roams about. In the middle courtyard, the water is deep; below the hall, boats embark.

VERSES

You must be cautious, guarding against the hidden and small,
Even the inner courtyard is not yet tranquil.
Within the family much clamoring and disruption,
Disputes given birth in the darkness.

Accumulated yin creates the harsh rain interminably falling,
Flooding waters embrace the mountainous terrain, inundating
the land.
If Great Yü hadn't implemented his plan to open and chisel,
How could all life have attained joyous hearts?

COMMENTARIES

YEN ∘ In this purely yin trigraph, the interior and exterior do not respond to each other. Disasters stemming from powerful ghosts also fall into the category of yin. All affairs will be like this; it is the image of baleful decline. Although the interior and exterior do not respond to each other, when official powers assist, the trigraph becomes auspicious. The pregnant will give birth to a female.

HO ∘ The traveler will encounter brigands. No affair will be advantageous. You must be very cautious about secret plots and disputes. One edition states this is the trigraph of enlightening the ignorant, that all affairs will be slightly auspicious. In front of the hall there is flowing water, "below the hall, boats embark." This trigraph is only appropriate to praying for rain. Formerly, when Chang Nan-hsüan divined about rain, he received these words as a response.

CH'EN ∘ The three positions are all yin; moreover, yin is increasing in extent. Yang *ch'i* is inevitably cut off. It stops in the middle of the Way, unable to do anything.

LIU ∘ "Heavy yin lies at the top"—the Tao of yang is stopped up. "In the middle courtyard, the water is deep"—one worries about being drowned.

This trigraph is purely yin, unresponsive—the image of disaster and misfortune. When the querent obtains it, hidden persons, thieves, and brigands may inflict harm. For the ill, it might be baleful. Moreover, it presages that there will be secret plots; curses being uttered; powerful ghosts; and disputes. The hundred affairs will all be baleful. Only praying for rain will be appropriate.

SAWYER ∘ Not only are the upper two positions dominated by mature yin, as in the previous trigraph, but the realm of Earth is also occupied by youthful yin. This implies a willful, energetic unruliness in a world filled with evil specters, an image created by the yin clusters in the realms of both Heaven and Man. Consequently, the time is not auspicious; behavior and expectations should be moderated accordingly.

63   *Tun Shih*

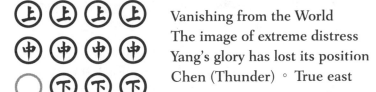

Vanishing from the World
The image of extreme distress
Yang's glory has lost its position
Chen (Thunder) ∘ True east

ORACLE

Distressed by baleful disasters, he closes his gate and sits alone. His disciples have separated and dispersed; there is no one from whom to get fire.

VERSES

A perverse destiny sustains great worry,
Amid grief and sorrow, spring turns to autumn.
Best to plot an escape northwest,
Seek nothing outside yourself.

Virtue solitary, without neighbors,
Who can be approached?
When the perfected lose the Tao,
The menial advance themselves.

COMMENTARIES

YEN ∘ Yang *ch'i* has lost its position; there is no one to be a disciple. Thus it says "sitting alone." Fire is of the category of yang and is the material for cooking and steaming. Clusters of yin have segregated it; there is no way to reach it. Remaining in residence will be disastrous and futile. Affairs will not accord with one's desires. Marriage arrangements will not result in descendants. The traveler is not yet returning. The ill might not yet recover. This trigraph is very baleful. It is absolutely necessary to be cautious about it!

Ho ∘ The ill might not yet recover. Official affairs will be difficult to resolve. The Tao of the family should be to accord with the old. In affairs, be extremely wary of secret plots. Commercial activities will not be profitable. If you employ the military, they will lose their discipline.

CH'EN ∘ Three yang lie below, the image of a Worthy in the wilds. A cluster of yin is at the top; the Tao of the petty excels. One cannot manifest oneself.

LIU ∘ "Distressed by baleful disasters"—yin takes advantage of yang. "There is no way to get fire"—the darkness cannot be made bright.

In this trigraph, yang has lost its position and lacks disciples. Yin is active above and cliques flourish. When the inquirer obtains it, it indicates there will be an unforeseen disaster. It is a very baleful trigraph.

SAWYER ∘ This trigraph depicts talents and ability frustrated by external hindrances and perversities, unable to advance or show itself. If one has inquired about external affairs, such as attempting new projects in the world, the moment seems very inauspicious. It may be that circumstances are simply adverse, but the trigraph might also be interpreted as suggesting that the project or activity should be reexamined. Further reflection might reveal a better approach, one that will meet with success (as then indicated by another trigraph). Conversely, if pondering psychological or spiritual states, the trigraph perhaps suggests someone beset by psychic obstacles, needing to retreat into contemplation in order to either vanquish or dispel them.

64 Chung Hsiung 眾 山

A Mass of Evils
The image of prosperity at the extremity
Pure yin manifest together
K'un (Earth) ∘ Southwest

Oracle

Baleful disasters brutally arrive; no affair whatsoever will be advantageous. There might be acute illnesses and official entanglements; actions will be marked by tripping and stumbling.

Verses

> Like the tip of a hundred-foot pole, the road is already
>   exhausted;
> Searching my thoughts, bereft of plans, I turn and wander
>   aimlessly.
> Engrossed by the white perch on my fishing pole,
> Unaware, I tumble into the waves.
>
> The mountains exhausted, the road becomes confused;
> The river rapid, the boat has difficulty crossing.
> Not one of the myriad things can be forcefully done,
> Everywhere one encounters the crafty and jealous.

Commentaries

YEN ∘ The three positions—all yin, black, and dazzling—approach together. Baleful disasters will inevitably arrive. Whether you go out somewhere or remain dark and silent, either will be auspicious or advantageous.

Ho ∘ Under this trigraph a mass of disasters arise together. For the ill, it might be especially baleful if they do not exercise care. Whatever is sought will not proceed expeditiously. The hundred affairs will not be advantageous. If you carefully avoid these disasters, then conditions will gradually revert to normal. Blossoms will open to frost the sky; smoky flowers will fill the eyes. Even though one exhausts the mind, human affairs will still continue indecisive.

CH'EN ∘ Twelve is the extreme number for Heaven and Earth. Yin thus is already at the pinnacle. The will to life being severed, one cannot again turn back. This trigraph is the last of the 124 trigraphs, the place where the myriad transformations stop. Its balefulness can thus be known!

LIU ∘ Extreme yin without yang, the pinnacle of being impoverished. "Actions are tripping and stumbling"—there is no place to employ one's power.

In this trigraph the three positions are all exhausted yin; a mass of evils arise together. Everything that is done is dangerous and obstructed; it suggests an image of awaiting a violent death, that's all.

SAWYER ∘ Anyone encountering this trigraph had best adopt a skeptical attitude in view of its dire characterization of the metaphysical moment. Ch'en's commentary, stating that this is the last or 124th trigraph, indicates that his copy of the text employed a different, more archaic order that may have proceeded from a single yang in the position of Earth through to twelve disks filling all the positions. (The 125th trigraph, all disks showing the obverse, unwritten side, was clearly appended as an afterthought but could equally be the starting point with a zero value.)

While the trigraph presages failure and misery, the wise person should regard the Oracle as simply warning of potential disasters that can be avoided by watchful waiting. Even though the last line of the second Verse, translated as "everywhere," literally states "Whether one goes out or remains secluded," maintaining a quiet, low profile continues to be advantageous. Accordingly, this would not seem to be a propitious time to initiate projects or undertake new efforts, especially those that require forceful action to wrest success under even the best of circumstances. Health should be focal and any present illness or discomfort aggressively treated. Moreover, inappropriate, stress-producing behavior and other bad practices such as inadequate sleep or poor diet should be appropriately modified to ensure that illness has no opportunity to gain a foothold. Furthermore, in this period of darkness one must be especially careful not to be mesmerized by small, glittering gains, such as the white perch mentioned in the first Verse, and thereby tumble headlong to be engulfed by an unseen but threatening morass. Fortunately, this being the absolute pinnacle of yin's manifestation in the trigraphs, it is also the most unstable. Consequently, movement through reversal should be almost immediate, and with it, the opportunity to be swept along toward the successful realization of projects and efforts.

65 K'U CHIEH 苦節

Bitter Constraint
The image of Heaven and yang
Two yang standing solitary
Ch'ien (Heaven) ∘ Northwest

ORACLE

Dwelling in poverty, experiencing the bitterness of suffering. Without any doors, going and coming are cramped and constricted. There is not enough land to stick an awl into.

VERSE

> Multihued clouds easily scatter, impossible to restrain.
> Forlorn, at twilight, affairs are troubling.
> Although hidden achievements secretly coalesce,
> Still must there be grief entailing sorrows of mind.

COMMENTARIES

YEN ∘ Distant and isolated, [the subject symbolized by the middle position] occupies a solitary position. From without, there is no response, while within, there is nowhere to dwell. In poverty, suffering, difficulty, and bitterness, one is sorely cramped and constricted. Under this trigraph, none of the hundred affairs will be advantageous.

Ho ∘ One lives without anything to rely on. Thus the Oracle says "there is not enough ground to even stick an awl into." Those suffering from illness may experience some difficulty. Whatever is sought will not proceed well. Official affairs will be difficult to resolve. The distant traveler will encounter brigands. It would be appropriate to quickly pray for the intercession of the spirits.

Ch'en ∘ Solitary yang lacks any response, while the Tao of Earth is empty and void. It is the image of poverty and suffering.

Liu ∘ "Dwelling in poverty, experiencing the bitterness of suffering"—one lacks the means to support a family. "Going and coming are cramped and restricted"—this also is lamentable.

In this trigraph the upper and middle positions are both singular, while the lowest position is absent. Thus it creates the image of being impoverished and cold, being without any land. Whatever might be inquired about will be baleful.

Sawyer ∘ This trigraph lacks any presence in the bottom position; therefore, the sole theme is the lack of support, the absence of any basis for sustaining onself and human affairs. While the image reflects the solitary householder dwelling in the poorest of shacks, a mere squatter likely tucked into the corner of some wasteland well apart from the village and society, it can be transposed into many realms to depict the image of a person isolated and alone—whether in business, the arts, or political office. Without a base of support nothing can proceed as desired. Consequently, the Verse suggests that yin (or inconspicuous) activities should be undertaken. They will eventually evoke a response, although worry and difficulty will continue. As Ho notes, the intercession of the spirits (or a powerful figure) is much to be desired.

66 *Huan Yüeh* 懽悦

○ ○ ○ 上
○ ○ 中 中
○ ○ ○ ○

Joy and Delight
The image of being matched
Yin and yang attain concord
Ken (Mountain) ∘ Northeast

ORACLE

Husband and wife in mutual intimacy, there are no others. Seated with their knees toward each other, great is their joy and happiness.

VERSES

Double layer of Heaven's great happiness,
Eyes and eyebrows cast open together.
The loneliness that long lingered now thrown off,
Hereafter unusual talents will unfold.

The Tao of Heaven is already established,
The Virtue of Earth is pliant.
She, beautiful and talented,
The true gentleman seeks her.
Forever united until aged,
Sharing virtue and blessings.

COMMENTARIES

YEN ∘ The firm and pliant respond to each other; it is the image of harmony and joy. Under this trigraph the hundred affairs will all be harmonious; marriage arrangements will be extremely auspicious. Commercial activities will be profitable.

Ho ∘ Remaining in residence will be peaceful and tranquil. Whatever is sought will be obtained. All affairs will accord with one's mind. Agriculture and sericulture will yield great harvests. Official affairs will dissipate; the ill will be cured. The traveler will return. It is an omen of auspiciousness and advantage.

CH'EN ∘ Yin and yang mutually gain each other, the image of husband and wife.

LIU ∘ "Husband and wife in mutual intimacy"—family affairs are appropriate. "With their knees toward each other, in joy and delight"—moreover, they find pleasure together.

Even though this trigraph lacks the lowest position, upper yang and middle yin have both obtained a match in each other. Furthermore, no harm intervenes. Divining about remaining in residence and marriage will be highly auspicious. All affairs whatsoever will be harmonious and untroubled. However, this auspiciousness is applicable to minor affairs, not great ones.

SAWYER ∘ Although one might expect the theme of trigraph 65, "Bitter Constraint," to also characterize "Joy and Delight" because both lack yin or yang in the bottom position, the natural harmony and mutual responsiveness of the yang and yin at the top and in the middle transcend the effects of such absence. This trigraph (and the accompanying Verses) presage marital bliss and supreme harmony in family affairs. Derivatively, harmony should accordingly prevail in most activities. However, perhaps because the trigraph lacks a firm basis, "great affairs"—meaning those of state, since marriage was apparently not considered a great affair by the *Ling Ch'i Ching*'s authors, contrary to Confucian attitudes—may not yet be promising.

67 FANG SUI 方遂

Just Completed
The image of birth completed
Two yang gain their positions
Ch'ien (Heaven) ◦ Northwest

ORACLE

He occupies an appropriate position and realizes his ambition in affairs. He settles his thoughts and quiets his mind; riches and blessings have just arrived. Celebrations and joy are increasingly to one's advantage.

VERSE

Rapid advance and leisurely pace each have their own meters;
The moon sinks into the western sea, the sun ascends in the
    east.
When fortune comes, why must you labor your mind?
The wind will waft you across the rivers and seas, ten thousand
    miles with ease.

COMMENTARIES

YEN ◦ Three yang dwell in the middle position and a single yang at the top responds to it, thereby realizing the proper order. The hundred affairs will all be auspicious. The ill will be free from suffering. Seeking bureaucratic office will result in great attainments.

HO ◦ All affairs will comply with one's heart. Marriage arrangements will result in a harmonious union. Official entanglements will be easily disposed of. Those remaining in residence will become rich and honored; those serving in bureaucratic offices will advance to high positions. The ill have nothing to worry about; someone is coming to treat them. Wealth sought will be obtained. Without being expected, the traveler will return. The myriad affairs are all very auspicious.

CH'EN ∘ In the Tao of Man, yang is just flourishing; there are no forces posed to conquer it either above or below. The thrust to life bursts forth.

LIU ∘ The Tao of yang just penetrated, so "one occupies an appropriate position." Above and below are free from preversity; riches and profits can be preserved. In this trigraph, since yang has gained its position, any affair divined about will be auspicious.

SAWYER ∘ This trigraph depicts yang having realized its active mode. Life is just being completed; the flow is therefore completely positive, without any hint of death or decay. Although the basis—the lowest position—is again lacking, there is no obstacle to yang's bespreading and extending. This outreach carries all things in its wake, bringing blessings and prosperity, presaging success in all things. Accordingly, the third line of the poem perhaps echoes Li Po's attitude—why trouble yourself?

68   *Kuei Ssu*   鬼伺

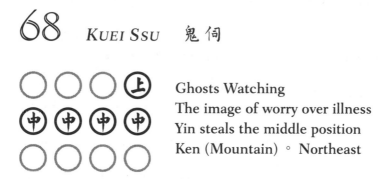

Ghosts Watching
The image of worry over illness
Yin steals the middle position
Ken (Mountain) ∘ Northeast

ORACLE

Food does not enter his mouth; *ch'i* does not exit his nose. The heart and stomach are knotted up with troubles, making it impossible to sleep.

VERSES

> Things of the same kind need to guard against times of discord;
> Previously intimate relations may change to perversity and
>   difference,
> When your monies are lost, you will sit alone;
> Along the river the luxuriant grasses still well ordered.

> Original *ch'i* has turned and dissipated,
> Essence and spirit are confused and flustered.
> Even though one might consult Doctor Pien Ch'üeh,
> His fate will still be overturned.

COMMENTARIES

YEN ∘ Yang weak, yin flourishing: a cluster of yin occupies the middle, unsubmissive to yang. Thus they lead to misfortune and harm.

HO ∘ For the ill, this trigraph might be inauspicious. It will be difficult for the imprisoned to get out. It would be appropriate to reproach yourself rather than blame others. The distant traveler will encounter brigands. Travelers voyaging by boat will meet with misfortunes of wind and water. The hundred affairs will all be inauspicious.

CH'EN ∘ The four yin are just flourishing; the single yang does not respond. It is the image of ghostly vapors at maximum.

LIU ∘ A single yang, four yin—the will does not penetrate. "The heart and stomach are knotted up with troubles"—illness lies in the middle.

In this trigraph, four yin have usurped the position of Man, while a solitary yang lies above without anything with which to be a companion. Above and below are not in accord: breath and *ch'i* do not penetrate. It is the image of worry over illness. One must cautiously guard against secret brigands. Going out to travel, there will be the worries of wind and water, thieves and brigands. Whatever might be inquired about will be inauspicious.

SAWYER ∘ This might well be the paradigm of the modern age— stress and difficulties leading to stomach disorders and ulcers. Unfortunately, no cure is immediately apparent because original *ch'i*, the primal life force, is being wasted and the body is beset with disharmony. Clearly the solution, although unexpressed, is to set forth on a more contemplative path, realize the nature of the difficulties, and wrest free of their emotional effects and control. However, while work on oneself is mandated, actions in the external world are momentarily contraindicated.

69 CH'IH CHI 遲吉

○○㊤㊤ Tardy Blessings
○○○㊥ The image of profit in the end
○○○○ Yin and yang overturned
            Chen (Thunder) ∘ True east

ORACLE

Seeking the intercession of others in your affairs, daily hoping for the realization of your thoughts, you have come to today, when you are about to attain resplendent happiness. Although you suffer delays, in the end matters will comply with your intentions.

VERSE

> Your career will have days of abundance and glory;
> Your plans and calculations eventually enable you to fulfill your
>   emotions.
> Moreover, you will gain the supportive eye of a noble person;
> All at once the hues of springtime will fill your courtyard.

COMMENTARIES

YEN ∘ Although the positions of yin and yang are inverted, through their interaction you will be assisted. "Seeking the intercession of others"—in the end you will realize good fortune. Since yang's position is solitary and slight, it is unable to achieve success by itself. Thus there will be delays before happiness. Under this trigraph the response will be slow but fortunate.

HO ∘ "Seeking the intercession of others in your affairs"—you must not be perturbed by the slowness of the response. Eventually matters will follow your mind. Outside there will be happiness and blessings. Illnesses of the heart and stomach should slowly recover. The traveler is about to return. Affairs are obstructed; each and every one of them will ever so slowly result in good fortune.

CH'EN ∘ Yang dominates speed; yin dominates slowness. The upper and middle positions inherently should respond to each other, but since the upper position is yin, the pliant, its response is somewhat slow.

LIU ∘ "Seeking the intercession of others in your affairs"—what is sought has not yet been attained. "After a delay, you will attain your desires"—in the end there will be the realization of what is sought.

In this trigraph, even though yin and yang form a match and the upper and lower positions interact, yang's position is singular and weak, unable to quickly achieve its goals. Thus it will be a long time before penetration. In all affairs there will at first be worry, later happiness. In the end you will realize what is sought. It is not appropriate to be hasty and impatient.

SAWYER ∘ Yin and yang are inverted from their appropriate positions of yang above, yin below. Moreover, the yin at the top occupies a yang position. In addition, the bottom line—the base—is missing, signifying that affairs lack substantiality and that assistance must be sought and goals attained through the intercession of others. (Surprisingly, the commentators do not concern themselves with the absence of a substantial basis, focusing instead solely on yang's weakness. Solitary yang here of course signifies the querent's situation and position.) However, as in the *I Ching,* yin being placed above yang is not invariably inauspicious, for the upper will naturally tend to sink, while the lower yang will naturally rise. It is through the interaction and intermingling of the two that affairs are engendered, that life is born. Therefore, since it is youthful yin at the top, and youthful yang below, even though youth may be marked by robust desire and energetic action, in the ancient world view they often lack the strength and direction of mature yin and yang. Therefore developments will be slow, contrary to contemporary phenomena, but eventually auspicious.

70 CHIEH SHEN 戒慎

Wary and Cautious
The image of worrying about separation
Two yin facing each other
K'un (Earth) ∘ Southwest

ORACLE

Although you may be secure, still there is danger; although you may be happy, still there is grief. There is a constant fear of separation and parting, of not being able to follow one another.

VERSE

> The myriad affairs never follow human intent,
> Grief and joy pervade each life.
> Guard against the minute, stifle the sprouts,
> Govern affairs with true mindfulness.

COMMENTARIES

YEN ∘ Two yin dwell facing each other; the trigraph has no yang position whatsoever, but there seems to be happiness. Their intentions do not cohere; separation constantly looms. Under this trigraph, whatever is done will not be advantageous. It will be difficult for marriage arrangements to be harmonious because the trigraph is purely yin. Every affair will be uneventful if you are wary and cautious.

HO ∘ Wanting to separate, they do not discriminate between good and evil. It will be difficult to obtain what is sought. Remaining in residence, it would be appropriate to be very cautious about family members; there might be a secret plot. It will be difficult to resolve official affairs. The ill might not yet recover. The traveler will not yet return. Commercial activities will not be profitable. If the army is sent forth on campaign, it will not be victorious. There is disaster without happiness.

CH'EN ∘ The two positions are both yin and weak; their intentions do not respond to each other. Thus it forms the image of separation and parting.

LIU ∘ "Although you may be secure, still there is danger"—the household is empty. "There is a constant fear of separation and parting"—their intentions are not the same.

In this trigraph, the two yin dwell outside and lack a house—they take themselves to be secure and fail to realize the danger. Moreover, their intentions do not cohere, so there is nothing to rely on. When the querent obtains it, whatever is attempted will not proceed well. The Tao of the family is dissipated and lacking. One will be constantly troubled by inescapable worries.

SAWYER ∘ Liu's commentary about the house—"in this trigraph, the two yin dwell outside and lack a house"—refers to the absence of a basis. From the perspective of Earth, there is an upper or outer shell but no foundation. Furthermore, the image consists of two yin, both passive and weak, marked by a tendency to separate rather than co-alesce and cooperate together. (If one of the two positions were yang, there could be interaction, as in the previous trigraph. Such interaction is precluded here, yet there need not inherently be the pronounced tendency to separation and disagreement envisioned for this trigraph.) Consequently, the situation is inauspicious, and care must be exercised because of the discord around you. Although things may seem secure, the present stability and tranquility may be illusory. Efforts should perhaps be directed toward forging a substantial foundation, a sustainable basis for constructing a more secure personal edifice.

71 *TA CH'ENG* 大成

Great Completion
The image of knowing to stop
Correct yang occupies the middle
Chen (Thunder) ∘ True east

ORACLE

Passing over our roads and byways, the wagons rumble along. What treasures do they convey? Gold and silver ever supplied in abundant sufficiency, one will never be troubled by poverty.

VERSE

You will receive Heaven's blessings,
It will certainly send down good fortune.
Concentrate on fullness, not excessiveness.
If you preserve them, you will prosper.
Do not be idle, do not be arrogant.
Forever maintain peace and vigor.

COMMENTARIES

YEN ∘ Although yin dwells at the top, yang dwells in the middle, so its intentions find a response from without. Great penetration, good fortune, and material blessings, all without any worry about poverty. This trigraph is extremely auspicious. Whatever you hope for ought to be distant; then there will be happiness and felicity.

HO ∘ Perhaps you will obtain things from people coming; perhaps you will go out to seek people and gain wealth. It will be like the ten thousand things being born—you will gain a double harvest, abundance, and sufficiency. Seeking office will result in harmonious union. The traveler will return after great gains. Official affairs will dissipate. The ill will recover. The hundred affairs are all very auspicious; it will be especially appropriate to seek wealth.

CH'EN ∘ In the Tao of Man, yang is flourishing and the two yin respond. It is the image of riches and sufficiency.

LIU ∘ "Passing over our roads and byways"—the firm and pliant respond to each other. "The wagons rumble along"—the middle position is correct. "One will never be troubled by poverty"—there will be great felicity.

This trigraph presages that whatever is divined about will be auspicious. But as it lacks the position of Earth, real-estate ventures and establishing a career will not be profitable in one's native village. However, they will prove advantageous outside. Whenever a trigraph lacks the lower position, it is generally like this.

SAWYER ∘ Great prosperity is in the offing, largely because of mature yang in the realm of Man. However, as the Verse admonishes, you cannot be dilatory just because Heaven promises its blessings! In fact, the more distant and perhaps ambitious your goals, especially financial and commercial ones, the greater the prospects. The eventual attainment of riches must not spawn arrogance, for Heaven—whether in Greece or China—abhors it and may brutally withdraw its favor.

72 *Fu Wei* 扶危

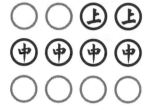

Supporting the Endangered
The image of maintaining constraints
Correct yin dwells in the middle
K'un (Earth) ∘ Southwest

ORACLE

Yesterday we traveled forth and confronted invading soldiers. A falling arrow struck my eye; tears flowed copiously.

VERSES

> Clouds stretch across the mountain ridges, the waters below are
>   boundless;
> For a thousand miles of a lengthy journey, I have looked
>   anxiously for my hometown.
> When difficulties and perversities arise, one should not detest
>   them;
> Dejected, I lean on a gate in the sun's slanting rays.

> Heaven gives birth to Sages and Worthies,
> Embracing the Tao they have no position.
> They travel about the four quarters,
> Taking the Tao for their nobility.
> Their adornment and substance refined,
> They are plucked out from among the masses.

COMMENTARIES

Ho ∘ Going places will not be auspicious. Perhaps you will meet invading soldiers and be shot in the eye. The traveler will not yet return. The ill may suffer somewhat. It will be hard for the imprisoned to gain release; it will be difficult to resolve official affairs. There will be the buzzing of disputes. If you seek blessings through prayer, you will be secure. It would not be appropriate to take a boat. If you preserve the old, you will obtain good fortune.

CH'EN ∘ In the upper position, yin is weak; the lowest position is fallen and empty. A cluster of yin dwells in the middle without any ground on which it can stand. This is the image of danger and chaos. "Support the endangered and maintain the constraints" and thereby encourage vigilance.

LIU ∘ "Going forth, one meets with disaster"—yin occupies the middle. "A falling arrow strikes my eye"—the top is similarly impoverished.

In this trigraph, the upper and middle are both yin; since there is no lower position, and moreover nothing to be a match, they harm and rob themselves. When the querent obtains this trigraph, it presages that there will be insults and offenses by the hidden and menial. The traveler will be worried about robbers. Official affairs will be difficult to resolve. Employing the army will result in losses and defeat. Marriage arrangements will not be harmonious. All affairs whatsoever are baleful.

SAWYER ∘ This trigraph unfortunately suffers from a corrupted text, even resulting in two different Oracles and Verses. The set provided in our translation accords with the trigraph's dynamics and the Commentaries. Since both positions are yin, and therefore fundamentally not interactive, the tendency is to dissension and chaos. Furthermore, the Tao of Man is mature yin and therefore overwhelmingly weak in the absence of any yang with which to mutually respond. The basis is also lacking, as the Tao of Earth is completely absent and therefore vacuous. It is an image of weakness and being overwhelmed, rather than eventual good fortune as suggested by the discarded Oracle.

73　*Fu Liu*　福流

Flowing Blessings
The image of gaining Heaven
Three yang at the top
Ch'ien (Heaven) ◦ Northwest

ORACLE

After repeatedly encountering misfortune, now you will meet a prosperous opportunity. It won't be for just a moment; the blessings should extend through generations.

VERSE

> The windblown waves now at rest,
> Your boat and oars will meet with tranquil passage.
> Hereafter achievement and fame will follow,
> Why must you sigh about white hair?

COMMENTARIES

YEN ◦ Three yang are at the top; nothing can encroach on them. The ruler is enlightened and the ministers excellent; the petty therefore retire from their positions. One can thereby attain good fortune and prosperity.

Under this trigraph, although in the beginning there will be worry, later there will be happiness. Remaining in residence will be auspicious and profitable. Moreover, affairs will begin to follow your mind. Salary and position are just about to be attained. The traveler is returning. The ill will recover. Whatever is sought will be highly auspicious!

Ho ∘ In the beginning there will be worry over affairs; later, good fortune will arrive. It would be advantageous to see a powerful figure, for then riches and things will be doubly obtained. Official affairs will be resolved. If the army goes forth, it will be victorious. A sealed official dispatch will arrive. Only marriage arrangements would not be auspicious!

Cʜ'ᴇɴ ∘ The Tao of Man is already correct; in the Tao of Heaven, yang's brilliance shines down. Those below receive Heaven's blessings.

Lɪᴜ ∘ "After repeatedly encountering misfortune"—at first there will be worry. "Now you will meet with a prosperous opportunity"—suddenly you will obtain what you seek.

In this trigraph, both the upper and middle positions are yang, while there is no opposition or obstacle. When intentions cohere and unite in the Tao, one can attain blessings and prosperity. It is the image of gaining Heaven. In all affairs, at first there will be regret, later happiness.

Sᴀᴡʏᴇʀ ∘ This trigraph is characterized by mature yang in the position of Heaven and youthful, energetic yang in the realm of Man— both appropriate, in accord with the basic theory underlying the *Ling Ch'i Ching*. Therefore, sagacious Heaven has a talented disciple to effect its mandates, and the prospects for worldly success should be good despite the absence of activity in the realm of Earth. Remarkably, "Flowing Blessings" portends even greater auspiciousness than trigraph 33, "Bright Yang," which is identical except for the addition of youthful yang in the position of Earth.

74 WAN CHIU 晚就

○ ⊕ ⊕ ⊕   Late Accomplishment
○ ○ ⊕ ⊕   The image of an omen
                 Yang arrayed above yin
○ ○ ○ ○   Ken (Mountain) ○ Northeast

ORACLE

Shouldering his plow, he tills the fields himself. Raising his foot to the task in the fourth month, he strives to accord with the time. The millet gradually appears.

VERSES

> Your career has a path, do not rail at its slowness;
> Sintering gold from amidst the sands awaits an opportune time.
> When sand and mud are completely washed away, the gold first
>   appears;
> Both name and profit will become greatly appropriate.

> The farmer tills the fields by himself,
> In his efforts there will be completion.
> Seeding and planting at the proper time,
> The hundred grains abundantly appear.
> Sated and drunken,
> Pleasure beyond compare.

COMMENTARIES

YEN ○ Three yang arrayed across the top, yin correct in the middle position, they realize the proper pattern. When you sow seeds at the appropriate time, there will be great profits. The fourth month is the time of correct (maturing) yang; the millet begins to flourish. Agriculture and sericulture are very auspicious.

Ho ∘ Every affair will be auspicious and profitable but somewhat slow. Seeking wealth, whether by remaining in residence or by going out, will be highly auspicious. Sending the army forth will result in victory. The traveler will arrive. This trigraph's image is free of internal conquest. It would be appropriate to commence the management of affairs after the fourth month.

CH'EN ∘ In the Tao of Man, yin is weak, still unable to quickly move to fruition. But with three yang above, it receives the blessings of Heaven and can thereby act as it wishes.

LIU ∘ Since yin follows yang, the positions are correct and appropriate. "Tilling the fields himself at the appropriate time"—one will achieve what is hoped for.

In this trigraph, the three yang at the top have attained their position while yin follows them. It is the image of complying without contradiction. But the trigraph lacks the position of Earth; therefore, you must exert great effort at the appropriate time to be able to harvest results.

SAWYER ∘ Although yin, rather than the appropriate yang, occupies the position of Man, the naturally envisioned order of yang over yin results in an image of principle and response. The theme focuses on late spring activity, requiring the energizing principle of yang to impregnate yin, bringing forth the fruit of the land. The only difficulty is caused by the continued absence of a basis, the ground for sowing. However, this may be overcome by effort, and the querent is therefore advised to be committed to the task, initiating it at the proper time. The "fourth month," possibly May in the Western calendar (depending on the *Ling Ch'i Ching*'s composition date), need not be understood too specifically. Simplistically, it is of course a particular time in the year, but the year is merely a descriptive matrix for event timing. Obviously, sowing seeds in the fall or winter could be foolhardly. Similarly, human activities have their appropriate moments for commencement—too soon and they are doomed, just as the early breaking sprouts that die in the next frost; too late, and they flourish gloriously but never ripen, perishing on the first frozen autumnal night. Great insight is required to successfully site actions in the unfolding pattern of existence.

75 Shih Chün 事君

Serving the Ruler
The image of uniting with Virtue
Two yang mutually productive
Ch'ien (Heaven) ∘ Northwest

ORACLE

An enlightened ruler above, no perversity or evil below. Those garbed in court attire are numerous and fine; demotions and promotions have been brilliantly effected.

VERSES

From low the dragon raises its horns on high, half breaking
    through the clouds,
Claws and teeth now complete, beyond hardship and suffering.
Henceforth it continually pursues thunder's transformations,
Shortly to become a man of Heaven in the human realm.

When Yao and Shun governed the world,
Ruler and ministers all excelled.
The chief of the four mountainous regions was accomplished
    and wise,
The prime minister approved the plans.
For three years they effected promotions and demotions,
The vile and malevolent were forever forced aside.

COMMENTARIES

YEN ∘ Above, there is an enlightened ruler, and below, there are worthy ministers; thus there is no evil or perversity, but a fine array of officials properly ranked and ordered. This trigraph is highly auspicious. It is appropriate to attaining official positions and emoluments.

Ho ○ At first there will be worry, later happiness. Assuming an official position would be especially excellent. The imprisoned will manage to get out. A sealed official document will arrive. In legal entanglements you will obtain the assistance of a noble person. Agriculture, sericulture, and raising livestock will be doubly profitable. If the army goes out on campaign, it will achieve great victories. This trigraph would not be auspicious for marriage arrangements; otherwise, the hundred affairs are all very auspicious.

Ch'en ○ Heaven and Man are pure yang—it is the image of an enlightened ruler and good ministers.

Liu ○ "The ruler is enlightened, the ministers good; there is no evil or perversity. Those garbed in court attire are numerous and fine"—it would not be appropriate to make many changes.

In this trigraph, mature yang dwells in the ruler's and minister's positions without the intercession of yin or menial persons. Thus the pinnacle of excellence is attained. All affairs whatever will be auspicious. It would be appropriate to preserve the status quo; it would not be appropriate to make changes. Only inquiring about marriage arrangements and rainfall will not yield results in accord with your wishes.

Sawyer ○ Ho's commentary is puzzling because the presence of mature yang in the top and middle positions is appropriate and correct. Only the basis, the position of Earth, is lacking, while the realms of Heaven and Man are both strong and active. However, the commentators simply ignore this deficiency in the foundation and the dangers posed by excessive, unbalanced yang. Although projects should be under the direction and influence of Heaven, some thought must be given to the risk posed by blundering ahead without foresight. Unrestrained, yang-fostered activities can become too swift, too direct, too forward moving. This might be appropriate to military affairs (which are normally considered to be of the category of yin), but not to activities requiring active harmony among parties, such as marriage and sexual partnerships. In the trigraph's image, the ruler—Virtue personified—is joined by his ministers; however, their role largely mirrors his Virtue, translating it into concrete measures in the human realm. While they are active, it is not a freewheeling, undirected thrust. The first stanza introduces the image of a young dragon pursuing self-transformation, descending from Heaven to the human realm. However, the second stanza is simply an allusion to the ideal government of the Sage Emperors, the progenitors of the ancient, semilegendary dynasties, and accords with the trigraph's imagery.

76 *PI TE* 必得

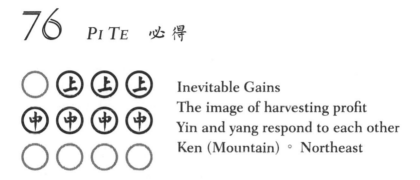

Inevitable Gains
The image of harvesting profit
Yin and yang respond to each other
Ken (Mountain) ∘ Northeast

ORACLE

The black dog of Han pursuing a rabbit, a flying falcon seizing a pheasant—in each instance they get what they go after. The results are easily seen.

VERSE

> A piece of jade from the Ch'u mountains,
> Must rely on a skilled artisan seeking it out.
> Cut and polished, it becomes a great vessel,
> In the end, meeting with kings and lords.

COMMENTARIES

YEN ∘ Three yang lie at the top, yin dwells in the middle; interior and exterior respond to each other. It is the image of compliant order. There is nothing that the racing dog and flying falcon fail to seize when they go after it. This trigraph is especially appropriate for hunting and punishing thieves. Seeking office and other hoped-for affairs will all be auspicious and profitable.

Ho ∘ The myriad affairs, although lacking a good beginning, will have an end. Official entanglements will dissipate. Agriculture and sericulture will enjoy great harvests. A sealed, official document will swiftly arrive. Military campaigns will result in great victories. Moreover, in the beginning, one's ambition must be great; then, in the end, if there are some minor losses, there still will not be any harm.

CH'EN ∘ Yin and yang are both flourishing; above and below respond to each other.

LIU ∘ "The black dog of Han pursuing a rabbit"—yang mounts yin. "His gains will be like this"—he achieves a great capture. This trigraph is highly appropriate for catching fugitives; extirpating brigands; real-estate transactions; and seeking office.

SAWYER ∘ Yang over yin appropriately mirrors the relationship of Heaven and Earth, presaging general auspiciousness. Yang is strong, robust, and mature, and therefore capable of acting as a sustained, driving force even in the absence of a true basis at the bottom. Mature yin is fully its counterpart, unlike the youthful partners found in trigraph 66, "Joy and Delight," although their relationship may be marked by conflict and enmity.

The black dog of Han appears as an allusion in a passage in the *Intrigues of the Warring States,* where the inevitability of one protagonist's victory is likened to "the black dog of Han pursuing a lame rabbit." Whatever one seeks should be obtainable, assuming sufficient effort is made. Therefore Ho, the only commentator to obliquely take cognizance of the missing earthly basis, advises aiming high. Racing swiftly, the target will be achieved, although only after some time. Any minor losses will pale in comparison to the gains realized.

77 HSÜEH CH'IH 雪恥

Avenging Insults
The image of bearing burdens yet riding
Yin occludes minute yang
Chen (Thunder) ∘ True east

ORACLE

Bearing food, I enter the fields but do not see the farmer. A thieving crow rudely pecks at the dried meat. Drawing my bow, I shoot it, hitting the left wing.

VERSE

Covering your head, you will not see travelers on the road;
Sitting alone in a darkened window, you will not discriminate
  clearly.
Below the mountain the water is deep, but boats have not
  set out;
Plans and plots put into action, unexpectedly difficult to
  achieve.

COMMENTARIES

YEN ∘ Yang's position is solitary and minute, occluded by the heavy yin. Affairs will meet with disaster. Thus the Oracle states: "The thieving crow pecks at the dried meat." However, yang forms the body, and from minuteness it will manifest itself. In the end, one ought to be victorious and thereby avenge earlier insults.

HO ∘ You are vexed by conflict with other people. This trigraph presages worry over distant travel. Those already traveling will encounter misfortune. Agriculture and sericulture will yield poor harvests. Whatever is sought will not prove profitable. Marriage arrangements will not be successful. Official entanglements will not be resolved. However, if you gain the powerful assistance of a noble person, in the end you can avoid great disaster.

CH'EN ∘ The Tao of Man stands solitary; a cluster of yin lies above. The *I Ching* states: "Bearing a burden yet riding in a carriage! It attracts brigands; it brings the arrival of thieves!" This refers to yin. Yet, since the Tao of Man is correct, in the end you should emerge victorious over the perverse and can thereby avenge any insults.

LIU ∘ "I don't see the farmer"—he is obscured by the verdant shade. My strength is small but responsibility heavy, thereby bringing about harm from thieves. "I shoot it, hitting the left wing"—thus I will yet be victorious.

In this trigraph, heavy yin dwells at the top, while minute yang lies in the middle. Accordingly, it ought to be the case that villainous robbers will, in the end, inevitably be defeated and captured. If one sends forth the army, at first they will suffer defeat, later be victorious.

SAWYER ∘ The title of the trigraph can be translated as "Avenging Insults" or, more literally, "Whitening Shame," for the first character is "snow." The basic theme focuses on talents or abilities being inadequate to a task, thereby encountering misfortune and failure at the initial stage. The *I Ching* reference is to the third line of hexagram 40, "Resolution," which the traditional commentators all understand as translated in Ch'en's passage above. In the hexagram, arrogance—overstepping the bounds of social convention (and probably the sumptuary regulations)—elicits the misfortune of being robbed because it was felt that the petty individual, despite great riches, would never have a sufficiently grave and self-possessed demeanor to intimidate common people. However, the feeling and image of this trigraph is distinctly different, despite Ch'en's interpretation. The inadequacy stems from a person—perhaps a wife, perhaps a small child—undertaking a necessary task by going out into the burgeoning fields where the farmer is not immediately apparent, no doubt being hidden by the green foliage. This can hardly be considered a disaster, for the difficulty arises from nature's growth and abundance rather than, for example, a cloud of deadly volcanic ash or ravenous insects. The uppity crow then seizes on the momentary confusion to quickly peck at the dried meat—certainly a hesitant, poking attack rather than a major onslaught. Yang, present in the Tao of Man, although still in its incipient stage, provides essential strength and the prospect of mounting what must be, in the context, considered bold, significant action. The bird is wounded—probably with a single shot—but not killed. It merely followed its nature to seize an opportunity and has now been driven off. Thus the immediate future is somewhat foreboding but clearly and equally promises the possibility of resolving the situation through decisive action.

However, note that the measure taken is essentially responsive: something appropriate to contextual demands rather than something initiated, despite the commentators' suggestions that military campaigns would prove successful. (The prospect of initial defeats would hardly seem to make the venture worthwhile. Sun-tzu would certainly deem such action imprudent, wasteful, and calamitous. A significant defeat at the outset might even reduce the army's strength so drastically that further engagements would become impossible.) Without any basis in the Tao of Earth, initiating major ventures of any kind may prove foolhardy.

78 CHIEH CHIN 戒 進

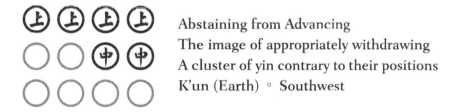

Abstaining from Advancing
The image of appropriately withdrawing
A cluster of yin contrary to their positions
K'un (Earth) ∘ Southwest

ORACLE

Quarreling and fighting in their drunkenness, both knives and staffs are drawn. Only when the host, becoming fearful, humbles himself does it cease.

VERSE

> Dwelling in prosperity, one should ponder and contemplate;
> Effecting plans lies in discerning the moment.
> When setting out the wine vessels, guard against uncouth
>   guests;
> By being humble and retiring, one can be free of anxiety.

COMMENTARIES

YEN ∘ Occupying a position beneath a cluster of yin, without any support from the absent position of Earth, guest and host become unruly. In their drunkenness they angrily clamor and fight. Only after the host humbles himself does it cease. This trigraph presages numerous calamities. Entertaining guests will be especially inauspicious.

HO ∘ At first there will be arguments, but if you accord with the antagonists in order to defuse them, in the end, there will not be any worries. Within the household, guard against secretive persons, stabbings, and bloody incidents. Official affairs, financial matters, and the problems of illness might all be disadvantageous. If you perfect yourself in prayer, it would be auspicious. The traveler will probably become involved in arguments and altercations. In everything it would be appropriate to be abstentious and cautious.

CH'EN ∘ The two positions are both yin; the host does not overcome his guest. This brings about the harm of thieves, but he avoids it.

LIU ∘ "Drunken from wine, they clamor and fight"—this is the balefulness of petty men. "The host humbles himself"—he avoids direct conflict. This is the image of numerous calamities. Under this trigraph it would not be appropriate to implement any affairs. If you preserve yourself, it will be all right.

SAWYER ∘ This is really a dark, miserable trigraph, overwhelmed by yin occupying the positions of Heaven and Man, where yang should prevail. Furthermore, there is no support in the Tao of Earth, nor any ruler of strength. The sky is dark and ominous; the realm of Man is filled with foreboding. Weakness and passivity induce arrogance and encroachment, both among states and in social relations. While the Confucians prized deference and yielding, they must always be founded on inner strength. Here there is none; only self-effacement and humbleness manage to get one through the gloom. Any presumptiveness derived from material wealth will simply invite robbers to throw the pretender from the car, as the ancients astutely observed and was mentioned in the previous trigraph.

79 CHIEH FENG 戒逢

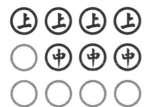

Abstaining from Encounters
The image of knowing to stop
Yang dwells below yin
Chen (Thunder) ∘ True east

ORACLE

Ahead there are bandits and robbers, to the rear no other travelers. Walking quietly, ceasing forward movement, one can be preserved.

VERSE

> Departing is not yet possible, numerous obstacles cause
> separation;
> Moreover, guard against the secretive and menial causing harm
> in the darkness.
> With a stick of bright incense you should pray and confess;
> Preserved by the spirits' blessings, with disaster mitigated, you
> will be hearty.

COMMENTARIES

YEN ∘ Three yang dwell together in the middle; below them the position of Earth is lacking. A cluster of yin lies above, like bandits and brigands being ahead. However, the three yang are just flourishing, so that if one "walks quietly and ceases forward movement," they will not be able to cause harm. Although the Oracle is not auspicious or felicitous, you can manage to preserve yourself. This trigraph presages that traveling about will be slightly auspicious. Moreover, since the lowest position is lacking, the Oracle states that "to the rear there are no other travelers."

Ho ∘ In the beginning, there will be disputes, and you will want to return to your native village. It would be appropriate to stop temporarily, for then you will avoid misfortune. The hundred affairs are somewhat calamitous. It is not appropriate to travel, only to stop. In everything it would be appropriate to proceed slowly.

Ch'en ∘ Yin and perversity lie above; the middle position, the ruler of this trigraph, is sufficiently firm and strong to govern them.

Liu ∘ A cluster of yin lies at the top—"ahead there are bandits." There is an upper but not a lower—there is no one to the rear. If you are aware of difficulty and stop, you can avoid calamity.

Sawyer ∘ Overwhelming yin again dominates the position of Heaven, giving rise to foreboding about bandits. Fortunately the position of Man is strong and robust, and therefore theoretically able to control evil and overcome perversity. However, this projected capability is undermined by the lack of a substantial basis, the absence of Earth's support. Thus the Oracle suggests that the querent is fundamentally vigorous and capable but needs to exercise restraint over immediate actions because of the obstacles apparently ahead and the insularity resulting from the emptiness of the trigraph's foundation. It counsels stopping and avoiding adversarial confrontations for the moment. Realizing the nature of the difficulty, calamity can thus be avoided. (Note the significant disagreement among the commentators regarding the auspiciousness of this trigraph's various aspects.)

80 *Pei Chiao* 被絞

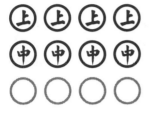

Bound Up
The image of speed being appropriate
Clusters of yin encroaching and
  flourishing
K'un (Earth) ∘ Southwest

Oracle

Suspended and anxious as if bound up, rescue cannot arrive. Even the case of the state of Lu looking to Kao-tzu for rescue is too weak for comparison.

Verse

> Yin at its pinnacle, balefulness and danger extreme;
> The living people are already overturned and suspended.
> Without some force to rescue and protect them,
> How could they preserve their lives intact?

Commentaries

Yen ∘ Yang's Virtue has withered away; "clusters of yin are encroaching and flourishing." It is the image of defeat and chaos, just like Duke Min of Lu meeting with inescapable death. Chi-tzu then brought the young Duke Hsi to the state of Chu; at the end of the year, Kao-tzu of Ch'i came to form an alliance. Subsequently, Lu's turbulence was quieted. This trigraph presages that military activities will at first result in defeat but later be auspicious. Moreover, it indicates that in everything one ought to be quick; long pondering will not result in harmonious cooperation.

Ho ∘ Disputes and arguments, turbulence and clamor! The ill will recover slowly. The traveler will not yet arrive. The army will not be victorious. Within the household be wary of female servants. Official affairs will at first be worrisome but later gain the strength of others. You should be quick in implementing plans if they are to succeed; otherwise, evil spirits and brigands will inevitably appear. Under this trigraph, every activity requires speedy rescue; it would not be appropriate to proceed slowly and leisurely.

CH'EN ∘ "Suspended and anxious as if bound up"—it is the pinnacle of exhaustion. "Rescue cannot arrive"—the disaster is already complete. As there is no lower position to provide rescue, the trigraph forms the image of being suspended on high.

In this trigraph, clusters of yin are active at the top, invariably bringing about defeat and chaos, spawning hope for rescue by other men. It is the extremity of hardship. When the querent obtains it, everything will be baleful.

SAWYER ∘ Darkness, weakness, and passivity strongly dominate the positions of Heaven and Man. The imbalance is extreme; there is absolutely no support from below. Clearly it forges an image that requires either precipitous action to extricate oneself from the morass, or dictates simply floating along in doomed anxiety until the moment changes and the threat of disaster has passed. The example of Duke Min, murdered while still small, is typical of the political intrigues found in the famous *Tso Chuan*. However, one wonders why this particular, fairly undistinguished example was chosen by the Oracle's creators. (For further details, consult the records for Duke Min's years.)

81   *Ching Shen*   敬 慎

Respectful Caution
The image of Virtue illuminated
Two yang ascending from below
Ch'ien (Heaven) ∘ Northwest

ORACLE

"Illuminate Virtue and repress the offensive"—affairs lie in according with the moment. Worthies are cautious about the beginning; the perfected guard against the minuscule.

VERSES

> There is another sandy path along the river;
> Don't follow women roaming about.
> Do not sigh over frequent stagnation;
> When you gain your ambition, you will flow with the wind.

> While dwelling quietly, guard against the minuscule;
> When risking danger, beware of tangents.
> Do not be dilatory, do not be hasty;
> Be cautious about the beginning, obtain what is appropriate.

COMMENTARIES

YEN ∘ Although it lacks the upper position, this trigraph has yang lines. They are sufficient to illuminate its flourishing Virtue and repress the incorrect and offensive. Moreover, the Oracle states that in everything it would be appropriate to accord with the moment and move, while simultaneously guarding against the minuscule. For the perfected it is auspicious; for the petty it is inauspicious.

Ho ○ In everything it would be appropriate to accord with the moment and move, for then you will attain your ambition. In the *Tso Chuan*, Tsang Ai-po said: "He illuminates his virtue and represses the offensive in order to illuminate and affect the hundred offices." Under this trigraph, undertaking official matters would be very auspicious.

Ch'en ○ The Tao of Man and Tao of Earth have each gained a single yang but are not yet able to flourish. However, the upper position lacks any support to lend the lower ones. You must be warily on guard and preserve yourself.

Liu ○ "Illuminate Virtue and repress the offensive"—they must accord with the time. Being cautious about the end lies at the beginning; one must invariably guard against the minuscule. Under this trigraph it is important to know the moment and recognize the time in order to effect public, upright affairs.

Sawyer ○ Another in a series of unbalanced trigraphs, here Heaven itself is neither yin nor yang, but simply absent. The two lower positions are both youthful, inexperienced yang and thus suggest rash action and easy misjudgment. Consequently, to ensure gaining one's ambition, it is necessary to be especially cautious when commencing any affair and recognize the potential danger inherent in the minuscule. However, Heaven will neither sustain nor impede your course; the effort and consequences lie with you alone. Thus it is important to recognize the "moment," the subtle point in time when affairs shift and good fortune germinates. Therefore, by according with the flux, prosperity and success should follow. As the Verse states, then you will "flow with the wind"—commonly understood in later times as excessively pursuing pleasure and indulging in debauchery.

82 *Ti Tao* 帝道

Tao of the Emperor
The image of Virtue arriving
Yin and yang mutually interpenetrating
Ken (Mountain) ○ Northeast

ORACLE

Heaven and Earth share achievements; yin and yang mutually interpenetrate. His activities and affairs are broad and vast. From west
to east, wherever he may come or go, it is difficult to tread in his
footsteps.

VERSES

> A young woman stands before the gate,
> In the end excellent affairs will come.
> Henceforth there will be neither danger nor obstruction,
> Enjoy the blessings of fortune, do not be doubtful!
>
> The Tao great, Virtue attained,
> The achievement cannot be compassed.
> The perfected advance in their employment,
> The petty retire in concealment.

COMMENTARIES

YEN ○ Heaven and Earth open and penetrating; grasses and trees
just beginning, but not yet easy to discern their traces. It would be
appropriate to accumulate Virtue, cultivate benevolence, and gradually attain glory. It is the image of a great ruler or sage. What is
planned is not yet fathomable; what is sought is difficult to respond
to. The distant traveler is not yet returning.

Ho ∘ Great ambition is difficult to attain; it cannot be measured.

CH'EN ∘ The Tao of Man is already correct; the Tao of Earth is also correct. Yin and yang gain each other; it is the image of All under Heaven being peacefully governed.

LIU ∘ "Heaven and Earth share achievements"—yin and yang gain each other. "His activities and affairs are broad and vast"—his advancement has not yet reached the pinnacle. "It is difficult to tread in his footsteps"—they cannot be fathomed. This trigraph presages that establishing achievements and implementing affairs will be very auspicious.

SAWYER ∘ Youthful yang in the middle and young yin at the bottom are both appropriate to their positions and hierarchically correct. Therefore, they suggest the interpenetration of Heaven and Earth which they respectively represent, thereby portending the growth of all things and the successful initiation of any undertaking that requires nurturing, such as embarking on musical or artistic endeavors. While this trigraph would be particularly appropriate in the spring, obtaining it in fall or winter will emphasize the opportunity for personal growth and success, contrary to the flux of yin without. The only troubling aspect is the absence of Heaven above, symbolizing a lack of support from superiors; the need for a mentor; or constant failure to be properly recognized by the established powers. (The trigraph notes "it will be difficult to fathom his tread"—your acts will not be easily appreciated.) The prospects for success are outstanding, but it should be noted that the gradual accumulation of virtue, synonymous with continuous effort and growing achievement, is required.

83 *Pu Ting* 不定

Unsettled
The image of suspicion and doubt
A mass of yang hasten to contend
Ch'ien (Heaven) ∘ Northwest

ORACLE

Suspicious and hesitant, unsettled within one's thoughts, advancing cannot be hoped for. Withdrawing to follow uprightness would be appropriate.

VERSES

Secret affairs emerge from darkened rooms,
Miasmic clouds seal the innermost chambers.
No possible ally being visible,
Solitary, alone, overwhelmed with melancholy.

Paths so numerous one forgets the direction;
Heaven expansive, Earth without any trace.
In advancing and stopping, you must be careful;
Make your body tranquil, in solitude adhere to poverty.

COMMENTARIES

YEN ∘ The upper position lacks a ruler, while a mass of yang contentiously arises. It is the image of not yet being settled. Interior and exterior are not responsive; thus there is hesitancy. Taking action when principles are obscure is not as good as retiring and preserving correctness.

Ho ∘ Advancing and withdrawing are not settled; it is difficult to follow one's heart. All affairs are thus. Moreover, this trigraph indicates that seeking office will eventually be auspicious. Illness might grow somewhat more severe before being cured. The traveler is not yet returning. Deploying the army will not result in victory. It is the image of withdrawing to contemplate and accord with the ordinary.

CH'EN ∘ The position of Man is singular and weak; in contrast, yang is flourishing in the position of Earth. A cluster of heroes, arising together, is flourishing, but they do not respond to each other. No one knows what to follow.

LIU ∘ "Suspicious and hesitant"—there is nowhere to go or follow. "Advancing cannot be hoped for"—the heart is irresolute. "Withdrawing to follow the upright would be appropriate"—then one will not enter into balefulness.

This trigraph presages a time without a ruler; thus the mass of yang below lacks any fixed direction. Accordingly, it creates the image of suspicion and hesitancy. Yang is present without any yin—"interior and exterior do not respond to each other." Thus "advancing cannot be hoped for; it would be best to retire to follow uprightness." If the querent preserves quietude, it would be auspicious.

SAWYER ∘ The Oracle envisions a theme of disunion and disharmony arising from the inappropriate presence of yang in the two lower positions. While other interpretations might be possible, the commentators naturally struggle to rationalize the interpretation. The weakness indicated by this trigraph is not an inherent weakness, for the active principle abounds, but rather a predicament of multiple choices and factors, as the Verses indicate. This suggests that the querent is at a turning point, with numerous possibilities and many talents, but lacks a clear indication or inner signal about which path to pursue. Although the military writers stressed that doubt and indecision doom people to fragmented efforts and inevitable failure, the Oracle counsels retiring to ponder and accord with the ordinary until the appropriate reality is revealed.

84   HSIEH NING   邪 佞

○○○○
○○○㊥
㊦㊦㊦㊦

Perverse Insinuation
The image of accumulating evil
A cluster of yin conquers yang
Ken (Mountain) ∘ Northeast

ORACLE

Disobeying Heaven; turning against the ruler, disregarding the principles of human relations; indulging in licentious excess; being perverse and insinuating—people all gnash their teeth.

VERSES

> No longer expecting the traveler, affairs gradually turn empty.
> Meeting on the bypath, we've already grown distant.
> Promises made in those years for life's fine plans,
> Till now haven't shown any greatness.
>
> Wickedness and perversity obscure the superior,
> Misfortune extends to the good and excellent.
> Turning against the Tao, going contrary to principle,
> The common people are resentful and expectant.
> When the menial obtain their ambitions,
> The Tao of the perfected is concealed.

COMMENTARIES

YEN ∘ At the top, the position of Heaven is absent; the middle, moreover, is singular and weak—a cluster of yin usurps the ruler's mandate. Thus the disciples of "disobeying Heaven," turning against principles, and acting perversely and insinuatingly appear. Hating the straightforward, ruining the upright, they harm the good. Undertaking bureaucratic office would be especially baleful. Lawsuits will be lacking in principle.

Ho ∘ When people indulge themselves in licentiousness, others must upbraid them. Thus when the Oracle says "gnash their teeth," it speaks of resentment and hatred growing deep. Under this trigraph, clandestine plots will negate each other. Disasters within officialdom will affect everything. It is extremely baleful. It would be appropriate for the ill to pray for blessings. If the army goes forth on campaign it will not be victorious. The traveler is not yet returning. It would be appropriate to cultivate virtue and accord with the old, for then one can get by.

Ch'en ∘ The Tao of man stands solitary; a cluster of perversities simultaneously arises. Clandestine plots ensnare those above.

Liu ∘ Solitary yang, a cluster of yin—the perverse occlude the upright. The petty indulge in licentiousness; no one is able to restrain them.

In this trigraph the upper position lacks Heaven. Moreover, the middle is singular and weak, while there is a cluster of yin below it. It is the image of acting to indulge one's desires, of "disobeying Heaven; turning against the ruler." For the querent, there is nothing that will not be baleful.

Sawyer ∘ Among the most ominous and pessimistic of trigraphs, "Perverse Insinuation" emphasizes the unruly nature of the mature yin massed at the bottom. Under other circumstances, mature yin's presence in the realm of Earth, being highly appropriate, would imply a strong foundation. However, in the absence of direction from Heaven, coupled with weakness in the Tao of Mean, the trigraph is envisioned as depicting a world filled with barbarians and indulgence. Pleasure grown extreme is considered inimical to society because hedonism and indulgence represses every individual's freedom to act in safety and strive for achievement. Clearly this is not a time either for becoming lost in pleasure or undertaking actions in a turbulent, threatening world. Pondering and self-cultivation provide the only paths to self-preservation, the means to avoid being swept away by the tide.

85 Shen Hui 慎悔

Caution over Regret
The image of being overturned and
  misplaced
Yin and yang misplaced in their positions
Chen (Thunder) ∘ True east

Oracle

Above and below contrarily misplaced, all affairs lack appropriateness. East and west perversely different, neither following nor approaching each other.

Verse

Heavenly affairs turn perverse and dangerous,
Human hearts likewise deceive themselves.
Investigate words, guard against the unrighteous,
Whether advancing or withdrawing, be cautious about the
  minuscule.

Commentaries

Yen ∘ Although you must take action, matters will not comply with your mind because "yin and yang are misplaced in their positions." Whatever one seeks will be without advantage. In affairs there will be a lack of cooperation.

Ho ∘ Yin dwells in the middle position. When interior yin dominates affairs, whatever is planned should incline toward yin, for only then will noble persons cooperate in managing affairs. Moreover, the Oracle indicates that seeking office will not yet be conducive, and striving for material wealth will result in numerous losses. It will be difficult to gain an interview with a noble person. Official affairs will not yet be decided. The ill might not yet be cured. The traveler will not yet return. Marriage arrangements will not result in harmony. Sending the army forth on campaign will not result in victory. It would be appropriate to preserve the old; perhaps good fortune will be found more than a thousand *li* away.

CH'EN ∘ Yin, contrary to its appropriate position, dwells above; yang, similarly contrary to its appropriate position, dwells below—inverted and perversely misplaced.

LIU ∘ "Above and below contrarily misplaced"—the pliant inclines to firmness. "East and west perversely different"—one will lose what was expected.

This trigraph lacks the position of Heaven; moreover, yin and yang have been turned upside down below. All affairs whatsoever will be reversed, contrary, and baleful. The querent must be cautious about this.

SAWYER ∘ This trigraph is inauspicious because of the reversal of positions in the only two elements—middle and lower. Thus Earth cannot sustain, Man cannot control. Affairs are beyond one's ability to manage; plans undertaken will not meet with cooperation. In the absence of direction from Heaven above, amid frustration and difficulty, the only alternative is to seek guidance from a mentor or powerful person, and they are difficult to find. However, Ho's commentary ("whatever is planned should incline toward yin") implies that women will exercise great power at this moment, and their intercession should be particularly sought. The Verse emphasizes the need to act cautiously in order to avoid incidents leading to regret.

86 *I CH'U* 宜初

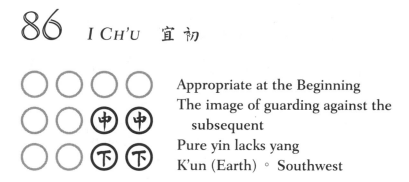

Appropriate at the Beginning
The image of guarding against the
   subsequent
Pure yin lacks yang
K'un (Earth) ∘ Southwest

ORACLE

Ponder deeply and think far off. Dwelling in security, contemplate danger. Although at present there aren't any difficulties, in the end there will inevitably be collapse and failure. Constantly implement the Tao of uprightness; be careful not to act deceptively.

VERSE

> Do not speak about minor affairs as if they were only trifling
>   matters;
> But greatly fear that through compliance affairs will turn
>   difficult.
> If you are not cautious about treading on frost, you will
>   eventually be upended;
> On solid ice you may then slip and be injured or maimed.

COMMENTARIES

YEN ∘ Since pure yin without yang cannot preserve good fortune in the end, one will certainly encounter danger and defeat. Under this trigraph, even though one might filch tranquility at the beginning, in the end calamity will inevitably be experienced.

HO ∘ In every affair whatsoever it would be appropriate to "ponder deeply and think far off." Although the present is peaceful and excellent, in the end it will not be advantageous. Moreover, one must be cautious about the distinction between the public and personal. As for official matters, if one seeks out a powerful person, they can be resolved. The ill will not encounter any baleful days. The traveler will not yet return. Other matters will not be advantageous.

CH'EN ∘ Above and below are both pure pliancy, but they have not yet reached their pinnacle.

LIU ∘ "Ponder deeply and think far off"—pliant and placid, dwell peacefully in one's place. "In the end there will inevitably be collapse and failure"—the top lacks a ruler. "Constantly implement the Tao of uprightness"—then you will not lose your place.

In this trigraph, two yin mutually associate below, while the top position lacks a ruler. Even one who manages to be tranquil at present, in the end will not be able to stand alone. However, if you adhere to uprightness, you can thereby preserve yourself. If you make wanton moves, you will inevitably bring about danger and defeat.

SAWYER ∘ This trigram continues the themes of the previous few, the prognostication echoing the absence of Heaven's position. The basis, being yin, is correct, so activities are sustained somewhat; however, the interior is also yin and therefore inappropriately weak. The trigraph thus exudes pliancy, without any firmness, and suggests that events—except the most conservative and righteous—may simply "get away from you" and prove overwhelming.

87 *Fu Hui* 福會

Confluence of Blessings
The image of respectful caution
Three yang assist yin
Chen (Thunder) ∘ True east

ORACLE

Virtuously pray for the elimination of the unpropitious; be respectfully cautious and appropriately reverent. Today, although you may be hidden away and constrained, blessings and riches will come by themselves.

VERSE

In autumn the osprey's power turns fierce,
Riding the wind, spreading its wings, it reaches the toad's palace.
As for glory and splendor, should you ask when they will come,
Sooner or later your fame will extend throughout the nine directions.

COMMENTARIES

YEN ∘ [Compared with the previous trigraph], this trigraph has changed its lower position from yin to yang. This then is sufficient for prayers to cast out the unpropitious. In the end, blessings and riches will be attained. All affairs will at first be somewhat worrisome, but later very auspicious.

HO ∘ Riches and blessings will certainly come but not quickly. Affairs will comply with one's heart. Moreover, in official matters at first there will be noise, later no competition. Worries about illness will at first be light, later perhaps heavier. It would be appropriate to cultivate yourself and pray. Traveling, sending the army forth on campaign, and commercial activities will at first all be disadvantageous.

CH'EN ∘ Although the Tao of Man is yin, yang is flourishing in the Tao of Earth. It presages the confluence of blessings and riches. Thus it states "confluence of blessings" and "respectful caution." Generally speaking, the pliant person of yin is unable to hold on and preserve them; therefore, there is the admonition of "wary caution."

LIU ∘ "Virtuously pray for the elimination of the unpropitious"— yang lies below yin. "Blessings and riches will come by themselves"—in the end you will obtain what your heart desires.

In this trigraph, although yin and yang have lost their appropriate positions, the three yang are firm and flourishing; yin is unable to overcome them. Thus it creates the image of "virtuously praying for the elimination of the unpropitious." Even though at their inception affairs will be inauspicious, in the end one will obtain great good fortune. The situation is naturally thus; it does not await being sought out. Whatever affairs are divined about will all be auspicious.

SAWYER ∘ The prognostication is essentially set by the presence of highly active yang in Earth's position, sustaining activities and bolstering the absent strength in the trigraph's ruler, the position of Man. The commentators are remarkably unperturbed by the voidness of Heaven and similarly ignore the interactive possibilities of yin falling and yang rising, generally considered auspicious in the *I Ching*. Consequently, although some worries will be unavoidable, it has become a somewhat auspicious time to initiate affairs and to witness projects already under way move toward fruitful completion. (The "toad's palace" in the Verse refers to the moon.)

88 YIN TSEI 陰賊

Secret Brigands
The image of subsequent balefulness
Yin flourishing; loss of yang
K'un (Earth) ∘ Southwest

ORACLE

Secret brigands make contrary plans; it will not be advantageous for later generations. Although things momentarily accord with one's intentions, later on they will actually not be prosperous.

VERSES

A single flower wants to bloom,
But meets with wind and rain.
The clouds disperse, deep blackness remains.
Gloom dissipates, but happiness and prosperity are void.

Danger and yin diminish good fortune,
One's power cannot long endure.
Disaster arises from a single person,
Then is bequeathed to later generations.

COMMENTARIES

YEN ∘ Changing yang, one obtains yin: this is the image of secret brigands. "Secret brigands plan harm"—your posterity will be reduced. Thus the Oracle states that "it will not be advantageous to later generations." This trigraph presages that all affairs, including commercial activities, will at first realize fortunate results, but later there will be harm.

Ho ○ A cluster of yin controls affairs; thus there are many hidden brigands. Their secret plans will harm people; however, these plans have not yet succeeded, so ordinary matters temporarily proceed as desired but later will actually not be auspicious. Moreover, "yang changes to become yin," signifying that the cluster of minor yin is plotting against its superiors.

CH'EN ○ The Tao of Man is already yin; the disciples of yin are numerous and furthermore flourishing. This portends contrary plans, secrecy, and darkness.

LIU ○ "Secret brigands plan contrary acts"—it is the time of the petty and despicable. In the end they too will not prosper and finally have no place to turn. Affairs being planned will at first be auspicious, subsequently baleful.

SAWYER ○ In Yen's commentary, "yang changing to yin" refers to the bottom position in comparison with the previous trigraph, the difference being that the three yang that occupied the lowest position in the former have now become four yin. The absence of formerly sustaining yang, which was still supportive despite its discordant positioning, engenders the voidness that appears in the Verse— "happiness and prosperity are empty"—and the gloomy outlook for forthcoming developments. While this might well be an image for contemporary urban life, where both secret and highly visible brigands plot against public welfare, one should also beware of more personally directed enmity. However, sinking into depression would be an inappropriate response. Rather, be conscious of the illusory nature of present success and thereby avoid being felled by wanton schemes and their progenitors.

89 *Fu Li* 福利

Good Fortune and Profits
The image of primal penetration
Two yang control affairs
Ch'ien (Heaven) ∘ Northwest

ORACLE

Going out the gate, one meets with good fortune and gains association with the virtuous. A bright pearl shines in the night, keeping one from being deluded.

VERSE

When fate arrives, achievement and fame are attained,
Imperial favor suddenly descends on the house.
Peach and plum trees, several years old,
With burgeoning spring blossoms fill the garden.

COMMENTARIES

YEN ∘ Yang's Virtue is just penetrating; moreover, one meets with good fortune. All affairs whatsoever are auspicious; whatever is done will be successful. For the traveler it is auspicious. Commercial activities, and agriculture and sericulture, will realize great profits. Those serving in bureaucratic offices will attain glory and prominence. It is a very auspicious trigraph.

HO ∘ One has already met with good fortune and is also illuminated by a bright pearl. Among the hundred affairs, not one is inauspicious. Whatever is undertaken will be accomplished. Legal suits will not be harmful.

CH'EN ∘ The Tao of Man is firm and correct; the Tao of Earth is also substantial. Blessings and riches will be cultivated together.

LIU ∘ "Going out the gate, one meets with good fortune" and obtains what it bestows. "A bright pearl shines at night"—although it is murky, one will not be blind.

In this trigraph, yang has gained appropriate associates and not lost the proper order. The firmness and brightness of the three yang are sufficient to illuminate the murky darkness. This can be referred to as "gaining association with the virtuous." Whatever affairs are divined about will be auspicious.

SAWYER ∘ This trigraph initiates the series of four marked by three yang dominating the middle position, the position of the trigraph's ruler as well as the realm or Tao of Man. (In this trigraph, these three yang are envisioned as a bright pearl whose radiance illuminates the realm of Earth below, where the single yang dwells. It is the latter that "goes out of the gate" in the Oracle.) The presence of mature yang in the Realm of Man signifies strength and the ability to control affairs in accord with established principles. Moreover, here the position of Earth is strong, even though somewhat inappropriate, because young yang's boundless energy validates the sustaining nature of present circumstances. Everything is auspicious, projects should flourish, and new activities can be undertaken. However, it would be well to remember that Heaven's guidance is still lacking; perhaps caution should not be totally abandoned.

90   *Fu Hsiang*   福 祥

Good Fortune and Happiness
The image of resting in prosperity
Yin and yang each at rest in its position
Ken (Mountain) ∘ Northeast

ORACLE

Heaven diminishing, Earth increasing—the Worthy rest in their occupations. Assuming office and retiring are both gloriously auspicious. There will be unbounded profit.

VERSE

A herd of wild, fabled horses, thunderously racing together,
By day startle the slumbering lakes and mountains.
Unimpeded, a thousand miles swiftly covered,
The verdant waves and fragrant grasses truly connect with
    Heaven.

COMMENTARIES

YEN ∘ "Heaven and Earth diminishing and increasing, yin and yang each rest in its position"—the perfected individual is quiet and self-satisfied. This trigraph presages that all affairs will return to their foundation. It is greatly auspicious and profitable.

HO ∘ Whatever is sought cannot be quick; the myriad affairs will by themselves comply with your heart. Seeking wealth and certain hoped-for matters will both be auspicious. The imprisoned and those involved in lawsuits will be rescued through the strength of others. The ill will obtain a skilled physician. Sending the army forth on campaign will result in victory. It is an omen of great auspiciousness.

C H'E N ∘ The Tao of Man is strong and flourishing; the Tao of Earth is pure and beautiful. Yin and yang mutually gain each other.

L I U ∘ "The Worthy rest in their occupations"—their positions are upright and appropriate. "Assuming office and retiring are both gloriously auspicious"—one is self-satisfied and untroubled.

S A W Y E R ∘ Both the positions of Man and Earth are appropriate: strong yang occupies the middle, controlling affairs, while yin lies below, signifying Earth's compliant yet sustaining aspect. The commentators again ignore Heaven's absence, although the Oracle notes that Heaven is diminishing while Earth is increasing, part of their constant cycle of ebb and flow. Simply phrased, things will go well, particularly if you are properly positioned at this time.

91 *YU HSÜ* 攸敍

Well Arrayed
The image of preserving tranquility
Two yang, purely firm
Ch'ien (Heaven) ∘ Northwest

ORACLE

Phoenix, carrying pearls in their beaks, gather in a corner of the courtyard. Good fortune is brought on my behalf; disaster is eliminated for me.

VERSE

> Auspicious and felicitous things arrive together,
> Bright and splendorous, the five hues anew!
> Heaven's grace descends today,
> Good fortune and riches lie with this person.

COMMENTARIES

YEN ∘ In an age in which the top position is lacking, being able to govern solely with the purely firm will be an omen of auspiciousness and blessings. Disaster will be dissipated, good fortune will arrive. The phoenix is foremost of the five spirits; pearls are treasured items for amusement. Whatever is sought will be very auspicious; moreover, there will not be any punishment or conquest.

HO ∘ Good fortune and riches have just arrived. It is a sign of great auspiciousness and profit, of riches and things being doubly weighed.

CH'EN ∘ The middle and lowest positions are both flourishing yang; there isn't any yin to conquer them. The hundred blessings naturally appear.

LIU ∘ "Phoenix gather in the courtyard"—the virtue of the worthy is glorious. "Good fortune arrives, disaster is eliminated"—innumerable good things accrue. For the querent, there is nothing that will not prove profitable. Only if seeking rain will events prove contrary to one's wishes.

SAWYER ∘ Strong yang in both the Tao of Man and the Tao of Earth—this imbalance should be inappropriate, with perhaps rule by central yang prevailing. However, the commentators envision it as strength sustaining but being controlled, necessary when Heaven's influence is absent. Consequently, virtually everything that might be undertaken in the human sphere will prove advantageous. It is an auspicious moment when even the seeds of indefinite disaster are vitiated. With firmness, what cannot be undertaken!

92 *P'I CH'ING* 否傾

Negativity Overturned
The image of entrusting affairs to the
  Worthy
Three yang lie above yin
Ken (Mountain) ∘ Northeast

ORACLE

The perfected wield authority; the petty prostrate their bodies. An enlightened ruler governs the age, dividing and apportioning the purple and red seals of authority.

VERSE

> Among the withered trees spring approaches,
> Amidst the mountains and rivers luxuriant *ch'i* overflows.
> Before the gate a pair of magpies chirp,
> Rewarded with happiness, profit and fame soon complete.

COMMENTARIES

YEN ∘ Dwelling in the tranquility of a secluded place, one obtains the radiance of the three yang. The *I Ching* states: "It is the time when the petty should not be employed." Seeking official position would be very auspicious. All other affairs will realize their principles.

HO ∘ When there is an enlightened ruler above, the perfected gain employment, and what they wish follows their hearts. The menial prostrate themselves; the principle is appropriate.

CH'EN ∘ Flourishing yang lies above; flourishing yin lies below. Yin and yang mutually respond to each other. The perfected and the petty each obtain their allotment.

Liu ∘ When the perfected gain their positions, the menial are submissive. "Dividing and apportioning the red and purple seals of authority"—each rests in their duties.

Under this trigraph, yin and yang each rest in its position. The firm and bright shine above while the soft and dark follow below. Affairs divined about will realize their principles. For both the perfected and petty it is auspicious.

Sawyer ∘ This trigraph echoes several themes from the *I Ching*, including the name itself, "Negativity Overturned." While Heaven continues to be absent, and therefore does not provide either leadership or beneficial influence, the remaining positions of Man and Earth are appropriate and mature. The four yin in Earth's position could prove unruly, reflecting a disorganized rabble, except for the presence of firm, flourishing yang in the Tao of Man to impose order and direction. In the *I Ching*—and particularly in hexagram 12, entitled P'i, or "Obstruction"—strong yang appearing over strong yin is considered inauspicious due to their directional tendencies: yang upward, yin downward, resulting in separation rather than the interpenetration necessary to create and sustain life and activity. Yet here they are said to be mutually responsive and therefore sustaining. This is all the more remarkable because hexagram 12 consists of the trigrams for Heaven (yang) over Earth (yin), exactly the situation created by the two positions in this trigraph. Furthermore, the trigraph's original Chinese title is "P'i Ch'ing"—where *p'i* refers to the negative, the polarity of darkness, a mass of evils, stagnation, and obstruction—and is the single character naming the *I Ching* hexagram. However, here the commentators all emphasize that an age of order has been achieved; therefore, the petty and despicable must withdraw for the perfected, their merit now recognized, are employed in the tasks of government. Accordingly, it portends an appropriate moment to seek new positions or undertake projects that can achieve their relative principles within a benign environment. The Verse designates the most fortuitous time as early spring, when the principles of growth manifest themselves.

93 WEI HSING 未形

Not Yet Formed
The image of a dragon ascending
A solitary yang ascends through yin
Chen (Thunder) ∘ True east

ORACLE

A hidden dragon is about to ascend, dark clouds are rising up. All under Heaven will receive good fortune. At first there will be obstruction, later happiness.

VERSE

The crescent moon restored to fullness,
On the flowered branches the colors renewed.
Along the road returning to T'ao-yüan,
Someday you will meet a spiritual immortal.

COMMENTARIES

YEN ∘ In the beginning, although things will not be outstanding, subsequently there will be great happiness. A single yang lies in the lowest position. The first yang line in the Ch'ien hexagram of the *I Ching* states: "A hidden dragon does not act." This trigraph embodies a dragon about to ascend; the clouds rise to accompany it. They fly up together into the empty void in order to govern All under Heaven. It is an omen of rulers and ministers gaining each other.

HO ∘ In the beginning, obstruction; later, prosperity. All affairs whatsoever will be auspicious.

CH'EN ∘ Flourishing yin lies above; a single yang lies below. It is the image of harboring an ambition to ascend and advance, of clouds above and dragons below. The Oracle states that things are not yet manifest in the world.

LIU ∘ A hidden dragon gains the clouds in order to go up to Heaven. "At first there will be obstruction, later happiness"—there is no forward movement.

In this trigraph, there is no Heaven above and only a single yang lying below. Four yin connect with it. Thus the trigraph creates the image of a hidden dragon gaining the clouds. In the beginning, even though there will be hardship and difficulty, subsequently one will overcome them and be successful. It is a trigraph of great auspiciousness.

SAWYER ∘ From an ostensibly dark and bleak trigraph, the Oracle wrests an image found in the first hexagram of the *I Ching*—a dragon, presently hidden, about to arise. Frankly, the absence of Heaven above, coupled with unruly strength in the four yin in the Tao of Man, might well have portended chaos and the tyranny of misfortune. However, the Oracle reflects the strength expressed by the hexagram Ch'ien, drawing its power from the potential of a dragon, long concealed, about to bestir itself and rise through the clouds up to Heaven. Thus the commentators interpret the single yang below as a hidden or concealed dragon, and the field of yin above as dark clouds hovering nearby. Among the commentators, Liu envisions the dragon ascending to Heaven through availing itself of the assistance of the clouds, no doubt because the two are always associated together in Chinese mythology, with the dragon frequently riding on them and bringing rain. Accordingly, the situation should be truly auspicious for undertaking major career activities and launching or bringing to fruition projects for which one exercises individual responsibility. Other affairs are auspicious, though to a lesser degree. However, as in all circumstances in which previously concealed power begins to manifest itself, initial difficulties and obstacles remain to be overcome. The title itself, "Not Yet Formed" rather than "The Unformed" or "The Formless," indicates that activities have yet to take shape and are therefore open to structuring and direction.

94 TANG FU 蕩覆

Unstable and Overturned
The image of disaster descending
Pure yin without any response
K'un (Earth) ∘ Southwest

ORACLE

The heavenly dragons are explosive and angry; the God of Thunder beats his drum, raising the clouds and bringing rain that flows down to Earth in torrents.

VERSES

Pondering the wine in a goblet,
Walking about midst the flowers beyond the rail,
In this place for feasting,
Unaware of evening's rays slanting down.

The sun dark and obscured,
Water transversely flowing.
Sowing and reaping are damaged,
Fish and turtles roam about.
When will the sun appear in a clearing sky?
Virtue lies uncultivated.

COMMENTARIES

YEN ∘ Dwelling in an unresponsive place, with pure yin one is unable to mitigate disaster and eliminate worries, but instead brings down calamity and misfortune. Thus the Oracle speaks about thunder and lightning striking across the Heavens. Water, being abundant, causes disaster. This trigraph presages that the hundred affairs will all bring regret. Travel, marriage arrangements, and commercial activities will all be inauspicious.

H o ० The rain flows, flooding and purging. All affairs whatsoever will bring about regret. It is the trigraph of being unsettled.

C h ' e n ० Below there are two yin ascending on high, but they are extremely obscured by the four yin in the middle. It is the image of floating and agitation, of being overturned.

L i u ० "The heavenly dragons are explosive and angry"—yin fulminates above. "Rain flows down to Earth in torrents"—nothing can overcome it. This trigraph presages that whatever is inquired about will be baleful. Only seeking for rain will be auspicious.

S a w y e r ० This trigraph is all yin; moreover, there is no ordering principle or influence from Heaven. Therefore yin is able to rise and exercise its dark effects above, being imagized as the dragon and thunder booming and blustering, sending down torrents of rain. Rain, while necessary and essential to the life of the world, harbors an inherent potential for disaster when it falls excessively or too intensely. Such is the case here, and everything is therefore in danger of being swept away rather than nourished. Affairs undertaken at this inauspicious time can only result in misfortune and regret. There is no basis for withstanding the momentary flux, although persevering and adhering to principle while reducing exposure should get you through. Actions in harmony with yin, such as clinging to the low, have some chance of persisting; however, care must be exercised that immersing oneself in the "valley spirit" doesn't make you vulnerable to accumulating water.

95 *Pi Shih*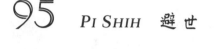

Shunning the World
The image of hiding far away
Insulting yang with yin
Chen (Thunder) ○ True east

ORACLE

The menial realize their ambitions, the perfected lose their Tao. Abandoning my thatched house, I enter the marshy grasses.

VERSES

Arguments come toward the gate,
The body suffers the misfortune of stagnation within.
In the human realm, guard against covert attacks,
The primary fear is damage to wealth.

The imperial carriage has departed from the vermilion steps,
Mountain finches have soared into the blue sky.
Perverse ministers increasingly usurp official position,
Worthy individuals find it advantageous to hide and flee.

COMMENTARIES

YEN ○ Those of enlightened, yang Virtue have withdrawn to dwell in a humble, inferior position. In contrast, the disciples of yin and darkness dwell in the middle position. It is the image of the worthy and the good bent and obstructed. Thus they abandon their houses and settle far off in the grassy marshes. Dwelling in gloom, they nourish their intentions and await their time. This trigraph presages that it would be appropriate to withdraw, inappropriate to advance.

Ho ∘ "To be insulted by yin" means the loss of the proper position. Moreover, the trigraph portends that the ill will be rescued and cured by a yin figure. The traveler is already en route. All affairs will proceed in normal fashion.

Ch'en ∘ A cluster of yin lie above; the menial realize their ambitions. Three yang, in essence complete talent, on the contrary dwell below. It is the image of the perfected in the fields. This trigraph's portents differ from those for the ninety-third—which has four yin in the middle and a single yang below—because the single yang can still advance, while three yang are already extreme and unable to advance. Thus it yields a different image and interpretation.

Liu ∘ "The menial realize their ambitions"—yin mounts above yang. "I enter the marshy grasses"—the position is not appropriate.

In this trigraph, yin and yang have lost their appropriate positions. In ordinary affairs, withdrawing would be auspicious, advancing baleful.

Sawyer ∘ While the main theme of this series of trigraphs continues to be gloom and darkness, the commentators differ on the extent of the impact. All four agree that the presence of strong, mature yin in the middle position indicates stagnation and the excessive influence of the powers of darkness; therefore, obstruction at best, perversity and misfortune at worst. However, the three yang at the bottom, while exhausted and therefore lacking any dynamic power—as well as being inappropriate in this position—do provide a basis in Earth. Accordingly, perhaps one can get by in ordinary affairs. However, generally speaking, it is a time for withdrawal, for avoiding foolish head-butting with the intractable. Conversely, it's an excellent time to cultivate virtue, skills, talents, and ideas.

96 Kuei Tung 鬼動

○○○○
⊕⊕⊕⊕
㊦㊦㊦㊦

Ghosts Stirring
The image of employing magical arts
Two yin positions battle for conquest
K'un (Earth) ∘ Southwest

ORACLE

Two ghosts dwelling together, constantly suffering, hungry, and vacuous. They want to enter my house but fear this spiritual talisman.

VERSE

In a dark place double yin ghosts
Are about to bequeath disease and grief.
Although talismans can ward them off,
Still one becomes frightened and worried.

COMMENTARIES

YEN ∘ It is a time when yin has accumulated and ghosts are about to do harm. Their sacrifices have lacked a master; thus the Oracle states that they are hungry and empty. "The ghosts dare not enter" only because they fear the spiritual talisman. Under this trigraph it would be appropriate to draw talismans and recite incantations in order to expel evil ghosts. By offering sacrifice, one will obtain good fortune.

HO ∘ Good fortune departs, disaster comes. It would be appropriate to cultivate meritorious virtue, to do good works and expel perversity. If the ill draw talismans and recite incantations, their treatments will be effective. Agriculture and sericulture will have sparse harvests and will not in any way accord with one's expectations. It is a trigraph of middling promise. The former ancestors of the land are not at rest. In affairs there will be many ghosts and brigands. As for illness, there will be many cases of ill temperament leading to depression, and fright leading to anxiety. Going out to avoid this would be auspicious.

CH'EN ∘ Yin is extreme in the two positions and cannot do anything. In situations where there are masses both above and below, it is appropriate to employ upright methods to control them. This trigraph differs from the eighty-sixth, which has two yin in the middle and two yin at the bottom, in that youthful yin is purely beautiful, while old yin is at its extremity and useless.

LIU ∘ "Two ghosts dwelling together"—an accumulation of yin results in secret evil. "They fear this spiritual talisman"—exhausted, they have nowhere to go.

In this trigraph, two yin dwell below while the top position is absent; there is no master for the sacrifices in the ancestral temple. For this reason they are what is referred to as ghosts with nothing to rely on. Although the position of Heaven is vacuous, where the high and clear should reside, the ghosts cannot go there. Moreover, there are spiritual talismans that prevent them from gaining entrance through the door into the house. Affairs divined about will encounter great difficulty. It would be appropriate for the ill to draw talismans and recite incantations to control them.

SAWYER ∘ This trigraph brings one into the realm of traditional Chinese beliefs about ancestors, sacrifices, and ghosts. The common people generally felt that if the ghosts of the departed were not properly propitiated through periodic ceremonies of remembrance and symbolic sacrifice in the ancestral temple, they would be cut off and unsustained, becoming troubled wanderers capable of wreaking evil. In this trigraph the sacrifices for these two ghosts have apparently been discontinued; there are no masters of ceremonies, no descendants to carry them forward. Perhaps the families have perished; perhaps they have just grown negligent. Other people are therefore affected and must swiftly act to deflect these pernicious influences. Thus one resorts to talismans and incantations, or to prayer and the practice of appropriate religious beliefs in a baleful time when yin has waxed strong and yang is completely absent. The Verse dramatically creates the image and conveys the tone of the moment.

97 *Wei Sün* 微損

○ ○ ○ 上 Slight Loss
○ ○ ○ ○ The image of seeking security
○ ○ ○ 下 Two yang separated from each other
           Ch'ien (Heaven) ∘ Northwest

Oracle

Climbing a tree to pick mulberry leaves, he falls to the ground and lies prostrate. Among neighbors to the east there is an herbalist. He goes in that direction to ask about a prescription and thus encounters an excellent physician. He manages to avoid injury.

Verse

Wanting to walk along a peaceful road, one yet encounters difficulty.
Seeking fame and profit is not as good as idleness.
Amid melancholy, you will fortunately benefit from the skills of an excellent physician,
And remain in this world for your twilight years.

Commentaries

Yen ∘ Yin has lost its position, and the yang lines thus lack any response. It is the image of ascending high and falling to the ground. Yet above and below are both yang without any yin. Although there is disaster, it will not be severe. The east is the beginning of yang. Thus "he seeks a prescription among neighbors to the east and gains a physician." Seeking wealth, commercial transactions, moving, and searching for what has been lost should all be directed toward the east. Then undertaking affairs will be auspicious. The traveler is not yet returning. Official entanglements will be difficult to resolve.

Ho ∘ He has fallen ill from going somewhere and taking things. If he returns to the former place and acknowledges his guilt, it will be auspicious.

Ch'en ∘ Above and below are solitary and single; moreover, the middle is vacuous. It is the image of someone above being overturned and falling. Yet when he reaches a lower position, he can be secure. This is probably because in the Tao of Earth security is provided by yang *ch'i.*

Liu ∘ "Climbing a tree, lying on the ground"—ascending heights is dangerous. "Asking about a prescription, he obtains medicine"—in the end there is no loss.

Sawyer ∘ This trigraph consists of youthful but solitary yang in the positions of both Heaven and Earth. The middle, or Tao of Man, is empty and void, and there is no yin anywhere about to respond harmoniously to the two yang. This emptiness in the middle portends misfortune, and the commentators foresee the solitary figure—yang that has perhaps foolishly ascended to Heaven—slipping and falling to Earth. However, there is youthful energy in Earth, so the final outcome will be reasonably pain-free. Thus the trigraph suggests an activity that overreaches one's skill but eventually results in no permanent loss. For curing illness the Oracle strikes an especially auspicious image.

98 *Ts'u Hsieh* 粗 諧

Coarse Harmonization
The image of prosperity in the end
Yin and yang gain their positions
Ken (Mountain) ○ Northeast

ORACLE

It is like a newly married wife dwelling in the family but not yet in harmony. Striving and exerting her own strength, their posterity and family name are soon continued.

VERSE

In whose family has the daughter taken up the halberd and
    spear?
One must know to seek profits and riches from them.
Venturing past the beginning, in the end they will live happily,
Unhindered in joyous love and tranquil wandering.

COMMENTARIES

YEN ○ Two yin at the bottom and one yang at the top—their Tao interacts gloriously. Even though the trigraph lacks the center line, yin and yang have gained their respective positions. Interior and exterior mutually respond to each other like the newly married beginning to unite harmoniously. In all matters, once they respond to each other, it will be alright. As for "exerting her own strength," the *I Ching* states: "He is constantly vigilant throughout the day, and in the evening maintains his alertness. Although there might be danger, there will not be calamity." Illnesses and official affairs will prove free from suffering. All affairs whatsoever will be auspicious.

Ho ∘ Marriage arrangements lack a harmonious beginning but will end well. Commercial activities will prove profitable, but it will be difficult to be successful in official affairs. Under this trigraph the hundred affairs will all be auspicious.

CH'EN ∘ Although yin and yang fundamentally respond to each other, the middle is void. Thus emotions are estranged and not yet united at the beginning. After some time they will be at ease.

LIU ∘ "A newly married wife dwelling in the family but not yet in harmony"—emotions are not yet attuned. "Striving and exerting her own strength"—the family's responsibilities are completed.

In this trigraph, yang lies above and yin below; each has obtained its respective place, but they are not intimate, just like a newly married wife who, although the couple's emotions interpenetrate, has not yet achieved intimate harmony. At the same time there is no obstacle in the middle position, so even though they are distant, eventually they will grow close. Thus she "strives and exerts her own strength," and in the end they are able to be harmoniously conjoined. Affairs inquired about will accord with one's wishes, but a resolute effort must be made. Sending the army forth on campaign will finally result in a peaceful resolution.

SAWYER ∘ This trigraph reflects the practice of arranged marriage found throughout Chinese history. The new wife, taken into the family after marriage, encounters onerous tasks and daunting obstructions, including the prejudices and whims of her mother-in-law. In the traditional context the burden of accommodation lies with her alone, and she must exert herself from dawn to dusk, as the *I Ching* citation originally describing the perfected man in his diligent pursuit of the true Tao indicates. However, the text speaks equally to today and to all persons, provided only that the original frame of reference is understood.

The situation depicted by this trigraph is one of parties suddenly brought together, finding themselves confronted by an unfamiliar but romantically interesting partner. Although China has a long tradition of romantic literature and abandonment to love and passion, generally speaking it was felt that the formal bonds of marriage would eventually lead to mutual respect and, for the fortunate, love. With a slight rotation of perspective, the situation equally expresses the unfamiliarity of a growing relationship, and the need for a period of mutual learning and emotional development. Neutralized, it can of course be envisioned as applying to any new social or business situation in which strangers gradually become friends, partners, or co-workers. Effort is required; subsequently, according to this trigraph, cooperation and harmony will follow. Heaven and Earth are appropriately yang and yin; the Tao of Man remains problematic, but at least being vacuous it retains the possibility of becoming filled rather than presenting an insurmountable obstacle.

99 *Pu Keng* 不 耕

Not Plowed
The image of the middle being vacuous
Two yang mutually separated
Ch'ien (Heaven) ∘ Northwest

ORACLE

The earth parched, the stones hard, raising their heads they rail against Heaven. Hoes and plows not being put to use, grains are in shortage.

VERSE

>Though I had a liaison, it was just a dream,
>Affairs not predestined are rarely successful.
>Thus I met with no human response,
>While the moon shone with a hollow brightness for a thousand
>   miles.

COMMENTARIES

YEN ∘ Interior and exterior are both yang; the middle lacks the *ch'i* of Man. Moisture does not penetrate; hoes and plows are all cast aside. Thus "they lift their heads and rail at Heaven," looking for rain.

HO ∘ All affairs require being sought before they will be obtained. If you do not seek them, they will not be completed. Without plowing there will be hunger; without rain there will be drought.

Everything will proceed in normal fashion, agriculture and sericulture even more so. One bends and sinks beneath official entanglements, for although rescue has been sought, still there has been no response. Even though illness might be severe, it can be treated. The traveler remains outside.

CH'EN ∘ In the Tao of Earth, yang is extreme. Above, there is no yin to respond, just like plots that are not plowed. Moreover, it is like drought-stricken fields.

LIU ∘ "The earth parched, the stones hard"—there is no harmony. "Raising their heads they rail at Heaven"—what has Heaven to do with it?

In this trigraph, three yang dwell in the position of Earth without any response. A single yang lies at the top, but the middle position lacks Man. They are separated and cut off, unable to give birth to things. Affairs divined about will all be vacuous; one will labor but without success.

SAWYER ∘ Although not explicitly stated, this trigraph symbolizes drought. There is nothing but the heat of yang, and it is most intense not in the Heavens above, but in the Earth below. Without the cooling effects of yin in the middle or at the top, without the presence of moisture or rain anywhere, affairs can only proceed in a desiccated, sterile fashion. The commentators still emphasize that without effort nothing will result—yet to plow parched and dusty soil seems fruitless, and perhaps even damaging. A more likely inference is that undertaking activities appropriate to the category of yin—to counterbalance the active, aggressive principle prevailing at the moment—should be appropriate. Since the Tao of Man is vacuous and empty, affairs are not promising, but exertions that maintain a low profile—self-cultivation, the enjoyment of music, and the pursuit of ordinary matters—rather than strong, herculean efforts, might prove fulfilling. Railing at Heaven much as Job did avails nothing.

100   *Kuei Tsai*   鬼災

Disaster from Ghosts
The image of vacuity and waste
Yin and yang mutually separated
Ken (Mountain) ∘ Northeast

ORACLE

The family has evil ghosts sitting about in opposite corners watchfully awaiting transgressions and errors. Cutting off water and severing fire, the spirits of Heaven and Earth are doing nothing but investigating human transgressions.

VERSE

> Dust has long buried the empty house,
> Each movement of residence led to stagnation.
> Only when a person's predestined fate is hobbled,
> Do yin and misfortune wind around the body.

COMMENTARIES

YEN ∘ Yin and yang resist their separation; they do not control or govern each other. Moreover, the position of Man is a wilderness; there is no one to be master of the family. This causes fierce ghosts to grow substantial and numerous. Under this trigraph the hundred affairs will all be inauspicious. Divining about houses and inquiring about illness might be somewhat inauspicious.

HO ∘ In everything it would be appropriate to be cautious. Abrupt movements will result in disaster. It would be appropriate to cultivate Heaven's blessings, offer sacrifice to dispel misfortune, and be careful about water and fire. Official affairs will not be auspicious. The traveler will not yet return.

CH'EN ∘ The middle position lacks Man, while a cluster of yin lies below. It is the image of ghostly *ch'i* overflowingly full. The single yang is incapable of controlling them.

LIU ∘ "The family has evil ghosts"—yin *ch'i* has accumulated. Yang, on high, is solitary and cut off, while the trigraph lacks the middle position. "Water and fire are cut off and severed"—the Tao of Man is distressed.

SAWYER ∘ Another of the really baleful trigraphs, this one perceives the malevolent influence of ghosts pervading the family. The Verse suggests ill fate has befallen the individual, though this should not necessarily be projected onto the querent. While yang is appropriate in the position of Heaven, and yin similarly appropriate to the position of Earth, difficulties arise because of the emptiness of the position of Man. Thus there is no response or fruitful interpenetration between the yin and yang, nor any activity in the human wasteland. Yin, being extreme, symbolizes willful activity. Any unbalanced, uncontrolled accumulation of yin bodes ill, for it indicates moisture, darkness, brooding, and discontent. Actions taken at this time must be spiritually generated, aligned with yang, and self-directed. Extroverted efforts will likely become excursions into the void, unsustained and unsuccessful. Particularly beware of projects or activities involving water and fire, whether actually or symbolically.

101 *K'UNG WANG* 空亡

Emptiness and Loss
The image of lacking expectation
Yin and yang opposed and overturned
Chen (Thunder) ○ True east

ORACLE

Going into rivers to cut trees, climbing mountains to catch fish—wasted effort and lost strength. Hands that are empty, mouths that are vacuous.

VERSE

> The treasured moon waxes full then wanes,
> The Yangtze and Yellow Rivers are muddy then clear.
> Even though there is neither calamity nor harm,
> There is also terror like an empty fear.

COMMENTARIES

YEN ○ The position of Man is already deficient; Heaven and Earth are opposed and overturned. Achievements cannot be realized; affairs cannot be completed. Thus the Oracle speaks about "going into rivers to cut trees, climbing mountains to catch fish." In the end, nothing can be obtained. This trigraph presages that marriage arrangements will be very baleful. Rescuing the ill might be somewhat difficult. This is because yin and yang are inverted.

HO ○ The traveler will not come. Illness may grow somewhat more serious. Marriage arrangements will not result in a harmonious union. Official affairs will be difficult to resolve. Neither seeking wealth nor obtaining office can be successful. This trigraph is really not advantageous.

CH'EN ∘ The Tao of Man is already empty, while above and below, yin and yang are mutually opposed. There is not anything that can be taken.

LIU ∘ "Going into a river to cut trees" is acting contrary to the Tao. "Hands that are empty, mouths that are vacuous"—there is nothing by which to live.

In this trigraph, yin and yang are opposed and overturned, while the position of Man is absent. Thus it forms the image of climbing mountains to catch fish and entering rivers to cut trees, thereby speaking about efforts that certainly cannot be fruitful. All affairs whatever are baleful.

SAWYER ∘ Another baleful trigraph, one symbolized by completely ineffective actions within a normal reality. The commentators are clear enough: almost any action undertaken *at this time* is doomed to failure. However, there may be a clue in the Oracle's choice of imagery—for it is not invariably true that one cannot catch fish by climbing mountains. In fact, the best trout are said to be found in the remotest, fastest-running streams. Similarly, cutting trees along a river provides the possibility of easily transporting them downstream merely by according with the Tao of things. So while these images initially suggest an inability to perceive and act within reality, imaginative efforts outside the normal frame of expectation might just work. However, caution is definitely indicated. (The image, translated as "lacking expectation," is also a play on the moon's fullness lacking.)

102 *Pu Hsieh* 不 諧

Uncooperative
The image of incompletion
Two yin not united
K'un (Earth) ∘ Southwest

ORACLE

Two women without husbands; wrangling and fighting, they dwell apart. Going in and out by different paths, they segregate their parts of the house.

VERSE

> Variegated clouds disperse in flight, water flows eastward;
> In the lonely twilight, affairs can be suffused with melancholy.
> Even if the present could be freed of all affairs,
> Annoyances will persist until the midst of autumn.

COMMENTARIES

YEN ∘ The interior and exterior are both yin, but their wills do not cohere with each other, just like two women without husbands. Principles will lead to wrangling and fighting. Remaining in residence will be increasingly baleful. Marriage arrangements will not result in harmonious union. This trigraph presages that the hundred affairs will not be auspicious because the two yin lack a ruler. Thus it says that two women dwell together, but their wills do not accord with each other. This trigraph is enormously baleful.

HO ∘ It is as if they have thoughts of separating. The situation is like one who wants to move out but doesn't fully move away. It will be difficult to resolve official entanglements. Illness will be cured slowly. The traveler is not yet returning. Such affairs as sending the army forth on campaign and seeking wealth will not be advantageous. All affairs whatever will certainly witness divisiveness.

CH'EN ∘ The middle position lacks Man, while the two yin in the upper and lower positions do not respond to each other. It is like two women dwelling together. They have the same form, but their wills differ.

LIU ∘ Above and below are two yin—"there are women without husbands." "They go in and out by separate paths"—the center of the house is empty.

In this trigraph the upper and lower positions are both yin, while the middle lacks a ruler. Thus it creates the image of two women without husbands, whose wills do not cohere, so they separate and dwell apart within the house. For the querent the hundred affairs will all go contrary to what is sought. It is baleful.

SAWYER ∘ This trigraph echoes two hexagrams from the *I Ching* in which the phrase "two women (daughters) dwell together" is found: number 38, K'uei, and number 49, Ke. The first is generally known as "Opposition," although "Separation" would also be appropriate, while the second is entitled "Revolution" (with "Sudden Evolution" or "Sudden Change" being equally possible). Both consist of the same two trigrams—Tui ("Lake" or "Marsh") and Li ("Fire"), but in inverted order. In K'uei the tendencies are toward separation, as fire above rises and water below drifts downward. Moreover, both trigrams signify daughters: Tui is the youngest, Li the middle of three. In K'uei, the elder of the two is above, the younger below, and therefore appropriate. Thus while there might be discord, separation, even opposition, there is still constraint. In Ke the relationship is reversed; the tendencies clash, and the youngest daughter dominates. This leads to real conflict rather than simply deferential separation. (The originators of the *I Ching* might well have seen the two coming together in cooperation but apparently felt the inappropriate dominance of the youngest daughter to be overwhelming.)

Although the basis for the trigraph's interpretation is thus fairly clear, the vision is perhaps less so. Commentators to the *I Ching* generally understand "two women" as "two daughters"; in traditional

China their interests would therefore diverge in accord with their husbands. The trigraph can be interpreted in similar fashion. However, within the formalized matrix of Chinese society, which made women subservient first to their fathers, then their husbands, and eventually even to their sons, the situation could simply be one without a dominant male figure. Any excess of yin without the counterbalance of yang is inherently unstable and disruptive—how much the more so a mother and willful daughter; a young woman and her stepmother; or perhaps a young bride left behind with her mother-in-law?

Transposing to the contemporary sphere, any self-contained situation with two (or more) women, whether voluntarily entered or not, is thus characterized as problematic. The trigraph of course provides an image for a general dynamic, not a mirror for an exact situation. The vectors of the moment are toward separation and disharmony, aligned with incompletion and conflicts of will. In concrete terms, any paired relationship that can be characterized as mutually yin-dominated will be difficult.

103 *Hsi K'an* 習坎

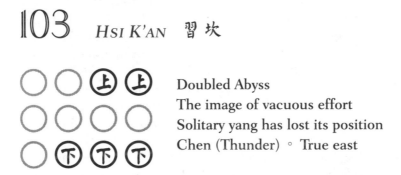

Doubled Abyss
The image of vacuous effort
Solitary yang has lost its position
Chen (Thunder) ∘ True east

ORACLE

Two travelers accompany each other, journeying to avoid danger. However, they encounter difficulty and fall into a well; the strength of their muscles avails nought.

VERSES

> Within the family there is much distress;
> Secret merit will facilitate the future.

Friendships focused on the superficial;
A lotus blossom flowers amid the fire.

Although guarding against subtle affairs.
Unexpectedly one still encounters danger.
Like walking into a well,
Or a movement releasing a trigger,
Misfortune cannot be avoided,
Blessings cannot be prayed for.

COMMENTARIES

YEN ∘ Wanting to avoid secret (yin) harm, they end up losing their positions. It is like "encountering difficulty and falling into a well." Hands and feet are as if nonexistent; muscular strength is ineffective. The hundred affairs are not completed. Business activities will mostly not accord with one's wishes. Undertaking a distant journey would be most baleful.

HO ∘ There is something that one wants to do, but nowhere to apply one's strength. Whatever is sought will not be obtained; whatever is done will be difficult to complete. Inquiring about illness might be somewhat baleful. Obtaining the wrong doctor might, to the contrary, witness increasing severity. The traveler will experience disaster. It is an image of great balefulness.

CH'EN ∘ Two yin are at the top, the middle is already vacuous, and three yang lie at the bottom. It is like being at the bottom of a well; there is nowhere to apply one's efforts.

LIU ∘ "Journeying to avoid danger"—they have doubt in their minds about each other. "They encounter difficulty and fall into a well"— this is equally grievous.

In this trigraph, youthful yin lies at the top, while firm yang dwells at the bottom. Their wills are not in accord. Thus at first they doubt each other; in the end they both fall into danger. The hundred affairs are all baleful.

SAWYER ∘ Youthful yin in the position of Heaven, old yang in the position of Earth—both inappropriate and separated by a gulf between them. In the *I Ching* the hexagram entitled "The Pit" is, surprisingly, highly auspicious, as is the one entitled "The Well." (The title of this trigraph, "Doubled Abyss," appears as the first words in the Judgment for hexagram 29; this is a reference not only to the great danger of the situation—abyss on abyss—but to the fact that the hexagram is composed of two identical trigrams that are also titled K'an, meaning "abyss" or "pit." It is only by passing through danger and challenges that the individuals attain an auspicious result according to the hexagram, a theme echoed in the Verse, which draws on the image of a lotus flower blooming despite passing through a scalding fire that must have desiccated the water essential to its existence.) However, in this trigraph one has the image of people beset by doubt and mistrust. Consciously striving to avoid the dangers they perceive about them, they manage only to end up falling into a well. Thus they are trapped, with no means to escape—clearly a valid characterization for many ancient and contemporary situations. Action in any direction is basically inadvisable; meditation and inward focusing are appropriate until the inescapably baleful is mitigated with the passage of time.

104   *Lai Ke*   來革

Coming Revolution
The image of hidden waste
Yin *ch'i* fully flourishing
K'un (Earth) ◦ Southwest

ORACLE

Icy snow heavily falling soaks my garments. The north wind blows so hard I cannot turn about and go back.

VERSE

Grief is born where joy grows extreme;
All his gold was expended last night.

Having already forgotten his future plans,
The road back is impenetrable.

COMMENTARIES

YEN ∘ "Yin *ch'i* fully flourishing"—interior and exterior lack a ruler. Windblown snow soars and swirls; the road back is vague and obscured. This trigraph presages numerous calamities. For the traveler it is especially baleful. Seeking office and commercial activities will mostly fail to accord with one's plans.

HO ∘ No affair whatsoever complies with one's thoughts. There are arguments and slanders; it is imperative to be wary of them. Moreover, guard against financial losses. Those serving in bureaucratic offices should retire and withdraw in order to avoid disaster. Be increasingly cautious in the hundred affairs.

CH'EN ∘ The upper and lower positions are both yin, the middle position lacks Man. The petty reign; the perfected have nowhere to stand.

LIU ∘ "Icy snow heavily falling"—yin *ch'i* accumulates. "I cannot turn about and go back"—there is no refuge. This trigraph presages that the hundred affairs will all be baleful. Distant travel would be especially inappropriate.

SAWYER ∘ Another in the series of baleful trigraphs resulting from a preponderance of yin, the absence of yang, and emptiness in the human realm. The connection between the trigraph's name and Oracle is unclear except to the extent that yin dominating in this fashion can (fortunately!) only be a temporary phenomenon. (Ch'en adds a cryptic comment that identifies the term "Coming Revolution" as a man's name, but this certainly seems spurious. More believable echoes can be found in the forty-ninth hexagram of the *I Ching*, usually titled "Change" or "Revolution.") The perfected have nowhere to turn; for all others it is like being lost in a blizzard, blown about in a sea of whiteness. Finding an appropriate path when Philistines reign supreme is much alike. Inner tranquility and self-distancing are perhaps the only refuge for the moment.

105 WU KUNG 無功

○ ㊤ ㊤ ㊤
○ ○ ○ ○
○ ○ ○ ㊦

Lacking Achievement
The image of laborious effort
Solitary yang loses support
Ch'ien (Heaven) ∘ Northwest

ORACLE

Journeying east to gather medicinal herbs, he ascends Mount T'ai. He does not obtain fragrant plants but discovers fragrant orchids. The orchid not being useful for relief, he returns empty-handed.

VERSE

> Hearing praise of the white peony,
> How can the human heart not extol it?
> When he left, he had great expectations,
> When he returned, he had already lost his family.

COMMENTARIES

YEN ∘ The interior and exterior, being pure yang, do not respond to each other. Heavy firmness lies at the top; it is the image of a mountain peak. The middle position does not cooperate with them; it is difficult to achieve anything. "Gathering medicinal herbs, he obtains orchids"—an image of vacuous beauty. All affairs whatsoever will have name but not substance. One will hear of joyousness, but it will not be joy; one will hear of sorrow, but it will not be sorrow.

HO ∘ Sending the army forth on campaign would not be auspicious. Whatever is sought will not accord with one's plans. Orchids not being usable, "he returns empty-handed." The hundred affairs will all be incomplete.

Cʜ'ᴇɴ ○ Three yang are at the top, signifying extreme but useless strength. A single yang lies at the bottom, solitary, weak, and unresponsive. Moreover, the middle position is vacuous. What results can there be?

Lɪᴜ ○ "Gathering medicinal herbs, he obtains orchids"—beauty without substance. "He returns empty-handed"—of what advantage is this?

In this trigraph, three yang are at the top, the image of a mountain peak. The interior and exterior are both yang, while the middle is lacking: there is nothing to respond to the yang positions. Thus there is vacuous beauty without substance. Even with persistent effort, it will be difficult to realize achievements. There is nothing that can be done.

Sᴀᴡʏᴇʀ ○ This trigraph has two elements that should symbolize good fortune: mature yang in the position of Heaven to provide energizing influence and direction, and youthful yang in the position of Earth which, although nominally inappropriate, frequently suggests sustaining power. However, the middle position continues to be vacuous; therefore, yang lacks the yin critical to counterbalancing its overwhelmingly active orientation. Thus there is the appearance of activity, the expenditure of effort, but no substantial achievement. The commentators are accordingly glum, but initiatives that are predominantly yin in character may prove more successful, perhaps providing the foundation so severely lacking.

The theme of medicinal plants is continued in the Verse, for tradition holds that the white peony was not known outside the great herbals for many centuries. Journeying to the east to find powerful herbs and the elixir of immortality was undertaken on a grand, imperially sponsored scale in the Han dynasty, while individual quests continued thereafter. Mount T'ai, one of the five sacred mountains of China, should have been an ideal place to find effective plants, yet the Oracle's subject discovered only orchids. (There is a word play on "fragrant plants," meaning "excellent plants" and "fragrant orchids.") Since the orchid's curative properties, as listed in the great herbals, are minimal, the search proved unexpectedly fruitless. The last two lines of the Verse perhaps conclude the Oracle's theme: the searcher went out on an urgent mission with great expectations but returned unsuccessful to find his family already felled by disease. (These lines may also echo the story of the wanderer who ventured into Shangri-la but returned to find generations had passed. Of course, orchids also being prized for their beauty and rareness, he erred again in not gathering them. Perhaps this suggests a need to be alert to simultaneously arising possibilities when an initial objective fails to be achieved.)

106 YÜ TSAI 雨災

Disaster from Rain
The image of difficulty in dwelling
Yin and yang slight each other
Ken (Mountain) ◦ Northeast

ORACLE

Torrential rains fall continuously; flooding waters overflow Heaven. The people live in tree huts, without fire or smoke.

VERSE

Everywhere thorns and brambles grow,
The phoenix has no treetop to alight.
Thought impoverished, mental strength stupefied,
How will we be sated on plump rice and grains?

COMMENTARIES

YEN ◦ Even though the interior and exterior are correct, the middle position is empty. "Yin and yang slight each other," thereby bringing about rain. This trigraph presages numerous calamities. Remaining in residence would be especially baleful. Agriculture and sericulture will have meager harvests.

Ho ∘ It is an omen of forthcoming chaos. None of the hundred affairs will be appropriate. Family members will not be harmonious because yin is small and not advantageous. Wealth sought will be difficult to obtain. The traveler will not yet return. Arguments will not yet be resolved. Sending the army forth on campaign would not be advantageous. It is highly appropriate to preserve the old.

CH'EN ∘ When yang becomes extreme, yin is born; the middle lacks Man. Yin *ch'i* will gradually flourish.

LIU ∘ Rainwater overflows Heaven, growing from below. "Dwelling in tree huts without smoke"—strength lies at the top.

In this trigraph the three yang at the top are strong, while youthful yin is growing below. The middle lacks a ruler; therefore, yin follows what it wants and sends down floods of rain. Yang is perched at the top but has nothing with which to fashion a house; it is the image of "dwelling in tree huts without fire." When the querent obtains it, it is baleful.

SAWYER ∘ The Oracle and the commentators emphasize yin's increasing strength and influence rather than the appropriateness of yang in Heaven and yin in Earth. They envision danger in the dynamics that arise once again because of the absence of the middle position, the Tao of Man. Accumulating yin—the torrential floods—overwhelm human capability, impelling civilization back to the earliest stages when, according to traditional Chinese belief, people lived in grass huts and nests and had not yet discovered fire. Not unlike in the great floods that inundated the American Midwest in the spring and summer of 1993, human response is limited to fleeing or climbing. Consequently, while activities characterized by yang seem to offer the best possibilities at this moment, the immediate future appears gloomy. (However, the commentators' interpretations seem somewhat forced, more appropriate to the presence of four yin in the position of Earth than the two in this trigraph. While the commentators can often be ignored, the Oracle and Verses comprise the core of the book, defining the interpretation.)

107 HAN TSAI 旱災

○ 上 上 上　Disaster from Drought
○ ○ ○ ○　The image of emptiness and exhaustion
○ 下 下 下　Fierce yang, lost yin
　　　　　　　Ch'ien (Heaven) ∘ Northwest

ORACLE

Blazing summer heat causes calamity; Heaven and Earth are scorched. One beseeches the dragons in Heaven above and enters Earth searching for springs. Trembling and fearful, the people are all uneasy.

VERSE

Wanting to advance on the path ahead, withdrawing proves
　difficult;
Often elated, many times displaying a sorrowful countenance.
As nebulous as grabbing the bright moon in an eastern sea,
With spiritual energy fully depleted, simply waiting in idleness.

COMMENTARIES

YEN ∘ Heaven and Earth are both yang; it is the image of fierce extremity. "One beseeches the dragons and seeks for springs"; in the end, there isn't any reaction anywhere. This trigraph is very baleful. Agriculture and sericulture will not yield any profits. Perhaps if you journey far away, a thousand miles, it will be auspicious.

HO ∘ The scorching drought causes disaster that stems from the upper position lacking beneficent moisture, thereby binding the people together in their annoyance. The hundred affairs are not completed. Marriage arrangements, undertaking projects, and seeking wealth will not be advantageous.

CH'EN ○ Above and below are both fierce yang, while there isn't any yin to respond to them. Moreover, the middle position is empty. This is the image of disaster.

LIU ○ Heaven and Earth are both yang; drought is fire scorching things. "Fearful and uneasy," the three yang at the bottom have lost their position.

In this trigraph, above and below are both yang, while the position of Man is lacking. Yang by itself does not give birth; therefore it creates the disaster of drought. Divining about the hundred affairs, none will be complete.

SAWYER ○ Yang not only excessive but also strong creates the impression of fierce heat charring Heaven and Earth. The position of Man, compressed between the two, lies empty; there is no obstruction to the confluence of desiccating effects. Thus, in contrast to the immediately preceding trigraph where the land was inundated with water, dryness reigns.

However, one might speculate that cleaving to yin locations—valleys, pits, caves—and minimizing the heat of human friction might prove palliative. Since both yang positions are mature, they are approaching or have attained their extremity and should quickly revert to yin. It's just a matter of time before activities can once more be undertaken in a conducive, moisture-laden atmosphere.

108   *YÜAN HSI*   遠襲

Distant Attack
The image of escaping and scattering
Yin and yang separated in their positions
Chen (Mountain) ∘ Northeast

ORACLE

Pursuing fleeing bandits, we catch them at Le-lang. We gather up our treasures and jade, lead back our cattle and sheep.

VERSES

A cow with two tails, something difficult to attain;
As for fame and profit, you must guard against them both
    proving incomplete.
Only after you bump into a wooden man will you have luck;
Perhaps you'll encounter water and earth that may also prove
    conducive.

Even though the mind feels no surfeit,
Who has known the full realization of two desires?
Although killing people requires hatred,
One is also reduced significantly.

COMMENTARIES

YEN ∘ Heaven and Earth mutually respond to each other; yin and yang have gained their positions. Thus one goes far beyond the seas, clearly flourishing an aggressive punitive expedition. But the middle position lacks a ruler; jewels and pearls, cattle and sheep do not escape being taken by brigands. This trigraph is slightly auspicious. Any punitive attacks undertaken will be victorious. Le-lang is on the Eastern Sea.

Ho ∘ Perhaps someone, through taking other people's things, has come to be in a disadvantageous situation. By quickly restoring them and apologizing, it will not be baleful. Perhaps someone has taken things from the house that should not have been taken; it is not auspicious. The traveler will suffer financial loss before returning. In all matters whatsoever, losing wealth will eventually be auspicious.

CH'EN ∘ Below, there is a cluster of yin, the image of robbers and brigands. The three yang are just flourishing, able to command the general to pursue and chastise, to destroy secret (yin) cliques.

LIU ∘ "Pursuing fleeing bandits, we catch them"—we go forth to complete the attack. "We reach Le-lang"—exerting ourselves, we go out far. "Leading back my cattle and sheep"—we regain our former possessions.

In this trigraph, yin and yang gain their appropriate positions and mutually respond to each other, but as it still lacks the middle position, the trigraph creates the image of things that have been lost to bandits. Only by exerting oneself to venture out far and attack them will they be caught. For the querent, success will follow the exertion of effort. Employing the military will at first prove difficult but will later achieve victory.

SAWYER ∘ The positions of Heaven and Earth are both strong and appropriate; they should interact and produce numerous blessings and great good fortune. However, the void in the Tao of Man precludes this realization, and the Oracle envisions not bliss and prosperity, but loss and annoyance. The warning to be heeded is that others presume to appropriate what is yours; remedial action, if not preventive measures, may be required. Expect difficulties; exert yourself fully to overcome them; success should follow. As the Verse advises, do not seek to complete more than one project or realize more than single desires, lest none at all be attained.

109 *Tao Ch'ieh* 盗竊

☒☒☒☒ Theft by Robbers
The image of being dragged in and
　　entangled
Yin suppressing, yang solitary
Chen (Thunder) ○ True east

ORACLE

Wanting them for themselves, they steal people's precious jewels. Officials investigate their villainy; ghosts bind their wrists.

VERSE

> It's unnecessary to sorely labor your body,
> You must guard against a moment of theft by robbers.
> If you pursue ends without regret,
> On the contrary, you will endanger yourself.

COMMENTARIES

YEN ○ Yin holds Heaven's position; yang, on the contrary, lies below. It is similar to the petty availing themselves of the talents of the perfected. Officials and ghosts interact to impose punishment.

HO ○ Illness, which arose from taking other people's things, had led to the present disaster. Those suffering from this sort of illness should urgently seek to resolve the cause. Moreover, be wary of arguments. This trigraph is extremely baleful. To the east it might be appropriate to seek out Buddhist priests and nuns, Taoist adepts, or female shamans to treat any illness, for then they will be cured. The traveler will not return until after the first of the year. If you seek for things that have been lost, they will be recovered.

CH'EN ∘ Four are at the top; robbers and brigands gain their desires. One lies below; it is the jewel that they want to steal. But the single yang lies in Earth, so Earth's power is still secure. The robbers can be pursued and the people put at ease.

LIU ∘ "They steal people's precious jewels"—certainly this is shameful. "Officials investigate, ghosts bind them"—they cannot keep any of them.

In this trigraph, extreme yin dwells in Heaven's position; it is a robber who dwells in an inappropriate place. Although yang is solitary and weak, it is not what can be long kept. Thus it results in officials and ghosts interacting and imposing inescapable punishments. Whatever affairs are divined about will be baleful. Only pursuing robbers will certainly result in their capture.

SAWYER ∘ Since the underlying image for the symbolism in this first of four trigraphs with four yin at the top is clear, it hardly need be recapitulated. However, note that the theme of theft found in the last trigraph is continued here and is inextricably bound up with temptation. The forces of the moment incline one to inappropriate actions. These need not be outright crimes but, rather, a succumbing to enticements that would best be forgone. Recriminations are certain to follow, whether from people or ghosts. Avoid offending and stepping on toes, justified or not! The Verse suggests that leading a purely circumspect life, without daring and challenge, might also be problematic. . . .

110 SHIH LÜ 失律

上 上 上 上
○ ○ ○ ○
○ ○ 下 下

Lost Standards
The image of reverting to calamity
Yin steals yang's position
K'un (Earth) ∘ Southwest

ORACLE

Offending the Tao and contrary to principle, yin and yang mutually injure each other. August Heaven doesn't provide assistance but, on the contrary, suffers calamity from it.

VERSE

Numerous nests overturned, misfortune growing deep.
Among troublesome affairs, guard against lawsuits and
  imprisonment.
If you want to journey out more than a thousand miles,
You'll have to worry about calamity striking your family.

COMMENTARIES

YEN ∘ "Yin steals yang's position"; thus the Oracle says "offending and contrary." Whenever affairs do not accord with principle, it is baleful; when they accord with principle, it is auspicious.

HO ∘ Illnesses inquired about might require concentrated attention. Official entanglements will not be dissipated. There are slanderers and backbiters. Conflict and lawsuits will bring harm. An army on campaign will lose its discipline. The traveler will not yet return. Commercial activities will not be profitable. The hundred affairs will muddle along.

CH'EN ∘ Two yin lie below; the Tao of Earth is fundamentally correct. However, four yin are at the top, so yin goes contrary to Heaven, which will certainly lead to defeat. This signifies the loss of the standards of yin and yang.

LIU ∘ "Offending the Tao and contrary to principle"—the position of Heaven is not appropriate. "Yin and yang mutually injure each other"—they will not go on for long.

This trigraph takes the extreme yin dwelling in the upper position as "offending the Tao." The middle position lacks Man, while the lower position does not respond. Thus, although the four yin usurp and hold the top for a moment, in the end, there will be disaster and misfortune. Affairs divined about will all be baleful.

SAWYER ∘ Another depressing trigraph in the series lacking the middle position or Tao of Man. Here the basis is secure—youthful yin in the appropriate position of Earth. Actions should be possible, but the Tao of Man is void and therefore unresponsive. Heaven, instead of sustaining, acts repressively, being itself beset by a cluster of yin. (Surprisingly, the Oracle doesn't envision a deluge.) No help from above means the inquirer must be self-reliant and, moreover, responsible. Then it might be possible to muddle through life's ordinary affairs, especially if care is taken not to offend anyone. It's hardly the time to attempt anything spectacular!

‖‖‖ CHIEN TANG   奸黨

Cliques of Villains
The image of repressing the Worthy
Yin advances, yang withdraws
Chen (Thunder) ∘ True east

ORACLE

Advancing the crooked, dismissing the straight, the performance of duties is lost. Worthies submerge themselves in hiding; the perfected sigh heavily.

VERSE

> According with proper custom, nothing is captured;
> Through crafty encounters, in the end many are caught.
> Golden pitch bowls lie buried in grassy weeds,
> While earthen cauldrons are sounded clackingly.

COMMENTARIES

YEN ∘ Yin advances into yang's position; thus the Oracle speaks about "losing duties." Worthies and the perfected are not entrusted with employment; thus it says they "submerge themselves in hiding and sigh heavily." The *Analects* states: "If you raise up the straight and put them over the crooked, then the people will be submissive. If you raise up the crooked and put them over the straight, then the people will not be submissive."

HO ∘ The hundred affairs do not proceed smoothly. It would be appropriate to withdraw oneself and preserve the upright. When the words of authorities are not obeyed, then following the times becomes auspicious. For the perfected it is baleful; for the petty it is auspicious.

CH'EN ∘ Yin and yang are both at the extreme of flourishing and contrarily opposed. It is the image of the perfected in the wilds and the petty holding positions.

LIU ∘ "Advancing the crooked, dismissing the straight"—principles are inverted. When the petty gain their time, the perfected avoid it.

In this trigraph a cluster of yin has usurped and holds yang's position in Heaven while yang occupies the bottom. Being far apart, they do not come close to each other, thus creating the image of "advancing the crooked and dismissing the straight, of Worthies submerged in hiding."

SAWYER ∘ Another in the series of trigraphs missing the middle position of Man and therefore highly problematic. However, the Oracle envisions a gloomy scenario deriving from the totally inappropriate presence of four yin at the top in Heaven's position. They are seen as strong, extreme usurpers that, in addition, repress the vital principle of yang sequestered below. Within a Confucian frame of reference, the crooked (or unqualified) have ascended over the straight (or competent) and are forming cliques contrary to the proper, public-minded behavior of the perfected. Sadly, this is a situation frequently encountered in life, and the querent perhaps feels stymied by people holding powerful positions. The best course is to persevere in self-cultivation while maintaining a low profile or searching for a more conducive environment in which to realize one's talents. Antagonizing others will not prove fruitful; it is better to soar dramatically at the proper moment than dissipate oneself prematurely and foster a negative image. Heed should be paid to the Verse which, apart from characterizing the decline of culture with its image of the golden pitch pipes abandoned in favor of common pottery, obviously suggests that adhering to rules and laws will prove frustrating. Rather than embracing the deviant behavior it implies, one should perhaps contemplate "unorthodox" ways, particularly as the Chinese military tradition emphasized the unorthodox in all difficult situations. This would avoid any descent into unlawful or immoral behavior, yet would probably yield spectacular results.

112 *K'ou She* 口舌

Disputes
The image of lacking auspiciousness
Two yin conquer each other
K'un (Earth) ○ Southwest

ORACLE

A family in the east is holding a ceremony to welcome a new bride; their neighbors to the west are also gathering guests. Trussed-up pigs squealing, beaten dogs yapping. Be warily cautious of misfortune and trouble; avoid completing external perversity.

VERSE

Arguments gravitate toward the gate,
To the end of one's life be wary of disaster.
Within the family, guard against secret arrows,
Being frightened, and suffering financial loss.

COMMENTARIES

YEN ○ Incidents arise in gatherings and assemblies. When in such gatherings do not be lax, then it will be auspicious. Perhaps there will be a ceremony to welcome a new bride. This will be auspicious because people harmoniously unite in it. Moreover, the Oracle states that the interior and exterior are mutual enemies. Even though the family in the east is holding a wedding ceremony, their neighbors in the west still want to gather guests for a feast. The two families roast pigs and beat dogs, thereby competing in boasting and forming factions that make comparisons. If they are small, it will be auspicious; if numerous, then insufficient.

Ho ∘ Under this trigraph, fighting and conflicts may incur legal action, affect marriage arrangements, and require payment of compensation before becoming auspicious. Riding horses may result in disaster. Legal entanglements will be marked by confusion. The traveler will not yet return. Within the family be cautious, taking precautions against fire from candles. It would be appropriate for the ill to cultivate good fortune through prayer. This trigraph is just middling.

Ch'en ∘ Clusters of yin, arrayed above and below, lack any response. Petty men gain their desires and do not unite. One can only see arguments arising like swarms of bees; chaos and dispersal are about to result.

Liu ∘ "Holding a ceremony to welcome a new bride and gathering guests"—the interior and exterior are enemies. Competing unyieldingly, there will certainly be evil.

In this trigraph, above and below are both extreme yin; their bodies are mutual enemies. One holds a wedding ceremony; the other gathers guests. They compete in joyous feasting, indulging in licentiousness without restraint. It is the nature of petty men that when their pleasure grows extreme, they will invariably become licentious and misfortune will result. Thus if one can be warily cautious, disaster can be avoided. Otherwise, there will certainly be incidents of fighting and conflict, discord and contrariness. The querent should be cautious about this.

Sawyer ∘ This trigraph is badly mangled in the various texts, and the meaning seems forced. The fundamental theme appears to be the dominance of petty men (symbolized by clusters of yin) in both Heaven and Earth. One might expect it to portend extreme disaster, especially since the Tao of Man is void and empty. Yin at its extreme in Heaven frequently represents torrents of rain, just as extreme yin does in the position of Earth. However, at least the latter is appropriate and therefore, in theory, strongly sustaining. Competition in licentiousness—or perhaps conspicuous consumption—certainly characterizes the present era. When the inquirer obtains this trigraph, it should perhaps be seen as warning against deepening involvement in such transitory and meaningless activities. While social gatherings are not inherently disjunctive, their propensity toward engendering chaos may prove overwhelming in a negative age and improper moment. (The title of the trigraph, translated as "Disputes," is literally "mouths and tongues." The two characters subsequently reappear as the opening words in the Verse.)

113   *WEI MING*   未 明

Not Yet Bright
The image of lacking brilliance
Solitary yang lacks assistance
Ch'ien (Heaven) ◦ Northwest

ORACLE

Primordial *ch'i* just born, the myriad things as yet unformed. Scintillating brightness not yet fused, going out and entering, murky and miasmic. The beginning is just being established, the hundred affairs are incomplete.

VERSES

> Relying on one's heart and depending on hope isn't a good
>   policy,
> As if halfway true and halfway not.
> The expected remains incomplete, the unexpected is attained;
> Determined to act, yet contrarily climbing trees to catch fish.
>
> A fire from one piece of wood, no man would raise.
> The courage of a single general, suddenly difficult to contain.
> Establishing a beginning, forging achievement,
> Things only the masses can complete.

COMMENTARIES

YEN ◦ "One" is the beginning of the myriad things. Yang *ch'i* has just been born; it is not yet able to be scintillating and bright. It is the image of interaction commencing from the single in search of the multitude. All affairs whatever will be slow and retarded, as yet unable to comply with one's thoughts. It would be appropriate to wait for the right time to move.

Ho ∘ Doing things will not result in their completion. Illnesses will gradually improve. The myriad things are all ordinary. What is sought cannot be completed. Neither official advancement nor seeking wealth will be realized. The army cannot be sent forth on campaign nor can criminals be apprehended. The traveler has been detained and will not return until the new year.

CH'EN ∘ Primordial *ch'i* has just divided; subtle yang is the first to be born. With just one, there is clarity; yin and turbidity do not yet balance it.

LIU ∘ "Primordial *ch'i* just born"—it does not yet have any companions. "Going out and entering, murky and miasmic"—in the darkness it is not possible to see. This trigraph presages that whatever is sought will not be obtained. The hundred affairs are all middling.

SAWYER ∘ This is the first in the final series of trigraphs, all of which are distinguished by the absence of both yin and yang in two of the three positions. Contrary to expectation, this does not simplify the explanations but does induce a certain precipitousness and ethereality.

This trigraph reflects, but does not completely accord with, the cosmogenic theory found in the Taoist classics and the *I Ching*. Normative theory holds that the void stirred and gave birth to the one, or unity. Then the one divided, giving birth to two, the interdependent polarities of yin and yang. However, here a solitary yang appears first, subsequently going on to engender the myriad things in conjunction with its counterpart yin that is yet to appear. Yang has thus become the generative force in the universe, empowering the coalescence of the myriad things.

In view of this vision, the trigraph can be understood as depicting the instant of inception, the time before which action is yet realizable. Thus it marks the most fruitful of moments in ultimate terms but also an amorphous stage that requires incubation. Actions cannot be precipitously pushed forward; events cannot be rushed beyond the ability of the environment to sustain them. It is this "sustenance" that is lacking; you should constrain and direct your enthusiasm appropriately. Although the Verses paint a somewhat pessimistic vision, ultimately, this trigraph is incipiently auspicious!

114 *CH'IEN LIU* 遷 流

Shifting and Flowing
The image of not yet being settled
Subtle yin contrary to its position
K'un (Earth) ∘ Southwest

ORACLE

The image is established from Heaven. *Ch'i* still floats and wanders, as yet unable to be decisively settled. It shifts and flows to the east and to the west, mostly without pursuing any objective, overflowing and extensive.

VERSES

Seeking official emoluments will truly not be advantageous;
Searching for wealth in business will also meet obstacles.
Although you attain prosperity and happiness,
When you see a tiger, you must be wary.

Solitary yin unassisted,
Earth expansive, fields vacuous,
Human affairs unsettled,
Impossible to dwell in peace.

COMMENTARIES

YEN ∘ From "one" to "two," the numbers engendered are just being nourished. Accordingly, the foundation's traces are beginning to arise; the Tao of Man is not yet established. Thus it causes "the *ch'i* to shift and flow." It is the image of "the not yet settled, of the extensive and overflowing, mostly without pursuing any objective."

Ho ∘ Human affairs are not yet settled. It is the omen of the not yet completed.

CH'EN ∘ "Two" is the beginning of yin *ch'i*; they lie in Heaven like floating, unsettled clouds.

LIU ∘ "The image is established from Heaven"—its Tao is subtle. "It shifts and flows to the east and to the west"—it has not yet formed the foundation. In this trigraph, human affairs are not yet settled; affairs attempted will not be completed.

SAWYER ∘ This trigraph is the corollary to the immediately preceding one defined by a solitary yang in Heaven. The classic's cosmogenic sequence thus envisions Heaven first spawning a single yang and then a single yin. Yin, however, represents an advance into the generative realm where the primordial *ch'i* spreads and unfolds, extending throughout the universe. Accordingly, it is capable of providing a foundation for things, evolving out of a beneficent Heaven even though yin is inappropriate in this position. Lacking any response from the positions of Man and Earth, Heavenly yin floats and diffuses free of obstacles.

The unsettled should perhaps be viewed as a field of possibility. Clearly there is nothing definite, no support from any position. At the same time, there is the possibility of defining and establishing, and therefore of realizing the moment of inception. The Verses depict as yet unfertile fields—and issue a warning for the time when success has been attained—but the image is not negative nor the tone one of gloom despite being marked solely by yin.

115 Wei Ning 未寧

Not Yet Peaceful
The image of deficient security
Three yang solely established
Ch'ien (Heaven) ◦ Northwest

Oracle

Only after Heaven and Earth have established their form is the Realm of Man transformed to life. Following *chi*'s turbulent movements, one is unable to realize peace oneself.

Verses

Startled into vacuousness, suffering loss, two severe disasters;
Be minutely cautious when acting and retiring, ponder the
    coming darkness.
If you manage to escape the tiger's tail and snake's head,
To attain tranquility you must sacrifice wealth.

The two poles establish the image,
The three yang are not vacuous.
When auspicious and baleful are not yet discernable,
What can one follow?

Commentaries

YEN ◦ Ruler and subjects confused and intermixed, as yet without any fixed abode. Tolerating those who should be dismissed and retained, they lack the means to impose order on each other. Even though this trigraph does not presage great calamity, it will be difficult to secure cooperation in any matter.

Ho ◦ Every affair will certainly encounter difficulty and hardship, and not yet be able to comply with your mind. Doubt will mark official entanglements; the ill will slowly recover.

Ch'en ◦ Three yang could fundamentally create the beginning for the Tao of Man, but they dwell in Heaven's position. Accordingly they have the image but not the position.

Liu ◦ "After Heaven and Earth have established their form"—this starts the birthing of things. "Following *ch'i*'s turbulent movements"—they still lack a settled abode. This trigraph has a definite tendency, but it still cannot strongly flourish.

Sawyer ◦ This is a rather unremarkable trigraph—even though Heaven is strong and appropriate—because Earth lacks the substantiality to respond. Heaven's positive influence thus radiates into the void, unable to shape the denizens of the realm into an integrated society. The human quest to establish hierarchies and impose order underlies the freedom of existence but also entails the obfuscation of spirit and individuality. At this stage in the cosmogenesis, tendencies to chaos still prevail. This is reflected by the indefinite floating that accompanies *ch'i*'s movements and is accordingly mirrored in the querent's situation at the moment. No doubt a certain indecisiveness prevails, whether in oneself or one's circumstances. However, the principle of mature yang suggests one can perhaps dictate an organizing principle, undertake action that will create a directional vector. Primordial chaos soon yields to impositions; why should they not be self generated?

116   *Ssu Hsiang*   死象

The Image of Death
The image of baleful omens
Double yin contrary to its position
K'un (Earth) ◦ Southwest

ORACLE

When human life approaches death, ghostly *ch'i* arises. The four seasons supersede each other; cold and heat succeed each other. Sunken and concealed, invisible, the body's yin congealing.

VERSES

> A swallow moves the curtains,
> Startled, my dream turns irrecoverable.
> In a darkened window I manage no affairs,
> But still incur right and wrong.
>
> Illness entering vital organs, *ch'i* will soon be depleted;
> *Po* dissipates, *hun* departs, the pulses are all exhausted.
> Schemes and plans of a hundred years will soon be abandoned;
> Even the great physician Pien Ch'üeh could not sustain life.

COMMENTARIES

YEN ◦ Above, yin doubled; below, no yang positions. This creates the image of death, for the dead are separated and severed from creative transformation. Yin and yang being perversely inimical, the four *ch'i* alter and change. The ill may feel increasingly worried; attention should be paid so that they don't succumb to dark weakness. Yin is the image of ghosts.

Ho ∘ In later years, as one grows old, numerous ghosts repeatedly appear. The four *ch'i* are not harmonious. It is a baleful omen.

CH'EN ∘ "Four" embodies yin at its extremity; moreover, it dwells in the position of Heaven. This then is the *ch'i* of death and severance among the four seasons.

LIU ∘ Double yin dark and obscure, exhausted above. Yang *ch'i* concealed and blocked, the Tao of Man is at an end. "Sunken and concealed, invisible," how baleful! This trigraph presages that one inquiring about illness should certainly focus on regaining health. All affairs whatsoever are baleful.

SAWYER ∘ Mature (or double) yin occupies the position of Heaven, creating a dark and gloomy image. The vital principle of life, yang *ch'i*, is depleted; it is the season when yin peaks—the heart of winter. Death wields its scepter and all succumb. The realms of Man and Earth are void and empty; no sustenance or energy is to be found. As the Verse foretells, even the two components of the soul, the *po* and *hun*, depart.

Metaphysically speaking, this is not an auspicious time for undertaking new projects or imaginative actions. Efforts should accord with the principle of "closure": self-constraint, hiding away, and avoiding entanglements (which the Verses indicate seem to arise in any event). Imagine the dark time of frontier existence; harmonize with the cold and starkness, and thereby be revitalized, for a spring of unconstrained growth is certain to follow past this ominous but integral time of enforced dormancy.

117 *FA YANG* 發 陽

Yang Developing
The image of life's inception
Solitary yang lacks a ruler
Ch'ien (Heaven) ∘ Northwest

ORACLE

Heaven's light overspreads below; the sun and moon manifest their brightness. The myriad things become active; those with feet all travel about.

VERSE

> Going south on a campaign of rectification,
> Heaven clears, the sun and moon are bright.
> Obstructions eliminated, disaster dissipated,
> With fame enhanced and profits, one returns to life.

COMMENTARIES

YEN ∘ A single yang, alone and bright—thus the Oracle states "Heaven's light." The birth of the myriad things depends on the sun (yang) and moon (yin). Under this trigraph, although affairs will all be somewhat difficult, in the end they will be hopeful. One should calculate measures carefully and not trust to others.

HO ∘ A single yang manifestly gives birth; the myriad things attain harmony among themselves and gain the Earth. However, since above and below are not substantial, things still cannot yet lightly arise. In all affairs whatsoever, one must be fully committed. Being entrusted with managing things would be auspicious. Seeking wealth will result in great profits. Trying to implement plans will definitely result in their compliance. Official entanglements will be free from suffering. The ill will probably recover largely by themselves. The traveler will return after a long time. Sending the army forth on campaign will produce great victories.

CH'EN ∘ "One" is Heavenly yang, but it dwells in the position of Man, just like humanity receiving Heaven's bright mandate to life.

LIU ∘ "Heaven's light overspreads below"—the Tao of Man is up-lifted. "Those with feet all travel about"—there is no dark or dim place.

In this trigraph a single yang dwells in the middle; it is the image of the glorious brightness of the sun and moon, the material basis that underlies humans and things. Expectations for affairs will be slowly realized.

SAWYER ∘ Although there is only a single yang dwelling in the position of Earth, it is envisioned as empowering the human realm, making activity and life itself possible. While this might have been expected were it in the position of Heaven, the Oracle focuses on the pervasiveness of its influence as existent rather than as emanating. Therefore, prospects for movement, projects, and activity are all excellent provided only that you remain self-reliant rather than looking to others. Innovation, conception, and renewal are all appropriate.

118   *Sui Teng*   歲登

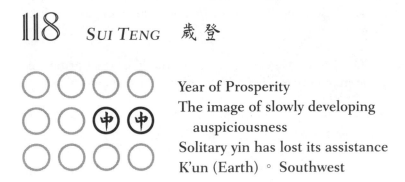

Year of Prosperity
The image of slowly developing
   auspiciousness
Solitary yin has lost its assistance
K'un (Earth) ∘ Southwest

ORACLE

Heaven and Earth opening and penetrating, the myriad things all exalted. Affairs have just been settled; great abundance at the end of the year!

VERSES

From the time you cling steadfastly to decisions,
Your achievements will surpass the common herd.
Moreover, you will experience extraordinary elation,
And accompany the dragons unto the Nine Heavens.

Although the merit of Heaven and Earth is great,
Still sustenance from rain and dew preceded them.
Awaiting the proper time will realize harvests,
Happiness and joy through years of abundance.

COMMENTARIES

YEN ∘ This trigraph is similar to the preceding one. The results of Heaven and Earth sowing and planting will be greatly realized in overflowing abundance. This trigraph is somewhat auspicious. Affairs being planned will achieve prosperity; clearly there will be neither doubts nor obstructions.

Ho ∘ All affairs will slowly become auspicious. It is not appropriate to quickly realize objectives, but rather to personally uphold correctness. The hundred affairs will all be similar. What has been lost can be regained.

Ch'en ∘ "Two" is yin, Earth, but it dwells in the position of Man, as if humanity had gained life through receiving the softness and pliancy of Earth. Moreover, it enjoys the beauty of Earth's advantages. "Two" is capable of uniting with yang.

Liu ∘ The Tao of Man is about to prosper. This trigraph imagizes things as progressing from "one" to "two," with the number of things being born incrementally increasing. Thus affairs undertaken will gradually become possible.

Sawyer ∘ This trigraph is likened to the preceding one which had a single, youthful yang in the position of Man, and the comments to it should be consulted. However, here the world is empowered by yin, which can sustain and support but lacks the energetic strength of yang. Rain and water, although unmentioned, fall within its domain and are crucial to farming and wresting abundant harvests. Thus they take precedence even over the efforts and merit of Heaven and Earth themselves, according to the last Verse.

Attention should be paid to the emphasis on gradual unfolding and the slow realization of projects and expectations. Youthful yin bridges the gap between Heaven and Earth, and mirrors their influence in the realm of Man, but in an evolutionary rather than revolutionary sense because of their absence. Just as a half-year's effort is required for a single crop, so must projects be incrementally matured and objectives creepingly attained.

119   Jen Shih   人事

Human Affairs
The image of great happiness
Flourishing yang occupies the middle
Ch'ien (Heaven) ◦ Northwest

Oracle

Human affairs have just arisen—auspiciousness and nothing that is not advantageous! Those remaining in residence obtain blessings; the traveler will certainly arrive.

Verse

> Remaining at home, numerous are the joyous occasions.
> Rich and honored, one attains tranquil ease.
> The myriad affairs commence in accord with your wishes,
> As they all appear, their advantages are perceived.

Commentaries

Yen ◦ Three yang dwell in the middle; the Tao of Man is just rising. Although it lacks responsive support, in the end great auspiciousness will be realized.

Ho ◦ All affairs and everything sought will penetrate and be successful. The traveler will certainly return at the appointed time. Seeking office, gaining an audience with a noble person, and making plans will all proceed compliantly. Those troubled by illness must await the next change in the two-week calendrical *ch'i* periods before they will recede.

CH'EN ∘ "Three" is yang flourishing; it dwells in the middle position, so the Tao of Man flourishes. Humanity was born in the first lunar month; this is also the time when mature yang intersects with prosperity.

LIU ∘ "Human affairs have just arisen"—yang is correct in the middle. "Auspiciousness, nothing that is not advantageous"—there will be a great conclusion.

In this trigraph, three yang issue forth from Earth and establish the first lunar month. It is the time when human affairs just arise. When Heaven and Earth interact to engender prosperity, it is auspicious. Everything will be advantageous!

SAWYER ∘ The great auspiciousness of this trigraph derives from the presence of mature yang in the position of Man. Energetic and strong, it bridges the gulf between Heaven and Earth, fully empowering human affairs. This may be understood cosmogenically, depicting a historical stage in the world's evolution, or in terms of the year's annual cycle. Humanity arose when yang provided the bright essence, but each year people arise from their winter slumbers to recommence social and agricultural activities. Accordingly, this is the time either for reviving projects or embarking on new, creative ones. Virtually everything should move toward a successful conclusion.

120 PAO SHEN 保身

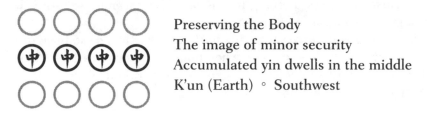

Preserving the Body
The image of minor security
Accumulated yin dwells in the middle
K'un (Earth) ∘ Southwest

ORACLE

Ghostly *ch'i* is not yet flourishing; cruel poisons have not yet taken shape. Preserve your nature, guard your life, then your gates and doors will be secure and tranquil.

VERSES

> Flowers encountering spring rain, difficult for their
>   voluptuousness to remain.
> Eastwardly inclined, water flows; how can the waves be
>   suppressed?
> Even casting aside profit and fame from future's path,
> One must still guard against numerous idle affairs and dark
>   worries.

> Blossoms open, spring departs;
> Butterflies come, flowers already decay.
> Only the green, green Cyprus
> Manages to endure the year's cold.

COMMENTARIES

YEN ∘ The middle position is the image of Man. Thus it says "ghostly *ch'i* is not yet flourishing." Still the middle is occupied by yin and is weak, without anything with which to interconnect. It would be appropriate to be warily cautious, to preserve your body and retire to secrecy, practicing uprightness and cultivating virtue. You should not do anything that will permit cruel ghosts to encroach on you. If you take action, you will invariably be defeated. It is impossible for this to be auspicious. Beware.

HO ∘ It would be appropriate to preserve your body and settle in quietude. On the whole this trigraph is inauspicious. Ghostly *ch'i* is rather heavy. It would not be very appropriate to divine about illness. As for official entanglements, at first you will suffer from defamation but later will escape when everything is cleared up. The traveler will arrive. The army will be victorious.

CH'EN ∘ "Four" is extreme yin, and it dwells in Man's position. Except for the elderly and dying, there must certainly be cruel ghosts. It is only appropriate to preserve yourself.

LIU ∘ "Ghostly *ch'i* is not yet flourishing"—it lacks companions with which to associate. "Preserve your nature, guard your life"—it would be appropriate to dwell quietly.

In this trigraph, yin occupies yang's position but lacks anything to rely on. Querents should be warily cautious and retire in secrecy in order to preserve themselves—then there will not be any calamity.

SAWYER ∘ Mature yin occupies the Tao of Man, while there is no other support or response from the positions of Heaven and Earth. Clusters of yin are frequently envisioned as symbolizing the presence of ghosts and spirits, particularly when the active, life giving principle of yang is either absent or depleted. The situation bespeaks potential difficulty and entanglements; the prudent course is to avoid actions that would facilitate their gaining a toehold and thereby prevent their potential dominance. Actions consonant with yin—cleaving to the dark, quiet, and valleys; maintaining a low profile; and dwelling quietly in seclusion—are deemed appropriate. Perhaps it should be seen as a time for preparation rather than some dank, externally imposed exile.

121   *Hua Yü*   化育

Transforming and Nourishing
The image of the *ch'i* of life
Solitary yang, not bright
Ch'ien (Heaven) ∘ Northwest

Oracle

Bright and clear, Heaven on high shines nurturingly on the Earth below. Transforming and nourishing the categories of life, it opens the gates and springs wide the doors. Affairs, all perceptive, in turn gaze on each other.

Verse

> Arriving on level, easy terrain,
> After ten thousand miles of rivers and hills;
> Along the road of green aspen and fragrant grass,
> The wind fresh, the horse's hooves light.

Commentaries

Yen ∘ The Virtue of Earth matches Heaven; there will certainly be glorious enrichment. It moistens the categories just sprouting, allowing them to grow large.

Ho ∘ All affairs will comply with one's mind, but there will be slight difficulties and delays. This trigraph does not entail any calamity. Inquiring about birth is highly auspicious and presages the birth of a male. Bureaucratic advancement, seeking wealth, hoped-for affairs, receiving officially sealed missives, commercial activities, and gaining audiences with noble persons will all be auspicious. As for official entanglements: laying accusations against inner-palace attendants, women, and Buddhist and Taoist monks will prove auspicious. The ill should not dwell in dangerous places but ought to stay within the house. The traveler has encountered obstacles and will not yet return. Sending the army forth on campaign will certainly result in victory.

CH'EN ∘ "One" is Heaven and yang; below, it becomes the power of Earth. When yang *ch'i* emanates from the Earth, the myriad things are transformed and born. A verse states: "It's the place where single yang first moves, the time before the myriad things are born." Solitary yin does not give birth; solitary yang does not stir things to development. Thus when yang *ch'i* lies in Earth, then the profits of Earth are beautifully abundant. Several trigraphs adopt this meaning.

LIU ∘ "Heaven on high shines nurturingly," thereby stirring things to life. "In turn they gaze on each other"—they are all glorious.

In this trigraph, yang has come to dwell in the position of Earth. For this reason it creates the image of "Heaven on high shining nurturingly." Affairs inquired about will begin to prosper and in the end will largely be free from calamity.

SAWYER ∘ Although this trigraph lacks the upper and middle positions, the Oracle emphasizes the initial generative aspects of yang, which has penetrated Earth, yin's realm. The field above is free of obstacles; growth can proceed unimpeded. For the querent this trigraph is completely positive and full of still unrealized possibility.

122 *Ti Li* 地利

◯◯◯◯
◯◯◯◯
◯◯ⓉⓉ

Profits of Earth
The image of settling in thickness
Yin dwells in yin's position
K'un (Earth) ∘ Southwest

ORACLE

The foundation established, affairs defined, people and things are ordered and correct. With liquids clear and food sweet, each preserves his nature and life.

VERSE

Almonds burgeoning, plums fragrant, luscious *ch'i* overflows.
Flower after flower blossoms forth anew.
Only when you encounter a double-mouthed man south of the
  Yangtze River,
Will you know that change and transformation lie with the
  Master of Men.

COMMENTARIES

YEN ∘ Heaven is "one," while Earth is "two" and the foundation. Thus the foundation is already established. People and things, relying on it, each correct their natures and lives. Every affair will be somewhat auspicious.

HO ∘ Human affairs are already defined; establishing the foundation binds them together. "Each preserves his nature and life"—all affairs become somewhat auspicious. Seeking official position and having an audience with a noble person are equally promising. The traveler will not return until autumn.

CH'EN ○ "Two" forms the purely beautiful body of yin *ch'i.* Dwelling in the lowest position, it makes the Tao of Earth correct. This is the image of tranquility and peace.

LIU ○ "The foundation established, affairs defined"—the Tao of Earth is complete. "With liquids clear and food sweet, each preserves his nature and life."

This trigraph presages that affairs sought after will be highly auspicious from beginning to end.

SAWYER ○ Although the upper two positions are void, Earth is appropriately empowered by youthful yin. This is not as auspicious as youthful yang dwelling below, as in the previous trigraph, but the basis is thereby correct. Youthful yin being energetic and the foundation being established because of the metaphysical value of "two" identified with Earth, actions, hopes, and expectations are capable of being sustained. The world is thus reasonably defined and settled; the frame of reference can therefore be known and efforts structured accordingly.

123 CHIEN HOU 建 侯

Establishing Lords
The image of achievement
Three yang provide assistance below
Ch'ien (Heaven) ○ Northwest

ORACLE

Affairs flourish, achievement arises. Valiant heroes establish the foundations; Sages and Worthies rescue the world; laws and commands realize appropriate principles.

VERSES

Crossing through the billowing waves in a leaflike boat,
I have just gained the sandy shore.
Affairs pondered for many years only now complete,
Counting them by fingers, most were impeded and worrisome.

Heaven gave birth to valiant heroes,
Who created foundations and expanded occupations.
Relying on the people's strength,
They spread kindness and distributed benefits.
The perfected are affably harmonious,
The petty are perversely vindictive.

COMMENTARIES

YEN ∘ Three yang dwell in the lowest position, the image of achieving merit and establishing affairs. As for creating the foundations, only valiant heroes could have overcome the difficulties and been successful. Thus they were able to illuminate the laws and rescue the world. The hundred affairs will all realize their principles. Human endeavors will also be auspicious.

HO ∘ People discuss every affair, assisting in deciding and analyzing. Planning affairs, advancing yourself, and seeking wealth are all auspicious. Official entanglements will be resolved according to principles. The traveler will arrive. Official seals and a letter of commission will arrive simultaneously. The ill should recover. Sending the army forth on campaign will result in victory. In the hundred affairs, change and movement will be auspicious.

CH'EN ∘ "Three" is flourishing yang, and it dwells in Earth's position. It is the image of a group of worthies establishing a state. This is because the Tao of Earth flourishes.

LIU ∘ "Affairs flourish, achievement arises"—the Tao of yang is established. "Sages and Worthies rescue the world"—they advance in order to complete their achievements.

In this trigraph, three yang lie in Earth's position, creating the foundation and establishing occupations. Their firmness and robustness are sufficient for taking action unimpeded and undisturbed. It would be highly appropriate to take action. The hundred affairs are all auspicious.

SAWYER ○ This trigraph is similar to the previous two—the upper two positions are void and therefore amenable to strong influence from below, while the active principle of mature yang dwells in Earth. Since its generative power is stronger than in "Transforming and Nourishing" (trigraph 121), the field of potential action is far more dynamic and can encompass radical changes and transformations. The Oracle emphasizes the creative acts underlying civilization and social order (including the position of lord or marquis, as suggested by the trigraph's name). These require sagacity, energy, and courage—in short, heroes willing to undertake great responsibilities and endure intense suffering. Perhaps they furnish an appropriate model for the present moment.

124 SUNG CHUNG 送 終

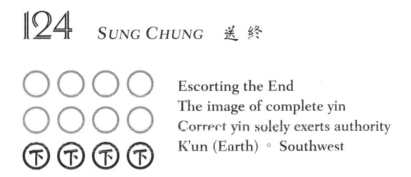

Escorting the End
The image of complete yin
Correct yin solely exerts authority
K'un (Earth) ○ Southwest

ORACLE

Nourishing the living; sending off the dead; sacrificial offerings clear and abundant—the filial son carries a staff; his clothes are rustic and coarse.

VERSE

Arguments among women presage worry and fright.
When a filial son approaches the gate, the sound of his weeping is moving.

When luck departs, even gold loses its luster,
With furrowed brow, matters lack completion.

COMMENTARIES

YEN ∘ In this trigraph, yin's number represents the myriad things at their extremity. Now one receives *ch'i* from Heaven, lives as a human, then dies and returns to the Earth. Thus it speaks of "nourishing the living and sending off the dead." Moreover, offering ancestral sacrifices at appropriate times is the way a filial son serves his deceased parents at the end.

HO ∘ Under this trigraph, if a filial son's parents are still alive, he should certainly behave most reverently. I'm afraid there might be a funeral; if not, there will be the external appearance of mourning. Divining about illness might be somewhat inauspicious. Everything else is inauspicious.

CH'EN ∘ "Four" is extreme yin which has submerged to dwell in the lowest position. This is the image of the dead entering the Earth. When yin is extreme, nothing else can be done.

LIU ∘ "Nourishing the living, sending off the dead"—the Tao of Man is fully realized. When the body and soul *(po)* return to the Earth, they dissipate.

This trigraph is the image of extreme distress. As for affairs inquired about, there aren't any that are not baleful!

SAWYER ∘ In several trigraphs "four yin" are identified with ghosts and spirits, an image that strongly influences the interpretation here. While the commentators emphasize the theme of the deceased returning to Earth, of being interred, the Oracle sets out what might well be termed the Confucian summation of life: nourish the living and reverently dispatch the dead. The duties of filial sons (and to a lesser degree, daughters) grew more onerous with the passing of centuries. However, the earliest impulse, from Confucius to the great classics on the rites and forms of social behavior, stressed felt emotion rather than mere formality. Respectful attention and obedience during life, strong grief at death, and the faithful fulfillment of sacrificial obligations marked filial behavior. However, when extreme *expressions* of grief came to merit official recognition and government rewards while the original spirit became ossified, the rites became mere formality for most, and charades for many. When the emotional content is appropriate, the forms of behavior circumspect, and actions timely, the "Tao of Man" is fully realized.

Yin in the position of Earth is of course appropriate and theoretically sustaining. However, it lacks any response from above, and being mature, finds its own energy waning. Thus the trigraph counsels that actions should not be undertaken at this time. However, the life work of mourning, whatever the cause, accords with the flux. Such "mourning" need not have been occasioned by the loss of living persons or pets, but might derive from projects, plans, ambitions, desires, dreams, or life-stage. The work of adjustment and reconciliation is vibrantly ongoing.

125 YIN MAN 陰 鏝

○○○○ The Mysterious Obverse
○○○○ The image of the formless
○○○○

ORACLE

The mysterious obverse, imageless—the omen's configuration as yet unformed. Movement forward will lead to regret; withdraw and preserve your purity.

VERSE

> Encountering a time of difficulties many and trembling fearful,
> Be as warily cautious as if treading on thin ice.
> Wanting to discern future threats and dangers,
> Is like hanging an open lantern in the wind.

COMMENTARIES

YEN ∘ The twelve disks are all overturned; no characters appear. This is the trigraph of the Mysterious Obverse. What originally had form has returned to the formless. The patterns of Heaven and Earth, yin and yang have reached their extreme. For this reason the *Ling Ch'i Ching* [once] began with a single line and ended with the imageless. It is a trigraph whose body lacks lines; therefore, it is not contained within the 124 trigraphs. This trigraph presages that you cannot yet initiate any of the hundred affairs. Retire to preserve darkness and purity in order to mitigate great calamities. Those who have long been ill will not die; after a period of time they should slowly be cured. For the traveler it is baleful. There is no advantage to anything being sought.

HO ∘ It would be appropriate to remain in residence and preserve your intentions. The hundred affairs should be stopped. If there hasn't been any offense, you will be spared from official entanglements. However, if some matter has already developed, it will be difficult to resolve. Deploying the military for an engagement would not be advantageous. Nothing sought will be obtained. This trigraph presages that remaining in residence will be tranquil and peaceful; it lacks predictions of gain and loss.

CH'EN ∘ The Three Realms of Heaven, Earth, and Man have not separated; yin and yang are not discriminated. This is the image of the primordial glob as yet undivided. There are not any characters that can be sought, no significance that can be determined.

LIU ∘ When the Great Ultimate had not yet separated, all was murky, dark, and black. Yin and yang being turbidly intermixed, no one could discern its shape. Withdraw to quietude; dwell in silence in order to preserve your purity.

In this trigraph the auspicious and baleful are not yet separated; you cannot do anything. If you remain quietly silent, preserving yourself, events will be auspicious and free from calamity. When the querent obtains this trigraph, it's like hearing of worries that are not worries, hearing of happiness that is not happiness. It is the trigraph of preserving the constant—one that lacks indications of gain and loss.

SAWYER ∘ This is perhaps the most amazing trigraph in the *Ling Ch'i Ching,* for it is beyond form as well as the categories of yin and yang. Unlike the *I Ching, T'ai Hsüan Ching,* and similar divination texts that employ dualities such as yin and yang, possibilities that fall into a simple "either/or" pattern, this book contains the possibility of reaching back to the formless, to the undiscriminated ultimate. Paradoxically, the trigraph is seen as concluding, rather than commencing, the cycle, but of course it represents the initial stage of the next progression. The most basic cosmogenic beliefs are reflected here; the implications are transcendent. (The Chinese title, Yin Man, entails a probable word play: yin referring to the yin of yin and yang, coupled with *man,* meaning "overflowing" or "unbounded," to yield "Yin Unbounded," and yin as "mysterious" coupled with *man,* referring to the back or obverse side of a coin or disk, as translated in the title "The Mysterious Obverse.")

If the querent should obtain this trigraph once in a lifetime of constantly consulting the Oracle, it would be considered remarkable, despite any claims of modern statistics. As for the implications, the formless is the ultimate labyrinth, for it lacks all indications and passages. The inquirer must establish orientations before embarking on interpretations; must conceive of directions before initiating projects. The Oracle counsels dwelling in dark solitude until the morass of unknowing has passed and discernment can begin. Truly a wise and conservative course for the moment, but doesn't the formless also posit ultimate freedom and possibility? Doesn't it imply a stage of heroic formulation rarely attained, when a person's will can be imposed on the unshaped clod?

Glossary

AGRICULTURE AND SERICULTURE ° The twin foundations of China's economic life. Agriculture was also the basis for the social order, being undertaken by the common people in the fields either on their own plots or in the service of extremely wealthy landowners. (In contrast with commercial activities, which were subject to official prejudice but private envy, agriculture was respected and respectable.) Sericulture, the various activities comprising the silk industry, encompassed the cultivation of the mulberry trees, essential for the silkworms to flourish; the raising of the priceless silkworms themselves; harvesting and unwrapping the cocoons; preparing the strands of silk thread; and finally weaving, considered in the Confucian vision to be the proper occupation for the ideal wife. From antiquity, Chinese sericulture produced the fine silks that were much desired throughout the known world, including ancient Rome.

"Sericulture" may also be understood in a more general sense as "cloth and garment production." The early stages are critical and therefore emphasized, just as agricultural work must precede eating. In a country extensively buffeted by natural disasters, with all the arable land under intense cultivation, the whims of nature and misfortunes such as droughts and floods, which were common from the uncontrolled Yellow and Yangtze Rivers, could mean the difference between life and death for millions, accounting for frequency of this topic in the *Ling Ch'i Ching*. References to agriculture and sericulture can be interpreted in the broadest sense, especially with respect to contemplated projects that require lengthy incubation and maturation periods.

ARGUMENTS AND DISPUTES ∘ Arguments and disputes were less likely to lead to violence in traditional China than today but are still issues to be aware of, particularly in large, clan-oriented social structures.

AUDIENCE WITH A NOBLE PERSON ∘ Also equivalent to "seeking the intercession of a noble person," echoing the ancient tradition of importuning nobles and officials wielding significant power whenever anything, such as an appointment, promotion, or the resolution of legal matters, was desired. However, in the period of this text, it can also be understood as currying favor or gaining the support of any powerful person, whether a member of the great families, the bureaucracy, or the ruling elite. Accordingly, the querent should seek out a mentor or advisor, a guru to provide enlightenment, or someone with the political or organizational power to smoothe the path and make projects possible.

AUSPICIOUS AND BALEFUL ∘ "Auspicious" describes favorable indications, presaging that within the querent's immediate circumstances and the flux of external factors, a contemplated activity might be expected to provide desired, superior results. Thus the commentators frequently speak about affairs complying with one's mind and proceeding well. However, it is important to note that neither the Oracle nor the Verse, presumably the classic's original core, often speak directly about concrete events, but instead tend to indicate situations or create moods depicting the flux of the moment or evoking less desirable conditions. Among the range of possible prognosticative evaluations—baleful, inauspicious, auspicious, and highly auspicious—baleful indicates that the portents are very inauspicious, that an activity is apparently doomed to failure as presently envisioned, structured, or contemplated.

BUREAUCRATIC OFFICE ∘ A major concern, the ultimate objective of the educated man, and the foundation for securing the family's fortunes, since wealth without political or official power could be easily confiscated by the government on one pretext or another. The examination system had long held sway by the time of the *Ling Ch'i Ching*; candidates had to vigorously pursue their studies for many years before even attempting the initial series of exams. However, at various times another route might be through local recommendation for good character or exemplary filial behavior. Presumably the lite-rati—those serving in the extensive bureaucracy of China—were the prime readers of this book, and the commentators directed their inter-pretations accordingly. Promotion and demotion at the local level was routine but uncertain, while serving in office at the highest level was fraught with danger because a careless act or single offense might result not only in personal execution, but also the extermination of one's entire family.

CH'I ∘ The pneuma of life, the essential constituent of human ac-tivity, *ch'i* is also the material from which the universe was fashioned, the primordial breath from which life emanated. A deficiency of *ch'i* is associated with weakness, difficulty, and sorrow; a surge with activity, success, and free passage. (*Ch'i* is a technical term of proto-scientific thought, with many ramifications for its circulation in the human body and stages of activity in the external world.)

COMMERCIAL ACTIVITIES ∘ The underlying Chinese term actu-ally implies retail activities, such as traditional street sales, village markets, or trading measures. However, the implications can be broadened to encompass modern stock and commodity transactions and similar retail-oriented or derived activities. (Occasionally the term "business enterprises" appears, obviously referring to major proj-ects; however, in the absence of it or other specific financial efforts, such as "real-estate transactions," "commercial activities" can be viewed as all-encompassing.)

GHOSTS AND SPIRITS ∘ These are distinguished in the text, with ghosts being viewed as the remnant energy of the deceased, and spir-its being associated with yang and Heaven. Much simplified, accord-ing to popular conceptions when the book was probably composed, if unpropitiated, these ancestor spirits could become troubled and in turn disrupt human life; therefore, the ancestral sacrifices—which bound the family together and gave it a sense of hierarchy and iden-tity—were considered to be extremely important. (Naturally, views varied across the spectrum of Taoism, Confucianism, and Buddhism, and the commentators reflect increasingly complex conceptions be-cause a simple idea evolved into two distinct souls, the *hun* and *po*. The former is identified as the yang component, the latter as the yin component that returns to the earth on death.) Whenever ghosts are mentioned in the text, it is because of the presence of mature yin, often spoken of as clusters of yin, and the pernicious effects they produce when unbalanced in the dynamics of the moment. However, there is no suggestion of the complex realms of Buddhist or Taoist heaven or hells here, nor of the various spirits and deities, except in passing. In contemporary terms, ghosts can also be understood as symbolizing neglected obligations, disquieting psychic energy in one's circumstances, or remnants of past events that have yet to be appropriately resolved within the unfolding context of personal life.

HUNDRED AFFAIRS ° The numerous affairs of life that the Oracle or commentators have not otherwise singled out for specific prognostication, such as commercial activities. The term "ordinary affairs" also appears, meaning the pedestrian affairs of life rather than sitting for imperial examination, assuming bureaucratic office, or getting married.

HUNDRED SURNAMES ° Originally a term indicating the nobility in the early Chou dynasty because only the nobles had surnames. However, with the passage of centuries and the dramatic economic and political changes that marked the Spring and Autumn and Warring States periods, the term came to refer to the people as a whole— the common people. Nevertheless, in many trigraphs of the *Ling Ch'i Ching* it still retains a slight aura of nobility.

ILLNESS ° Another paramount concern in both traditional and contemporary life, the nature and course of illness always entails severe psychological implications. Even today, with routine treatment available for most infectious diseases, plus the modern techniques of diagnosis and surgery, people are still easily troubled by even the most minor discomforts. Accordingly, the commentators inevitably turned their attention to this category, deriving concrete implications from the Oracle, especially when yin tended to dominate. However, even if there were a basis for ascribing validity to the *Ling Ch'i Ching's* prognostications, the commentators' statements should be understood in the broadest context, not as specifically bad implications, but rather as positive encouragements to devote proper attention to self-care and the management of any health problem within the context of modern modes of treatment. If the commentators suggest that an illness might grow more severe, it implies that this will happen if the present circumstances continue to be maintained. Therefore, the wise will pay heed to the body's demands; consult their physicians; embark on appropriate, mindful body work; and make every effort to improve their health and maximize the certainty for recovery by altering the immediate situation. (The implication might well be that insufficient psychic energy has been directed toward the body, that cues have been ignored or treated offhandedly, such as by routinely ingesting antibiotics while vigorously pursuing normal activities. The Oracle can be viewed as perhaps indicating that such practices are inimical to health and a more serious and solicitous attitude should be adopted.)

LEGAL ENTANGLEMENTS AND OFFICIAL AFFAIRS ° The latter of course being broader, but generally any conflict with others and especially the offices of government, including permits, payments, and permissions, is inferred. Mainly framed as legal actions in which one becomes involved, the prospect is couched in terms of their possible resolution. (A more extreme case is "the imprisoned," whose prospects for release are sometimes indicated. Under China's severe legal system, it was easy to become implicated and difficult to escape punishment once charged or imprisoned.)

MARRIAGE ARRANGEMENTS ° The emphasis falls on the arrangements being initiated rather than the ceremony itself, although marriage and the consequent course of events are implied, because in traditional Chinese society, marriages were largely arranged either directly between families or through appointed intermediaries. Once the arrangements were concluded, the affair was deemed permanently settled; only the unfolding of marital life might hold personal surprises.

THE MOMENT ° The Oracle indicates that at the "present time"— which may be more or less extensive but should be assumed to be momentary—certain conditions obtain and must be immediately acted on. This emphasis on grasping a moment of opportunity probably stems from the ancient belief in the point of the ever-changing flux when actions will suddenly have the possibility of being determinative. As seen in the early military thinker Wu Ch'i, the "moment" is fleeting, subtle, imperceptible, and ineffable; difficult to grasp, elusive to exploit; and irrecoverable. The moment must be seized; otherwise, it is immediately lost. However, in some cases a more extended time frame is indicated by the *Ling Ch'i Ching,* such as a single *ch'i* period (one of twenty-four equal phases of *ch'i* activity into which the year is divided), a season of the year as commonly conceived, or even an agricultural season of more than several months during which fruits and vegetables ripen. Actions have their formative periods, their latent stages, and finally their moments for realization, and cannot be forcefully hurried.

PERFECTED MAN or INDIVIDUAL ∘ The classic Confucian model of self-cultivated perfection—in antiquity, a man of Virtue, wisdom, courage, responsibility, duty, and natural compassion. His actions are always altruistic, guided by a concern for the common good, while his highest aim is to serve gloriously in the realm of a moral ruler. The literati, who attained appointments in the bureaucracy through rigorous examination and selection procedures, espoused this as their ideal, but according to Confucius himself, perfected men are exceedingly rare. (In Confucian-influenced writings and popular culture, the perfected man is generally contrasted with the petty or menial man. Over the centuries in China the ordinary reader consulting the *Ling Ch'i Ching* would probably have considered attaining the ideal of the perfected man beyond his ability but would still have at least nominally aspired to it and identified with it.) The perfected individual is morally contrasted with the petty person, discussed next.

PETTY INDIVIDUALS ∘ Often termed the "small man," "common man," or "menial man" by earlier Chinese translators, it is a decidedly pejorative term reflecting not evil or perversity, but simply base, selfish interests being allowed to dictate behavior, resulting in a person oriented toward self-satisfaction and the constant fulfillment of the desires. In short, the petty individual is simply governed by wants and emotions rather than altruism and morality. The theoretical moral spectrum, from good to evil, that evolved in early Confucian texts, might be envisioned as follows: Sages—Worthies—the perfected—ordinary literati or cultivated individuals—common people (including peasants)—the petty—the crafty—the perverse—the outright evil. The "evil" include "brigands," who commit crimes of violence against people of rank and property, including robbery and murder, and also robbers and thieves, who steal by violence (or threat of violence) and clandestinely, without violence respectively.

PRAYER AND SACRIFICE ∘ Admonitions to pray or offer sacrifice are frequently encountered when circumstances are deemed inauspicious or there are pernicious, even baleful influences about. No particular God or spirit is normally designated. For the querent, it essentially implies a ritual act within the framework of one's beliefs, perhaps as simple as lighting incense and meditating, or as formal as active prayer within a sanctified religious structure. (As commonly practiced in the modern Far East, sacrifice no longer entails any vestiges of the ancient meaning, but instead consists of such simple symbolic acts as offering fruit or other items to the spirits and subsequently consuming them within the family. It is the sincere performance of the ritual—the attitude, emotional, and psychological experience—rather than the items offered that is focal. Because prayers and rituals are personally empowering, a detailed religious pantheon is unnecessary to their recommendation.)

THE PREGNANT WILL GIVE BIRTH TO A MALE ∘ In a male-oriented, male-dominated agriculturally based society, the birth of a male was of course much desired and therefore highly auspicious. (The sorrows of wives giving birth to unwanted females, both in traditional and contemporary Asian societies, need hardly be mentioned.) Women prayed in temples for a son even before seeking their own health and safety in the difficult and dangerous course of childbirth, while wives might be displaced if they bore only daughters. However, note that this concern with a child's sex appears only with the commentators rather than the Oracle and Verse.

PRESERVE YOURSELF, CULTIVATE PURITY ∘ The recommended course for times of difficulty, when the tides of change and flow of events are inimical. This approach presumes that virtuous behavior and maintaining a "low profile" will be sufficient to avoid being overturned and crushed by adverse circumstances, whereas high-profile behavior and aggressive actions would evoke disaster. Since self-cultivation is assumed to be an ongoing practice and the basis for all life and action, any explicit recommendation to "preserve oneself" only emphasizes the imperative need to dwell apart, beneath the prevailing dark clouds. However, these times of enforced contemplation need not be viewed negatively, but rather as the incubation periods inevitably required for future success and tranquil existence.

REMAINING IN RESIDENCE ∘ Not simply "staying at home," which tends to connote a lack of initiative and a fear of facing challenges, it is translated in this somewhat formalistic way to emphasize the conscious aspect of forgoing any temptation to go out, to undertake external activities, or to travel. The querent should deliberately remain at home or on the family estate to cultivate personal virtues, manage family or clan affairs, and devote oneself to business enterprises and agriculture.

SAGES AND WORTHIES ∘ The terms *sage* and *worthy* refer to two special classes of superior individuals within the Confucian conception, each possessed of surpassing moral virtue, self-perfection, and wisdom. However, innate wisdom is perhaps the Sage's hallmark, while the Worthy are relatively more defined by their unsullied moral purity. Worthies are of course perfected individuals, but their attainments exceed those of the simply perfected. However, in a somewhat eclectically oriented text such as the *Ling Ch'i Ching*, Sages may also be Taoist beings, in which case their lifestyle would not have been marked by a commitment to the Confucian virtues and practices, but to Taoist values, such as contemplative studies, extensive meditation, abstract wandering, and the development of natural harmony.

SENDING THE ARMY FORTH ON CAMPAIGN ∘ Military questions numbered among the very oldest subjects for divination and constituted the greatest affairs of state. From the querent's frame of reference, some moments are more auspicious than others, for even though the engagement begins at the same time for both sides, only one emerges victorious. Modern interpretations can be imagined, such as business conquests or other personal activities that employ a military theme for their conceptualization.

SPIRITUAL IMMORTALS ∘ Sometimes seen in the Verse, the term refers to people who have perfected themselves through self-cultivation in the Taoist arts to the point of enjoying great longevity or even becoming ethereal, capable of floating on the wind and living on air. Their appearance symbolizes an alluring path in an unfettered world.

THE TRAVELER ∘ The commentators frequently indicate whether or not "the traveler" is about to return. In an era lacking modern telecommunications, the fate or progress of family members away on a distant journey, whatever the reason, would obviously be a matter of great anxiety. Divination about their return provided a temporarily reassuring answer, although not necessarily an accurate one. By implication, the response encompasses planned travels, pondering whether they will be free from difficulty and if one will return safely. (In the modern age, only in rare circumstances does one not return. However, some modern prognosticators in China view this response as indicating whether a plane or boat voyage would be risky or not, or even if the querent should consider driving somewhere.)

VIRTUE ° Although encompassing the basic meaning of moral virtue, Virtue *(te)* was the object of much complex thought in ancient China and came to have numerous nuances and technical meanings, including the two most important: "power" and "potency." Capitalized, it refers here not just to the ordinary, commonplace "virtues" espoused by most religious and ethical systems—although they are certainly subsumed by the term and taken as fundamental—but rather the transcendent, numinous *power* developed through their intensive, conscientious cultivation. Moreover, the term *te,* similar to the ancient concept of *virtus,* means the power inherent within a person, force of nature, or object, as found in the title of the famous Taoist classic, the *Tao Te Ching,* often known as *The Way and Its Power.* (Within the context of Taoist texts the term *te* particularly indicates inner potency, or power, generally as contrasted with and distinguished from the moral and ethical realm because the artificial constraints of the rites, morals, and ethics were anathema to most Taoist-oriented thinkers.) Accordingly, throughout this translation of the *Ling Ch'i Ching* the term *virtue,* uncapitalized, refers to morals and ethics, while *Virtue,* capitalized, connotes surpassing moral achievements and the attainment of special, virtually transcendent moral status through Confucian practices. However, it should be noted that the forces of nature and other animate forms are also perceived as possessing power, the latter also being spoken of as their "Virtue."

Shown below are all of the possible trigraphs, keyed to the trigraph number. The chart is arranged in five groups, based on the top row of the trigraph, which is shown at the upper left of each group. The five possibilities for the middle row are shown at the column heads to the right and the five possibilities for the bottom row are shown to the left.

○○○●

	○○○○	○○○●	○○●●	○●●●	●●●●
○○○○	113	65	66	67	68
○○○●	97	1	5	9	13
○○●●	98	2	6	10	14
○●●●	99	3	7	11	15
●●●●	100	4	8	12	16

○○●●

	○○○○	○○○●	○○●●	○●●●	●●●●
○○○○	114	69	70	71	72
○○○●	101	17	21	25	29
○○●●	102	18	22	26	30
○●●●	103	19	23	27	31
●●●●	104	20	24	28	32

○●●●

	○○○○	○○○●	○○●●	○●●●	●●●●
○○○○	115	73	74	75	76
○○○●	105	33	37	41	45
○○●●	106	34	38	42	46
○●●●	107	35	39	43	47
●●●●	108	36	40	44	48

Consultation Chart

●●●●					
	○○○○	○○○●	○○●●	○●●●	●●●●
○○○○	116	77	78	79	80
○○○●	109	49	53	57	61
○○●●	110	50	54	58	62
○●●●	111	51	55	59	63
●●●●	112	52	56	60	64

○○○○					
	○○○○	○○○●	○○●●	○●●●	●●●●
○○○○	125	117	118	119	120
○○○●	121	81	85	89	93
○○●●	122	82	86	90	94
○●●●	123	83	87	91	95
●●●●	124	84	88	92	96

Shambhala Dragon Editions

(*Continued on next page*)

Mastering the Art of War, by Zhuge Liang & Liu Ji. Translated & edited by Thomas Cleary.

The Myth of Freedom and the Way of Meditation, by Chögyam Trungpa.

Nine-Headed Dragon River, by Peter Matthiessen.

Rational Zen: The Mind of Dogen Zenji. Translated by Thomas Cleary.

Returning to Silence: Zen Practice in Daily Life, by Dainin Katagiri. Foreword by Robert Thurman.

Seeking the Heart of Wisdom: The Path of Insight Meditation, by Joseph Goldstein & Jack Kornfield. Foreword by H. H. the Dalai Lama.

Shambhala: The Sacred Path of the Warrior, by Chögyam Trungpa.

The Shambhala Dictionary of Buddhism and Zen.

The Spiritual Teaching of Ramana Maharshi, by Ramana Maharshi. Foreword by C. G. Jung.

Tao Teh Ching, by Lao Tzu. Translated by John C. H. Wu.

Teachings of the Buddha, Revised & Expanded Edition, edited by Jack Kornfield.

The Tibetan Book of the Dead: The Great Liberation through Hearing in the Bardo. Translated with commentary by Francesca Fremantle & Chögyam Trungpa.

Vitality, Energy, Spirit: A Taoist Sourcebook. Translated & edited by Thomas Cleary.

Wen-tzu: Understanding the Mysteries, by Lao-tzu. Translated by Thomas Cleary.

Worldly Wisdom: Confucian Teachings of the Ming Dynasty. Translated & edited by J. C. Cleary.

Zen Essence: The Science of Freedom. Translated & edited by Thomas Cleary.

The Zen Teachings of Master Lin-chi. Translated by Burton Watson.